HOW TO LEGALLY COLLECT YOUR CHILD'S FAIR CHILD SUPPORT DUES, OR TO FIGHT ITS PAYMENT WHEN YOU NEED TO.

The National Child Support Collection Enforcement Manual

By **Benjamin Anosike, Ph.D.**

Copyright © 2007 by Benji O. Anosike

Printed in the United States of America
ISBN: 0-932704-91-3

Library of Congress Catalog Number:

NOV 1 3 '07

Published by:
DO-IT-YOURSELF LEGAL PUBLISHERS
1588 Remsen Avenue
Brooklyn N.Y. 11236

The Publisher's Disclaimer

To be sure, this publication is designed to provide, and to the best of our knowledge and ability, does provide, accurate and authoritative information in regard to the subject matter herein covered. It remains for us, the Publishers of this manual guidebook, to assure our readers that, upon credible information and honest belief, the author of this publication has diligently researched, checked and counter-checked, every bit of information and claims contained in this manual to assure its accuracy and up-to-dateness. And, that it is herewith absolutely assured. Nevertheless, we humans have never been noted for our infallibility or perfection, no matter how hard the efforts! Nor, is this relatively short manual conceivably intended to be an encyclopedia on the subject, containing the answer or solution to every issue on the subject.

THE READER IS THEREFORE FOREWARNED THAT THIS MANUAL IS SOLD AND DISTRIBUTED TO ALL WITH THIS DISCLAIMER: The Publisher (and/or the author, or any persons or entities involved in any way in the preparation, publication, sale, or distribution of this manual) make NO guarantees of any kind or nature whatsoever on the actual outcome of the application of the recommendations, strategies, or remedies outlined in this book for child support collection or enforcement, or for modification or challenge of child support, and herewith absolutely disclaim, for one and all, any and all responsibility for the effects, consequences, outcome or results from any action taken in reliance upon information contained in this book. Nor, does the Publisher (and/or the author or any others) purport to engage in rendering professional, legal, family or marriage counseling or other services, or to substitute for   a family counselor, a lawyer, or accountant, or the like. Where such professional advice or expert assistance or other help is legitimately required or called for in your specific or other cases, it should be readily sought accordingly. *Again, to the reader: YOU and only you, are responsible for whatever the result for whatever you choose to do based on what you read in this manual*

— DO-IT-YOURSELF LEGAL PUBLISHERS

ACKNOWLEDGMENT

The author is deeply grateful and indebted to many persons and entities or institutions without whose help or contribution the research and writing of this book would not have been possible. They are responsible in large part for the manual's truths, but for none of its errors. Of particular mentioned, is the U.S. Department of the Health and Human Services, whose publication, the *Handbook on Child Support Enforcement,* constitute a great inspiration for, and a substantial part of, this present manual.

TABLE OF CONTENTS

CHAPTER 5
ESTABLISHING FATHERHOOD: **PATERNITY**

CHAPTER 6
ESTABLISHING ORDER FOR CHILD SUPPORT: **FINANCIAL OBLIGATION**

CHAPTER 7
MAKING SURE SUPPORT PAYMENT IS PAID: **ENFORCEMENT**

CHAPTER 8
DISTRIBUTION: HOW THE STATE DISBURSEMENT UNIT (SDU)
DISTRIBUTES PAYMENT COLLECTED TO THE CUSTODIAL PARENT

CHAPTER 9
ACF HEALTHY MARRIAGE INITIATIVE

FOREWORD:

WHAT THIS GUIDEBOOK IS ALL ABOUT

A. CHILD SUPPORT PAYMENT IS NOW A SERIOUS BUSINESS

After some three decades of federal and state legislations and "reform" efforts, it has become true, as of today, that there are a variety of state tools and remedies, including civil and criminal judicial remedies, available to parents and interested parties for collecting child support, in addition to assistance in locating parents who fail to make court ordered child support payments. In each state there are agencies, known as "Title IV-D" agencies, which are required by Federal law to provide child support enforcement services to anyone who requests such services.

In a word, today, family law and social services experts assert, not meeting your child support obligations is a very "serious business" in the American society. No more is it just a matter of your being "harassed" or even being occasionally arrested to coarse payment. But you can lose many of your prized citizenship rights and privileges, including having a criminal record and being put in jail for up to six months for "contempt of court" (not paying child support). You may also be fined for each violation and have to pay attorney's fees and court costs as well.

B. THE CONSEQUENCES TO PARENTS AND FAMILIES OF NOT MEETING CHILD SUPPORT OBLIGATION

In deed, in many states, the court can, among other things:

- Order that your picture be posted in private and public locations and in the newspapers;

- Revoke or suspend your driver's license;

- Take the tax refunds that are due you;

- Garnishee your wages

- Add interest to past-due child support

- Deny you occupational or business licenses;

- Deny state loans or grants;

- Revoke your passport to travel, or refuse its renewal

- Refer your case to private collection agencies

- Report you to a consumer credit reporting agency;

- Direct you to skills training and job placement services.

- Refer or direct you to education or literacy classes and counseling services (substance abuse, parenting skills, etc.), or for you to take part in these services.

- Deny you some basic judicial and administrative rights. (For example, under federal law, the adjudication process in court and administrative proceedings have been streamlined so that in paternity cases, for example, your right to a jury trial is generally eliminated).

- Place you in jail for "contempt of court" and nonpayment (for up to 6 months or more).

- Even pursue you to a foreign country your state might have concluded a reciprocal agreement with to which you might have fled to avoid payment, and file claims to compel you to make payment of your child support obligations.

C. THE PRACTICAL CONSEQUENCES OF CHILD SUPPORT ENFORCEMENT POLICIES ON PARENTS, FAMILIES AND THE SOCIETY

According to family law experts, such as Carl E. Schneider, Margaret F. Brinig, Laura W. Morgan and others, the two principal "traditional" goals of family law are protecting family members (the children) and preserving marriage and family stability. The whole design of the past three decades of federal and state legislation and policies in family law, experts note, has been "to reduce welfare costs and improve conditions for custodial mothers and children through more rigorous establishment and collection of child support."

BUT, HERE'S THE CENTRAL QUESTION: Have these laws and policies met these desirable vital goals – of protecting children and preserving family stability in America over these years? At best, experts assign a "mixed result" grading to that exercise. Stricter child support enforcement, it is generally agreed, has resulted in increased substantial child support collections and outcome for many women and children. However, they say, those measures have also, "for a substantial and immeasurable number of men, women and children, inflicted unintended and undesirable harms that we would regret...negative consequences [that] would be borne disproportionately by the poorest persons and by persons of color." The negative consequences of stricter child enforcement collection policies which have been identified by experts and critics, include the following:

- Because of the fact that frequently the present child support enforcement system increasingly reject fatherhood based on marriage or caretaking in favor of fatherhood based solely on paternity or biology, children are becoming fatherless and losing the emotional connection, companionship, nurturing and economic support that fathers provide.

- The aggressive pursuit of welfare-driven child support policies against fathers of children receiving public benefits, the substantial majority of whom have been found to be poor and low-income, is pushing those fathers to resist and seek disestablishment of paternity for children

- The current policy defines fatherhood almost exclusively in economic and biological terms that ignores other potential bases for fatherhood-based caretaking, and a result, children are becoming fatherless and the state's and society's stated interests in collecting child support, which is to preserve families and protect children, are frequently undermined

- Child support policy which limit the meaning of fatherhood to biology and financial support, have had an adverse impact on low income families, particularly the relationship between fathers and children in those families

- A primary assumption and expectation of the present child support law was that improved child support collection would reduce poverty in low income custodial homes. Experts have found, however, that while there has been some success in improving child support collection, "there is considerable evidence that [the] reforms have failed to accomplish one of the most important objectives of child support, that of reducing child poverty."

As another expert put it, "There is some evidence that the receipt of child support may be critical to non-welfare custodial households. But the same research shows that aggressive child support enforcement has not reduced poverty for welfare families."

- Whereas the common assumption is often made that fathers of children on welfare who are frequently the target of some of the most aggressive child support enforcement efforts, are all 'deadbeats,' credible research on the matter show that a substantial number of such men who owe child support, are in fact dead broke. Consequently, the desperate economic circumstances of most fathers of children on welfare almost immediately ensures the inevitability of the failure of the child support system to effectively address child poverty.

D. IS HE A 'DEADBEAT DAD,' OR A POVERTY-STRICKEN DAD WHO'S TRYING TO SURVIVE?

Keen observers and experts of modern family law have noted that the stereotype of the "deadbeat dad" who deliberately shirks responsibility to live up to his legal and moral duty to care for his children, is long-standing and common in our popular culture, and that propping up the straw man of the "deadbeat dad" often seems especially tantalizing among politicians and some social writers who seek an easy whipping boy for what ails the American family.

One observer, Tonya L. Brito, a family law expert, sums it up this way in a 1999 essay:

> "The public's anger has spread to all non-custodial fathers owing support. These fathers have emerged as the new villains in our culture. 'The irresponsibility' of fathers takes three forms: they bring into the world 'illegitimate' children they do not intend to support; they leave marriages they should remain in; and, whether married or not, they fail to pay support for the children they leave behind. It would be an exaggeration to say that politicians of all stripes have taken up a moral crusade against non-supporting fathers, condemning their immorality and selfishness."

Another observer, Laura Morgan, strongly agrees. "The image of the 'Deadbeat Dad' is well-entrenched in American culture," Morgan says, "[and] evokes an image of a non-custodial father who has impoverished his children while improving his own standard of living after separation from the family…[while] ignoring his children's needs and enjoying a prosperous lifestyle." However, says Morgan, while such stereotypical 'deadbeats' do exist, they are largely uncommon and untypical. Citing various studies and research support for virtually every individual assertion she makes, Morgan adds as follows:

> "While these stereotypical 'deadbeats' exist, many of the men owing child support are in fact dead broke. Researchers estimate that as many as 33.2% of young, non-custodial fathers are unable to pay child support due to poverty. Many low-income fathers have substandard education, lack marketable skills, and often have criminal histories that hinder employment. Many are minors, and are without strong family support. Many are substance abusers, have mental and physical disabilities which can contribute to economic and family instability. They are often immigrants for whom English is a second language. All of these circumstances have created a substantial group of non-custodial fathers who are subject to child support obligations they are simply unable to meet. They accrue large arrears, are subject to sanctions, and fall further into the cycle of poverty."

E. HERE'S THE CENTRAL POINT HERE

The point of this guidebook, *How To Collect Your Child's Fair Child Support Dues, Or To Fight It When It's Unfair,* is that on the issue of parents making a reasonable child support payment, or its collection, there is not necessarily a 'bad guy' or 'good guy' on either side of the issue, and there is not necessarily a 'villain.' The Non-custodial parent, especially when he/she is able and capable, should reasonably be expected to make reasonable payment of financial support for the care of his or her children. The custodial parent and dependent child, should reasonably expect to collect such support from the other parent, and should have available the tools and the assistance, including the services of the State's Child Support Enforcement office, to enforce the collection of such payment from the obligated parent when the obligated parent proves unduly delinquent or uncooperative in making payment.

There is merit on "both sides" of the issue. True, there is good cause, as the welfare costs have soars over the years, for the federal (and state) governments to have increased their powers of recovering these costs in the form of child support from the fathers, and to engage in somewhat aggressive paternity establishment and child support enforcement policies to ensure collection. However, by the same token, there is also good cause on the part of the non-paying or delinquent parents, mostly men, undereducated, poverty stricken and largely ill equipped to meet such obligations, who must, in response, often seek to defend against arrest or incarceration and other severe sanctions for failing to pay child support. They may, for example, out of necessity rather than choice, rightly need to question, say, the legitimacy of a paternity order that's established against them by default without a personal appearance in court or a hearing, or genetic testing, or to question a child support amount that is way out of proportion to what they actually earn or can reasonably afford, or out of proportion to the other family or financial obligations and necessities they may have, etc.

This manual simple seeks to provide the basic "equalizer," the essential information and knowledge, by which any parties in interest – the custodial parents of children who receives or is entitled to child support, or a parent who pays or expects to pay child support, or a person in interest who operates in the child support enforcement machinery, etc – could be well informed and properly equipped as to his/her rights and obligations in such capacity, and where or how he or she can get affordable assistance in enforcing his legitimate rights.

Thank you.

The Publishers,

DO-IT-YOURSELF LEGAL PUBLISHERS

INTRODUCTION

In this manual you'll hear (or read) a lot about the "IV-D Program" or the "Child Support Enforcement Program."

What is the IV-D Program?

The IV-D program (pronounced Four-D) is the technical name for government administered Child Support Enforcement (CSE) Programs. The term 'IV-D' comes from Title IV-D of the Social Security Act, which is the federal enabling statute (law) that brought it into being. Put simply, a IV-D or Child Support Enforcement Program is a Federal/State/Local partnership to collect child support.

Each state, as well as the District of Columbia, Puerto Rico and other territories, has a IV-D program. In most states, a case is considered a IV-D case if the family has received public assistance benefits or if an application is filed with either the Department of Social Services or the Support Enforcement Unit asking for its assistance in obtaining or enforcing a child support order.

All IV-D programs perform following activities:

- Locating Non-custodial parents
- Establishing support orders, both financial and medical
- Enforcing support orders, collect and distribute support payments
- Reviewing and adjusting support orders to ensure that the orders are appropriate
- Providing payment processing services

Is The IV-D Program the Only Way You May Go?

As a custodial parent of a child, you may establish paternity or support, or enforce court orders, without the assistance of the IV-D program; and as a non-custodial parent seeking modification of an aspect of a child support order, you may also seek to do so without the assistance of the IV-D program. The point is that it is not mandatory that you must use the Child Support Enforcement office. Basically, in order to receive child support, you must first obtain a court order. And basically, there are three ways to get a court order for child support.

- Hire an attorney to pursue your case in court and paying him/her out of your pocket.
- Represent yourself in court (at no charge to you).
- Apply for child support services (IV-D) offered by the State. (Free of charge, as child support services are free).

This guidebook, *How To Collect Your Child's Fair Child Support Dues, Or To Fight It When It's Unfair*, is a guide to help you get the child support payments that your child needs and deserves, if you are a custodial parent seeking child support, and to help you pay the fair and proper child support amounts that you need and deserve to pay, if you are the non-custodial parent desiring to pay but are only seeking a fair shake and reasonable treatment. Although you'll hear a lot in these passages about the government-sponsored Child Support Enforcement (CSE) program and how to work through it, this guidebook is designed for use by parents, custodial as well as non-custodial, who seek to get the task performed, either on their own, or through a private family law attorney, and/or through the CSE.

Who Will be interested In This Guidebook?

Would your answer be a YES to any of these questions (and other like ones)? If it does, or would be, then the contents of this guidebook should be of direct interest – and value – to you. You'll find in this guide the basic answers to the questions outlined below, as well as the practical steps to follow by which to tackle, or resolve, or be informed about the issues. undertake such vital matters as establishing paternity, getting a child support order, collecting child support from a parent, modifying an unfair or unreasonable child support order based on your current income and the necessary expenses you'd need to live, knowing and securing your rights and responsibilities, etc., etc.

- Are you a parent (divorced, separated or never married) with children to support?
- Do you wish to get child support or a child support court order?
- Are you seeking to collect child support from a parent, or to establish father or non-fatherhood of your child
- Are you having trouble paying your current child support?
- Are you behind in your child support payment because you're out of job or it's too high?
- Are your child support payments making it difficult for you to support your new family?
- Is the Child Support Enforcement Agency of your state after you for back child support or AFDC welfare repayments?
- Have your wages been garnished, or about to be?
- Has your driver's license or passport been suspended, or about to be?
- Is the State caseworker involved in your child support case giving you the run-around?
- Has a child support-related warrant been issued for your arrest?
- Do you believe that the child support order you received is an unjust or unfair order, or that it's not reasonable based upon your current income and necessary expenses to live, and would like to reduce it?
- Do you believe that your ex-wife or ex-girlfriend, for example, is seeking an unreasonable increase in your current child support payments?
- Do you need to know (using, perhaps, the same kind of child support computer program that the judge uses) the approximate or actual amount of child support you will be obligated to pay before you even step into court?
- Would you like to obtain an audit of your child support account to determine the actual child support arrears you ought to pay, plus interest thereon and, perhaps, to arrange a reasonable repayment plan with your child support agency?
- Do you believe that your ex-wife or the mother of your child (or the father, in your case) is brainwashing your children against you, and wish to get information on how to counteract that to maintain your bond with your children?
- Has your ex already moved your children out of state, or is planning to move away taking your children with her, and you wish to remain active in the lives of your children, even if your children live far away or in another state, or it would mean having to engage in "long distance parenting" by you?
- Is your ex attempting doing something you think is designed to frustrate or eliminate you from the lives of your children?
- Are you a frustrated custodial parent of a child who's interested in information on collecting unpaid child support payments from the father (or mother) of your child?
- Are you interested in information about matters like reducing your child support-related wage garnishments, about keeping your driver's or business license, or a release of your driver's license that has already been suspended?
- Are you interested in knowing your legal rights as a father or mother in Child Support issues?

6

- Are you interested in making modifications of your current child support?
- Are you interested in disputing your back Child Support?
- Are you interested in challenging any false charges of child abuse and/or domestic violence against you as a non-custodial father (or mother)?
- Are you interested in finding out when you child's child support can be terminated according to your State's "Age of Majority" rules or statute of limitations?
- Are you interested in learning whether or not under your state's rules, child support obligations end if the child leaves the household, and whether support is ever paid beyond the child's age of majority? Or, in learning what your State's Statute of Limitations are for enforcing child support orders, or how it applies in paternity issues in your state?
- Is the father of your child located in a foreign country and you want to enforce child support court order against him to collect support?

If you answer YES to any one of the above questions (or questions similar to them), then this manual should certainly be of immense interest, and usefulness, to you. JUST READ ON.

How to Collect Your Child's Fair Child Support Dues, or to Fight It When It's Unfair, will provide you with the basic tools and information, and the steps, to get the tasks done, whether you're doing it working with your state or local Child Support Enforcement (CSE) program, or by yourself or your own private attorney. To be sure, the central function of the CSE program is to collect and distribute child support payment. However, the essential message and effort of this manual, is that all concerned and interested parties in child support - the custodial parent, the non-custodial parent, the government, the society, and particularly the children - fare and benefit best when both parents play an active, supportive role in their children's lives, and that this is much more likely to happen when the child support the parents are asked to pay is reasonable and fair.

How the Guidebook Is Organized

FIRST: In Chapter I, you are given the HISTORY of how the all-pervasive national Child Support Enforcement program we've come to have today started and developed. Then in Chapter 2, you're given a grand tour of the Child Support Law of each state in the nation, and your parental and child support rights and responsibilities under your particular state's law. These first two chapters are the "informational background chapters"– to provide you with some helpful background details on the history and the law and evolution of child support enforcement.

The rest of the Chapters, the PRACTICAL chapters, are organized simply so that you can refer directly to the specific child support or family law NEED you wish to address. They go as follows:

- Know Some Preliminary Helpful Information You'd Need, To Pursue a Child Support-related Case (Chapter 3): **BASIC INFORMATION YOU NEED**
- Find a non-custodial parent (Chapter 4): **LOCATION OF PARENT**
- Establish legal fatherhood for a child (Chapter 5): **PATERNITY**
- Establish and maintain a fair financial and medical support order (Chap. 6): **OBLIGATION**
- Enforce a support payment or order (Chapter 7): **ENFORCEMENT**
- Distribute money that is collected (Chapter 8): **DISTRIBUTION**

- With Intestate, Tribal and International Enforcement (Chapter 9): **ENFORCEMENT ACROSS BORDERS**
- The Child Support Program and Healthy Marriage (Chapter 10): **HEALTHY MARRIAGE INITIATIVE**
- Rights and Responsibilities of the non-custodial parent (Chapter 11): **WHICH PARENT PAYS THE SUPPORT?**
- Child Support Program Progress (Chapter 12): **LESSONS LEARNED.**
- Sources of Information & Materials for Parents (Chapter 13): **INFORMATION & HELP SOURCES**

CHAPTER 1

THE HISTORICAL DEVELOPMENT OF THE NATIONAL CHILD SUPPORT ENFORCEMENT PROGRAM

Here, we look at the historical development of the government child support enforcement program under Title IV-D of the Social Security Act. In particular, we will identify ways in which federal mandates that arise out of Title IV-D legislation, have fashioned child support enforcement under state laws over the decades.

A. THE CREATION OF THE GOVERNMENT CHILD SUPPORT ENFORCEMENT PROGRAM.

The Social Security Amendments of 1974.

Signed into law by President Gerald Ford on January 4, 1975, this law provided for, among other provisions, the following:

1. The creation of a state-federal child support enforcement program under a new part D of title IV of the Social Security Act - now generally referred to as the "IV-D program."

2. Was to be a new partnership between the states and the federal government, whose purpose was directly tied to the existing federal program of cash assistance, or "welfare," under the Title IV-A, "Assistance to Families with Dependent Children" (AFDC).

3. Specifically, the new IV-D program was designed to accomplish two welfare system-related goals through the enforcement of child support: (1) "cost recovery" or the recovery, for the state and federal governments, of the costs of public assistance paid out to families; and (2) "cost avoidance," or to help families on welfare leave the public assistance rolls and help families not yet on welfare avoid having to turn to public assistance.

4. By and large, all applicants for, and recipients of, AFDC would have to accept IV-D services and cooperate with the state IV-D agency as a condition of initial and continuing eligibility for public assistance, and in order to limit the growth of the public assistance rolls, the IV-D services would be available to families not on AFDC. These non-public assistance families could voluntarily apply for IV-D services; they could, also, close their IV-D cases at any time.

5. It assigned specific roles to the state and federal governments in the operation of the new program. In order to receive federal AFDC funding, each state was to designate an agency to administer the IV-D child support enforcement in the state. It could be an entirely new agency or an existing agency (e.g., the state human services agency), but the state's IV-D agency had to be "a single and separate organizational unit," wherever located. Moreover, the state IV-D program had to be statewide, although it could be administered on the county level.

9

6. While the primary task of the states was to administer the child support enforcement program, the primary role of the federal government, through a federal Office of Child Support Enforcement (OCSE) in the, now, Department of Health and Human Services, was: to share the costs of the state's administrative expenditures for the program; to award states with incentive payments for program performance; to provide technical assistance; and to exercise regulatory oversight, which limits included making recommendations to Congress for legislative changes to strengthen the IV-D program and auditing state program performance on a triennial basis.

7. Provisions establishing a Federal Parent Locator Service in the Department of Health, Education, and Welfare with access to all Federal records, and which would draw upon various data resources of the federal government to locate "absent" parents for the purpose of establishing paternity and/or establishing and enforcing a child support obligation.

The 1974 Act stated the mission of the IV-D program as: "enforcing the support obligations owed by absent parents to their children and the spouse (or former spouse) with whom such children are living, locating absent parents, establishing paternity, obtaining child and spousal support, and assuring that assistance in obtaining support will be available . . . to all children (whether or not eligible for aid under [the AFDC program], for whom such assistance is requested." Thus, President Gerald Ford, very reluctantly, and while expressing the concerns of many both inside and outside Congress at the time about "injecting the Federal government into domestic relations [law]," did sign the H.R. 17045 into law on January 4, 1975, and the Title IV-D program was born.

OTHER RELATED LAWS & ACTIONS PRIOR TO THE 1975 LAW

Although the IV-D program was the principal law that established a new kind of state-federal partnership in child support enforcement, the IV-D program was not without its antecedents. The other significant laws that preceded the 1975 law include the following:

1. Social Security Act Amendments of 1950

Nearly a quarter of a century earlier, Congress had enacted the Social Security Act Amendments of 1950 which added § 402(a)(11) to the Act, 42 U.S.C. § 602(a)(11), requiring state AFDC agencies to notify appropriate law enforcement officials when a child received AFDC because of abandonment or desertion by a parent. The central intent was that these parents be held responsible for the support of their minor children, not thrusting that cost upon the government and, ultimately, the taxpayer.

2. Uniform Reciprocal Enforcement of Support Act (URESA) of 1950.

Also in 1950, the National Conference of Commissioners on Uniform Laws and the American Bar Association approved the Uniform Reciprocal Enforcement of Support Act (URESA) for the interstate enforcement of child support. URESA, a model act, was in time adopted by 48 states, with 2 other states, Iowa and New York, adopting something closely related to it. Under the Act's provisions, states could pursue either civil enforcement, by petition, or by the registration of an existing order or criminal extradition. And under the provisions of the 1996 Welfare Reform Act, Congress mandated that all states adopt verbatim the Uniform Interstate Family Support Act (UIFSA), a replacement for URESA providing greatly improved interstate procedures, in the form approved by the National Conference of Commissioners on Uniform Laws and the American Bar Association.

3. The Social Security Amendments of 1965. In spite of these laws, there continued to be a steady growth in the number of families turning to AFDC, due, in large part, to the desertion of children by their parents, combined with an increase in out-of-wedlock births. This growth of the welfare rolls led Congress to enact further legislation designed to make parents responsible for the support of their dependent children. Thus came the enactment in 1965 of the Social Security Amendments. This law allowed state and local welfare agencies to obtain the home and/or employment address of an absent parent from the files of the Department of Health, Education, and Welfare (the HEW, or the Department of Health and Human Services, today) under certain conditions (e.g., if the address could not be obtained from other sources and the child was an AFDC applicant or recipient).

4. 1967 Amendments. Further amendments to the Act in 1967 required the following:

a) The Secretary of HEW to provide a court having jurisdiction with the home and/or employment address of an absent parent for the purpose of issuing a child support order. b) The establishment in a state or local welfare agency of a single organizational unit responsible for the establishing paternity and collecting support from absent parents for children receiving AFDC.

c) To facilitate this child support effort, states were to enter into cooperative agreements with court and law enforcement officials, including financial arrangements.

d) Authorized the Internal Revenue Service (IRS), under statutory procedures, to yield information from its files for the purpose of locating an absent parent subject to a child support order or named in a petition for support.

Nevertheless, none of these legislative efforts made up to that point, had produced the results sought by Congress, as a 1972 report of the General Accounting Office (GAO) showed. Among the shortcomings reported by the GAO, were the following:

- States had failed to implement successfully the requirements of the 1967 amendments, but this failure was largely the result of bureaucratic ineptitude on the part of HEW.
- HEW was approving state AFDC plans without carefully scrutinizing state mechanisms for enforcing child support in AFDC cases or monitoring results.
- HEW was providing no guidance to states in pursuing ways to strengthen their child support activities to yield greater results.

The response of Congress to the GAO report was to seek to develop a national program with a significant federal oversight and direction designed to reduce dependence upon the government welfare program whose caseload, by 1971, had grown to 10 million, double what it was in 1967. One notable leader in that national effort, was Senator Russell Long, the then Chairman of the Senate Finance Committee. In 1971, Long offered the Bill, S. 3019, proposed as a reform of the AFDC system whose thrust would be to shift responsibility for the support of minor children from the taxpayer to the parents whom, in floor remarks on his legislation, Long characterized as "deadbeats." After several years of repeated failures to get a comprehensive child support enforcement bill adopted by both chambers of Congress, in 1974 the proposed child support provisions were finally incorporated into the H.R. 17045, a bill which redesigned federally funded social services. Thus, *the Social Services Amendments of 1974* were enacted with provisions creating a national child support enforcement program under part D of title IV of the Social Security Act. And, very reluctantly, and expressing the concerns of many both inside and outside Congress about "injecting the Federal government into domestic relations [law]," President Gerald Ford signed H.R. 17045 into law on January 4, 1975 as the Social Services Amendments of 1974, and the Title IV-D program was born.

B. THE HISTORICAL DEVELOPMENT OF THE NATIONAL CHILD SUPPORT ENFORCEMENT PROGRAM

As has been pointed out by several family law experts such as Laura W. Morgan and others, the enactment of Title IV-D represented a bold step of Congress into the arena of family state law, an area that Congress could constitutionally contend to go into only on the basis of there being a "nexus" that presumably exist between such a legislative act and the enumerated powers of Congress under Article 1, section 8, of the U.S. Constitution and other categories of congressional authority under the Tenth Amendment. That "nexus" with respect to the establishment of the Title IV-D program lay in the spending powers of Congress in funding the AFDC cash assistance program under Title IV-A. Says Morgan:

> "Although traditionally the domain of the states and beyond the reach of the federal government, child support became a concern of Congress to the extent that the location of absent parents, the establishment of paternity, and the establishment and enforcement of child support obligations had an impact upon the federal purse through the financial assistance paid families under the Title IV-A entitlement program. While participation in the AFDC program was voluntary on the part of the states, their participation in it, and the receipt of federal funds through it, was conditioned upon their meeting various federal requirements, including establishing child support enforcement programs under Title IV-D."

The 1975 Act laid the foundation for a program that, within a few years, grew in complexity, both with respect to its regulatory mechanisms and the statutory mandates it imposed upon the states, changing the character of family law in most matters affecting the parent-child relationship. As noted above, as a condition of receiving federal AFDC funds:

- States had to establish a child support enforcement program meeting federal requirements under Title IV-D of the Social Security Act. This meant operating the state program according to a "State plan" approved by the Secretary of, now, the federal Department of Health and Human Services, through the Office of Child Support Enforcement (OCSE).
- The Secretary, that is the OCSE, was responsible for establishing and operating the FPLS drawing upon information available from federal agencies, while state IV-D agencies had responsibility for maintaining a State Parent Locator Service (SPLS) drawing upon various state sources (e.g., drivers' licensing bureaus).
- The Secretary establishes standards for the operation of state IV-D programs, conducting audits of state program performance, providing states with various kinds of technical assistance, and certifying cases to the IRS for services to collect support delinquencies where the collection efforts of the state IV-D agency failed.
- For their part, state IV-D agencies had to provide enforcement services to all AFDC applicants and recipients, who, in turn, had to accept these services unless there was a finding of "good cause" for not doing so (e.g., potential harm to the custodial parent and/or child).
- The enforcement services provided by the state agency included locating the absent (non-custodial) parent, using the resources of the FPLS and SPLS, and, as needed, establishing paternity and establishing and enforcing a support obligation.
- In providing these services, state IV-D agencies were to enter into cooperative agreements with appropriate courts and law enforcement officials and to cooperate with the IV-D agency of any other state in locating absent parents, establishing paternity, and securing support.
- The wages of federal employees (including members of the military) could be garnished for child and spousal support; the federal courts were given jurisdiction to hear and determine any civil action in any interstate child support cases certified by the Secretary.
- Prescribes procedures for the distribution of support collections in both AFDC and non-AFDC cases.

1976 - The Unemployment Compensation Amendments.

This Amendment made by Congress, required state employment security agencies to provide state AFDC and IV-D agencies, upon request, with information concerning the address of any non-custodial parent, as well as concerning such a parent's receipt of, or application for, unemployment insurance benefits and response to offers of employment.

1976 - Tax Reduction and Simplification Act.

Under this Act, the conditions and procedures for garnishing the wages of federal employees were clarified and extended by Congress to include employees of the District of Columbia. Also, state plan provisions, 42 U.S.C. § 654, were amended to require IV-D agencies to provide bonding for employees receiving, handling, and disbursing cash and to separate accounting and collection functions within the state IV-D agency.

1977 - The Medicare-Medicaid Anti-Fraud and Abuse Amendments.

Congress provided for a medical support enforcement program enabling states to require Medicaid recipients to assign their rights to medical support to a state as a condition for receipt of benefits. Moreover, a state's Medicaid agency was authorized to enter into cooperative agreements with other appropriate agencies of the state, including the IV-D agency, to help enforce assignments and collect medical support amounts. This set the stage for the later (1987) requirement that state IV-D agencies provide enforcement services to Medicaid families with an absent parent, regardless of whether or not they also received AFDC (so-called "Medicaid-only" cases).

1978 - An Act to Establish a Uniform Law on the Subject of Bankruptcies.

The provision under the Social Security Act, 42 U.S.C. § 656(h), barring the discharge in bankruptcy of assigned child support rights was repealed and placed instead in the provisions of the new Act. In addition, specific exceptions to discharge in bankruptcy were identified, including maintenance or support due a spouse, former spouse, or a child of the debtor under a separation agreement, divorce decree, or property settlement.

1978 - The Financial Institutions Regulatory and Interest Rate Control Act

Financial institutions were authorized to disclose account information to a governmental authority where there was a possible violation of any statute or regulation, thus enabling OCSE to again further locate information on delinquent obligors.

1980 - The Social Security Disability Amendments.

Extended the use of "full collection" services of the IRS to non-AFDC cases enforced by the state IV-D agency. It also made federal matching funds at the rate of 90 percent available for the enhancement of automated systems used by state IV-D programs, subject to an approved "advance planning document." Most importantly, it authorized access by state IV-D agencies to wage information held by state employment security agencies and the Social Security Administration to assist in establishing and enforcing child support obligations.

1980- Adoption Assistance and Child Welfare Act

Made the federal cost-sharing and matching funds for the administrative expenditures of state IV-D agencies in providing services to non-AFDC families, permanent. Up to this point, such funding had been tentative, being periodically renewed, because of the belief that, in time, services to non-public assistance families could be entirely funded out of fees for services. By 1980, it had become apparent that without guaranteed, continuing federal sharing of the costs of providing enforcement services to non-AFDC families, state IV-D agencies would be less than fully committed to providing those services.

1981 - The Omnibus Budget Reconciliation Act.

- Congress provided the IV-D program, through the so-called "IRS intercept" mechanism, with an enforcement tool that has proved to be one of the most effective means of collecting past-due child support the program has ever; it required the Secretary of the Treasury to withhold from refunds of annual personal income taxes, any amounts certified by the Secretary of Health and Human Services owed as past-due child support. (The "IRS intercept" procedure has enabled state IV-D agencies to collect effectively on support delinquencies in both public assistance and non-public assistance cases.)
- Withholding was provided for child support from unemployment insurance benefits, either through an agreement between the IV-D agency and the support obligor or by legal processes.
- The Act also required state IV-D agencies to collect spousal support for AFDC families and re-instituted under the Social Security Act the non-dischargeability in bankruptcy proceedings of any child support amount assigned to the state (which provision had been repealed in 1978). Three years later, under the Bankruptcy Amendments and Federal Judgeship Act of 1984, any debt for court-ordered child support was made non-dischargeable, whether or not the debtor parent had ever been married to the child's other parent.

1984 - The Child Support Enforcement Amendments.

- These Amendments dramatically increased federal oversight and control of the child support enforcement program and brought some major changes to both the IV-D program and to state domestic relations law - propelling the process of "federalization" vastly forward. A major objective of Congress in drafting the 1984 Amendments was to achieve some degree of uniformity among the states in the enforcement of child support, to see that "best practices" were used by all states, as well as to ensure that state IV-D programs served public assistance and non-public assistance families equally well.

- There were to be specific requirements for state law, not just state IV-D procedures. States were required to have "statutorily prescribed procedures" under which all new or modified child support orders issued in a state on or after October 1, 1985, included a provision for income withholding when an arrearage occurs
- . In IV-D cases, state law had to allow the interception of state income tax for the enforcement of child support obligations.
- State law had to provide for the imposition of liens against real and personal property and of security or bonds to ensure compliance with support obligations.
- State law must allow for the bringing of a paternity action until a child's 18th birthday, and states had to establish administrative or judicial expedited processes for establishing and enforcing child support orders, and, at the option of the state, establishing paternity.
- Title IV-D agencies were required to report to consumer credit bureaus the names of the delinquent obligors and the amounts of past-due support.
- Both AFDC and non-AFDC cases were made subject to the same mandatory practices and case processing standards. The interception of federal income tax refunds for past-due support was extended to non-AFDC cases, federal incentive payments were authorized for collections in non-AFDC cases (although limited under a "cost-effectiveness" ratio of collections to administrative expenditures)
- Interstate enforcement of child support was strengthened through new enforcement procedures, federal incentives, and federal audits.
- The further development of automated data systems by IV-D agencies was encouraged through 90 percent federal match rate for the acquisition of computer hardware.
- Finally, parent locator services were strengthened by allowing state IV-D agencies to access the FPLS directly, without first having to exhaust state locator resources, and the social security numbers of absent parents were made available to state IV-D agencies either through the FPLS or the IRS.

- States were required to formulate discretionary guidelines for the setting of child support obligations by courts and other tribunals authorized to issue support orders.
- To increase the use as well as the credibility of objective criteria for the setting of support amounts, the Act required each state, by October 1, 1987, to establish "by law or by judicial or administrative action" guidelines for determining support award amounts within the state.

States and their IV-D agencies had scarcely begun to deal with the many requirements under the 1984 Amendments, before Congress enacted the next major piece of legislation affecting child support enforcement: the Family Support Act of 1988 (FSA).

1988 - Family Support Act (FSA).

- While most of the child support enforcement provisions directly related to the operations of the state IV-D program, some had an impact on ALL child support cases, both IV-D and non-IV-D. One of these was the requirement that the hitherto discretionary guidelines for setting current support amounts be made mandatory and that such guidelines be reviewed by the state at least once every four years. The primary rationale behind that was the wide belief that if a case were packed within the guidelines, it had a high presumption or probability that the amount of support awarded through that would be just and appropriate in the case. State IV-D agencies were required to review each support order in their non-AFDC caseload every 36 months and, if necessary, adjust the support amount in accordance with the state guidelines. They were also required to "review and modify" in non-AFDC cases at the request of either parent.
- The FSA made significant changes to state income withholding procedures. In cases being enforced by the state IV-D agency, orders issued or modified on or after the 25th month following enactment of the FSA (November 1, 1990) had to provide for immediate income withholding unless (1) one of the parties demonstrates, and the court finds, that there is good cause not to require such withholding or (2) there is a written agreement between the parties with respect to an alternative arrangement. Furthermore, under state aw all child support orders initially issued in a state on or after January 1, 1994, had to provide for immediate income withholding, whether or not the order was enforced by the IV-D agency.
- While the FSA "encouraged" states to adopt simple civil processes for the establishment of paternity, it set new performance standards for establishing paternity in cases being enforced under Title IV-D. With respect to locating parents in a child support action, state law dealing with the issuance of a birth certificate had to require each parent to furnish a social security number, unless the state found good cause in a particular case for not doing so. Although not appearing on the birth certificate, the social security number(s) had to be made available for child support enforcement purposes.

OTHER CHILD SUPPORT LAWS WHICH PRE-DATE THE 'BIG ONE' – THE 1996 LAW

The next major federal child support legislation was the one which came in 1996 (see the PRWORA laws below). However, in every year intervening between the enactment of FSA and PRWORA, except for 1991, Congress passed one child support enforcement legislation of one sort or the other.

1992 - Child Support Recovery Act of 1992. This Act imposes a federal penalty for the willful failure to pay a past-due child support obligation with respect to a child residing in another state where the obligation has remained unpaid for longer than one year or is greater than $5,000. For a first conviction, the penalty is a fine of up to $5,000, imprisonment for not more than 6 years, or both. A second conviction carries a penalty of a fine up to $250,000, imprisonment for up to 2 years, or both.

1992 - The Ted Weiss Child Support Enforcement Act. This amended the Fair Credit Reporting Act to require consumer credit reporting bureaus to include in any consumer credit report information on child support delinquencies that is provided by IV-D agencies and that antedates the report by seven years.

1993 - Omnibus Budget Reconciliation Act of 1993.

Among other child support enforcement provisions of this law, is the provision that the federal "encouragement" in the FSA with respect to states' development of simple civil procedures for paternity establishment, became a federal mandate by way of requiring states to adopt laws under which paternity may be voluntarily acknowledged (including through hospital-based programs). This Act also mandated state laws (1) ensuring compliance by health insurers and employers in carrying out court or administrative orders for medical child support and (2) prohibiting health insurers from denying coverage to children who are not living with the covered individual or who were born outside marriage.

1994 - Full Faith and Credit for Child Support Orders Act. This law required each state to enforce a child support order issued by a court or other tribunal of a sister state, and laid out conditions and specifications for resolving issues of jurisdiction.

1994 - The Bankruptcy Reform Act of 1994. It provided that the filing of a bankruptcy does not "stay" (stop from execution) a paternity, child support, or alimony proceeding; that child and spousal support payments are priority claims; and that custodial parents may appear in bankruptcy court to protect their interests, without the requirement of paying a fee or meeting any local rules for attorney appearances.

1996 - The Personal Responsibility and Work Opportunity Reconciliation Act (PRWORA), which ended the cash public assistance entitlement and transformed AFDC into TANF: "Temporary Assistance for Needy Families."

Simply stated, with the enactment of the PRWORA laws in 1996, the long-standing scheme for "federalization" of state domestic relations law moved to a point that even the legislative founders of the IV-D program could not possibly have imagined. Title III of the voluminous 1996 Act contains literally dozens of new federal mandates, most of them affecting the procedures and operations of the IV-D program, but many of them transforming state child support enforcement mechanisms in general.

The extensive PRWORA child support enforcement provisions include the following:

Requirement for the establishment at the state level of a "State Case Registry" and a "New Hire Directory," with federal counterparts ("Federal Case Registry of Child Support Orders" and the "National Directory of New Hires") within an expanded FPLS. The case registries contain information on all child support orders being enforced by the IV-D program and all other orders established or modified in a state on or after October 1, 1998. The new hire directories contain information reported by all employers (including state and federal governments) on all newly hired or rehired employees, beginning October 1, 1997. Information comparisons are conducted within the FPLS between the national case registry and new hire directory for the purpose of identifying parents who are subject to child support orders and reporting pertinent data (including locate information) to appropriate state IV-D agencies for the purpose of establishing and/or enforcing support obligations.

✓ States must also operate a "State Disbursement Unit" for collecting and disbursing child support payments in all IV-D cases and in non-IV-D cases with support orders initially entered in a state on or after January 1, 1994, under which the non-custodial parent is subject to income withholding. In addition, each state IV-D agency must enter into arrangements with all financial institutions in the state for quarterly data matches to identify and seize any assets of delinquent obligors in cases being enforced by the IV-D agency.

✓ It mandates numerous changes to state laws relating to paternity establishment, down to the last detail, including the denial of the availability of jury trial in a contested paternity action.

✓ It prescribes matters of notice and due process requirements in child support actions and requires the use of new enforcement remedies, including the suspension, denial, or limitation of professional, driver's, and recreational licenses and (in IV-D cases) passports for support delinquency.

✓ It requires Social security numbers on applications for every sort of license issued by a state, as well as in records for divorce decrees, support orders, paternity determinations or acknowledgments, and death certificates.

✓ It requires Child support liens to arise by operation of law and be enforceable across state lines, and standard forms promulgated by OCSE are to be used for interstate income withholding, liens, and administrative subpoenas.

✓ Other provisions of the Act greatly expand the state and federal data resources to which a state IV-D agency may have access for child support enforcement (including public and private records of various kinds) and bestow upon the IV-D agency administrative authority to undertake a number of legal actions "without the necessity of obtaining an order from any other judicial or administrative tribunal."

CONCLUSION

Summed up simply, with the enactment of the extensive child support enforcement provisions of PRWORA, the movement of federal law in the direction of "federalization" of state family law not only reached its highest historical heights in the nation's history, but become all pervasive in the lives of the American families. The central idea which powered this whole movement, was the belief shared by the President (Clinton), Congress, public policy groups, and special interest organizations, that there could be no real reform of the welfare system without an overhaul of the child support enforcement system. As these advocates saw it, the requirement that custodial parents move from welfare to work in order to support their families, had to be accompanied by the requirement that non-custodial parents pay child support to supplement the family income.

Surely, with this law, almost all child support orders became subject to IV-D enforcement services. And clearly, with this law, today's Congress no longer has any of the qualms about the intrusion of the federal government into domestic laws which the Congress of twenty-five years or so ago had. As Prof. Laura W. Morgan, a leading expert on the subject, sums it up, noting that historically Congress had deferred such domestic issues to the States, "In time, particularly from 1984 onward, this congressional acknowledgment of the historic primacy of states in family law matters was eroded by a succession of federal Acts mandating changes to state laws relating to the parent-child relationship, culminating in the 1996 welfare reform Act (PRWORA) which instituted far-reaching changes." Today, there's hardly any aspect of American family life or parent-child relationship, which is not deeply impacted and dramatically affected by pervasive federal intrusion and presence in family law matters, and the child support and collection enforcement operations of federal and state governments and courts on American parents.

CHAPTER 2

SUMMARY OF THE CHILD SUPPORT LAWS FOR EACH STATE, AND EACH STATE'S SUPPORT RIGHTS AND RESPONSIBILITIES OF THE PARENTS

Here in this Chapter we outline each State's specific provisions of the relevant child support laws, and how you may use them to gauge your rights and responsibilities as a parent, a custodial parent, or actual or potential child support payer.

ALABAMA: HOW CHILD SUPPORT IS DETERMINED

Alabama child support laws provide guidelines designed to be in the best interest of the children. Unless the parents have a written agreement stating a different amount, as well as a reasonable explanation for the difference, child support will be based on a percentage of the disposable net income of the parent responsible for support. Percentages of net income used to determine child support amounts in Alabama are outlined below. Other factors including second families, insurance and day care costs, may also be considered. Number of children to support from the marriage:

1 = 20%; 2 = 25%; 3 = 30%; 4 = 35%; 5 = 40%; 6 = 45%.

At what age does child support payments end? Generally, at 19 years of age.

Custody guidelines: Since January 1, 1997, Alabama officially favors joint custody if it is in the best interest of the child, and the parents agree. However, when parents disagree, custody may be granted to either parent with the following factors considered by the court in determining who is awarded custody:

- the age and sex of the child; the safety and well-being of the child; the moral character of the parents; the wishes of the child..

Medical insurance guidelines: Generally, a determination about who is going to provide medical health care insurance for the children and how uninsured medical bills will be paid is part of the marital settlement agreement set out in the divorce process. However, if a medical insurance plan is available through a parent's employment, they are required to cover their children on this plan.

How permanent are the provisions for Alabama child support and custody? As in most states, court orders providing for support and custody of children are subject to modification after a divorce if there is a substantial change in either of the parties' circumstances. For instance, a substantial increase or decrease in income could be reason to modify a court order. While all orders concerning the children are modifiable in the future, you are not encouraged to enter into an agreement based on the idea that it can always be changed or modified later.

Wage garnishment for child support payments: Alabama has a provision for withholding child support directly from the earnings of the parent who has been ordered to provide support. Withheld support is sent to the state agency authorized to receive and disburse payments and once verified, sent to the custodial parent.

How does joint custody work? Joint custody requires both parents to share the responsibilities for the children, and approve all major decisions related to the children. It rarely works out to be a 50-50 sharing of time with the children. Usually one parent is named as the primary joint custodian and the other parent is granted visitation "at all times mutually agreed" upon, and failing an agreement, the terms of the state's standard visitation policy is used

How Alabama determines child visitation: Alabama, like most states, use a standard visitation schedule that provides a safe and acceptable solution for those times when parents cannot mutually agree to a schedule of their own. With some minor differences, the standard visitation schedule includes: every other weekend; four to six (4-6) weeks during the summer; alternating holidays.

ARKANSAS: HOW CHILD SUPPORT IS DETERMINED

Either parent may be ordered to provide child support. Court order for a reasonable amount of child support is based on the following factors: the circumstances of the parents and the child; and the nature of the case. Arkansas has official state Child Support Guidelines that determine child support paid based on the parent's income and other financial factors. These guidelines are aimed to be in the best interests of the child. When the payer's income exceeds that on the state guideline chart, the following percentages are used:

One dependent: 15%; Two dependents: 21%; Three dependents: 25%; Four dependents: 28%; Five dependents: 30%; Six dependents: 32%.

The state Child Support Guidelines will be used by the court to determine the child support payments unless this amount is determined to be unjust, and the court makes written findings on the record that the application of the support chart would be unjust and inappropriate.

At what age does child support payments end? Generally, the obligation ends when the child reaches 18 years of age or the child graduates from high school, whichever occurs later. A child will also automatically be ineligible for child support if that child marries, is removed from disability status by a court order, or the child dies.

Custody guidelines: When it comes to awarding child custody in Arkansas, the decision will be made without regard to the sex of the parent. Joint custody may be awarded if it is found to be in the best interests of the child. The court considers the welfare and the best interests of the child, as well as the following factors:

- the circumstances of the parents and the child
- the nature of the case
- which parent is most likely to allow frequent and continuing contact with the other parent
- and any acts of domestic violence

Arkansas's medical insurance guidelines: Generally, a determination about who is going to provide medical health care insurance for the children and how uninsured medical bills will be paid is part of the marital settlement agreement set out in the divorce process. There is a standard medical order which requires both parents to carry medical insurance at their place of employment if it is available at a reasonable cost. Also under this order, each party is required to pay half of the medical expenses of the minor child not covered by the insurance. If the non-custodial parent has been ordered by the court to pay medical support or to maintain health care coverage, this parent is subject to income withholding for the health care coverage in Arkansas.

A court may issue an income deduction order to insure that the required health care coverage is being provided for the children of the parties. The income withholding order will become effective as soon as the child or children are enrolled in a health insurance coverage plan. Once activated, income withholding shall apply to current and subsequent periods of employment. Furthermore, income withholding for health care will have priority over all other legal processes against the earnings of the non-custodial parent except an income deduction order for child support.

How permanent are the provisions for Arkansas child support and custody? As in most states, court orders providing for support and custody of children are subject to modification after a divorce if there is a substantial change in either of the parties' circumstances, such as a significant increase or decrease in income. The criteria for a modified court order includes:

- both parents offer their consent for a modification
- there is a 20% or a $100 change per month in the payer's gross income

Reviews of court orders occur once every 36 months from the date of the most recent order or the most recent review. While all orders concerning the children are modifiable in the future, we encourage you to not enter into an agreement based on the idea that it can always be changed or modified later.

Wage garnishment for child support payments: Almost every state, including Arkansas, has a provision for withholding child support directly from the earnings of the parent who has been ordered to provide support. In fact, in Arkansas, all child support orders issued include a provision for immediate implementation of income withholding, barring any good reason not to require immediate withholding. The way money is withheld is very similar to the way income tax is withheld.

This way of paying and receiving child support is generally easier for both parties and considered a very dependable solution. The way it typically works is, once the support is withheld, it is then sent to the state agency authorized to receive and disburse payments. Once it has been verified that the support was paid, it is then sent to the custodial parent.

How does joint custody work? Joint or shared custody may be awarded if the court determines it is in the best interests of the child. Specifically, joint custody is a form of custody of minor children that requires both parents to share the responsibilities of the children, and for both parents to approve all major decisions related to the children.

While it is a 50-50 sharing of responsibilities and major decisions affecting the children, it rarely works out to be a 50-50 sharing of time with the children. Usually one parent is named as the primary joint custodian and the other parent is granted visitation. The primary joint custodian typically retains the decision making power to determine the child's primary residence and school and to designate things such as the child's primary physician.

How Arkansas determines child visitation: The state guidelines assume that the non-custodial parent or the parent who is not the primary joint custodian, has visitation rights every other weekend and for several weeks in the summer.

Is there a statute of limitations on collecting unpaid child support? Yes, prior to 1998 the statute of limitations was 10 years. In 1998 a change was made to the statute lowering it to 5 years, and was not retroactive. In other words, the custodial parent still has 10 years to collect those missed payments if the cases is prior to 1998. For all cases after 1998, the custodial parent only has five years.

In some instances, interest is applied to unpaid child support. There is a 10% interest penalty applied to missed child support payments. There is also a 10% interest penalty applied to adjudicated arrearage – in other words, past due child support payments for which there was a court order. There are, however, no interest payments applied to retroactive child support. The primary joint custodian typically retains the decision-making power to determine the child's primary residence and school and to designate things such as the child's primary physician.

ALASKA: HOW CHILD SUPPORT IS DETERMINED

Either or both parents may be ordered to provide child support. Alaska has set guidelines for child support, designed to be in the best interest of the children. Unless the parents have a written agreement stating a different amount, as well as a reasonable explanation for the difference, child support will be based on these Alaska guidelines. The only reasons to deviate from these standard guidelines would be:

- especially large family size
- significant income of a child
- health or other extraordinary expenses
- unusually low expenses
- the parent responsible for support has an income below poverty level

For non-custodial parents with income over $72,000, the above factors do not apply. In those instances, support ordered is based on:

an increased award that is just and proper in relation to the NCP's income; the needs of the children; the standard of living of the children; the extent to which the standard of living of the children should be reflective of the parent's ability to pay.

Each parent must file a verified statement of income. Support payments are based on a percentage of disposable net income of the parent responsible for support. Other factors including second families, insurance and day care costs may also be considered. Percentages of net income used to determine child support amounts in Alaska are: Number of children to support from the relationship:

- 1 = 20%; 2 = 27%; 3 = 33%; 4 = 36%; 5 = 39%; 6 = 42%.

At what age does child support payments end? Generally, the obligation ends when the child reaches 18 years of age.

State's custody guidelines: Neither parent is considered to be entitled to custody. Custody is determined with the best interests the child in mind. The factors the court in Alaska considers include:

- the capacity and desire of each parent to meet the child's needs;
- the physical, emotional, mental, religious and social needs of the child
- the preference of the child if considered old enough to make that decision

- the love and affection between the child and each parent
- the length of time the child has lived in a stable environment and the desire to maintain continuity
- the desire and ability of each parent to allow an open and loving and frequent relationship between the child and the other parent
- any evidence of domestic violence
- any evidence of substance abuse that affects the emotional or physical well-being of the child
- any other relevant factors

Alaska's medical insurance guidelines: Generally, a determination about who is going to provide medical health care insurance for the children and how uninsured medical bills will be paid is part of the marital settlement agreement set out in the divorce process. However, if a medical insurance plan is available through a parent's employment, they are required to cover their children on this plan. When one parent provides the medical insurance, credit is usually granted, and the amount used to pay for the medical insurance is subtracted from child support obligation.

How permanent are the provisions for Alaska child support and custody? As in most states, court orders providing for support and custody of children are subject to modification after a divorce if there is a substantial change in either of the parties' circumstances. For example, in Alaska, the child support agency or the courts can modify the court order if the non-custodial parent's income has increased or decreased by at least 15% since the last order. This is just one example. There are other reasons that could qualify an order to be modified. While all orders concerning the children are modifiable in the future, we encourage you to not enter into an agreement based on the idea that it can always be changed or modified later.

Wage garnishment for child support payments: Almost every state, including Alaska, has a provision for withholding child support directly from the earnings of the parent who has been ordered to provide support. It is very similar to the way income tax is withheld. This way of paying and receiving child support is generally easier for both parties and considered a very dependable solution. The way it typically works is, once the support is withheld, it is then sent to the state agency authorized to receive and disburse payments. Once it has been verified that the support was paid, it is then sent to the custodial parent. If a non-custodial parent can show that they are providing more than 50 percent of the support for dependents not included in the court order from a second marriage, and is not in arrears, no more than 50% of their disposable income can be attached if they cannot pay the full court-ordered amount of both orders.

That number goes to 55% if the non-custodial parent is in arrears, 60 percent for a person only providing support to dependents under the current order, and 65% for a person who is in arrears and paying only on the current order.

How does joint custody work? If parents do not agree to joint custody between themselves, the court can award joint or shared custody. Most all states are now encouraging parents to work together for the benefit of the children and agree to joint custody. Specifically, joint custody is a form of custody of minor children that requires both parents to share the responsibilities of the children, and for both parents to approve all major decisions related to the children.

While it is a 50-50 sharing of responsibilities and major decisions affecting the children, it rarely works out to be a 50-50 sharing of time with the children. Usually one parent is named as the primary joint custodian and the other parent is granted visitation "at all times mutually agreed" upon, and failing an agreement, following the terms of the state's standard visitation policy. The primary joint custodian typically retains the decision making power to determine the child's primary residence and school and to designate things such as the child's primary physician.

How Alaska determines child visitation: Through the years, a standard visitation schedule has emerged that most states, including Alaska, consider being in the best interest of the children. Although parents are generally free to visit with their children at all times mutually agreed to by the parents, this standard visitation schedule provides a safe and acceptable solution for those times when parents cannot mutually agree. With some minor differences, the standard visitation schedule includes: every other weekend; four to six (4-6) weeks during the summer; alternating holidays.

ARIZONA: HOW CHILD SUPPORT IS DETERMINED

Child support is based on the "Income Shares" model. The court will approximate the amount that would have been spent on the kids if the parents and the children were living together. Then each parent will be ordered to contribute a proportionate share of the total child support.

Because the custodial parent's support obligation is satisfied by the daily care of the child, he or she is not required to render payment to the child support registry. The court is also responsible for including in the record a finding of gross income, adjusted gross income and the total child support order. However, if the court makes the determination to deviate from the "Income Shares Model," the factors listed below provide the framework for the child support order:

- financial resources and the child's needs
- financial resources and needs of the custodial parent
- child's standard of living during the marriage
- child's educational and physical needs
- possible fraudulent dispositions of community property
- duration of visitations and related expenses

The child support obligation has priority over all other financial obligations. Non-support related expenditures and the support of step-children and parents do not justify a deviation from the "Income Shares Model" support guideline.

At what age does child support payments end? Generally, when the child reaches 18 years of age or graduates from high school, whichever occurs later. A child automatically becomes ineligible for child support if he/she marries, is adopted, or dies.

Arizona's custody guidelines: No preference is given based on the sex of the parent. The court considers the best interests of the child, and the following factors:

- the preference of the child
- the desire and ability of each parent to allow for an open and loving and frequent relationship between the child and the other parent
- the wishes of each parent
- the child's adjustment to his/her own home, school and community
- the mental and physical health of the child and both parents
- the relationships between the child, the parents and any siblings
- evidence of significant physical abuse
- any coercion or duress in obtaining a custody agreement
- who has provided primary care of the child

23

- any evidence of drug abuse

Arizona's medical insurance guidelines: Generally, medical health care insurance and uninsured medical bills will be decided as part of the divorce agreement. However, if a medical insurance plan is available through a parent's employment, they are required to cover their children on this plan.

How permanent are the provisions for Arizona child support and custody? Court orders for support and custody of children are subject to modification if there is a substantial change in either of the parties' circumstances, such as a significant increase or decrease in income.

Wage garnishment for child support payments: Arizona has a provision for withholding child support directly from the earnings of the parent who has been ordered to provide support. Typically, the support is withheld and then sent to the state agency authorized to receive and disburse payments. Once verified, the support is sent to the custodial parent.

How does joint custody work? Joint custody requires both parents to share the responsibilities including approving all major decisions related to the children. Joint or shared custody may be awarded if both parents submit a written agreement providing for joint or shared custody, and the court determines it's in the best interests of the child. The court can order joint custody over the objection of one of the parents. The primary joint custodian typically retains the decision making power to determine the child's primary residence and school and to designate things such as the child's primary physician.

How Arizona determines child visitation: Arizona uses a standard visitation schedule considered to be in the best interests of the children. Although parents are generally free to visit with their children at all times mutually agreed to by the parents, the standard visitation schedule provides a safe and acceptable solution for those times when parents cannot mutually agree: every other weekend; four to six (4-6) weeks during the summer; alternating holidays.

CALIFORNIA: HOW CHILD SUPPORT IS DETERMINED

The father and mother have an equal duty to support their child in a manner suitable to the child's circumstances. There is a mandatory minimum amount of child support outlined in the state guidelines, and this amount will be used unless there is a reasonable agreement between the parents. Often today, parents make an agreement as to an amount of child support that is reasonable as part of their parenting plan or their marital settlement. These stipulated agreements are usually recognized by the court.

However, agreements and stipulations between parents to compromise the parents' child support obligations or remove the case from the court's jurisdiction are void. Such agreements contradict the public policy to maintain the child support obligation of the non-custodial parent. Some counties may order mediation to reach an agreement between parents. All agreements and stipulations for child support must be in writing. Stipulation forms provided by the court should be used and must contain all information, including a statement of the guidelines of support and the "agreement language." IF AFDC is owed for public assistance, the representative of the DA office paying the assistance must sign the agreement. California's state child support guidelines consider such thing as the current income of both parents and the amount of time the children spend with each parent.

At what age does child support payments end? The child support obligation continues past 18 years of age, as long as the child is unmarried, is a full-time high school student and is not self-supporting.

24

In this case, the child support obligation will end when the child reaches 19 years of age or graduates high school, whichever of these occurs first.

Custody guidelines: The California courts may award joint or sole custody based on the best interests of the child. The following order of preference is given to the different types of custody:

1. joint custody or sole custody to one parent based on the best interest of the child; preferences will not be made based on the sex of the parent
2. custody to neither parent; custody would go to the person where the child has been living in a stable environment
3. custody to any other person or persons deemed, by the court, to be suitable and able to provide adequate care and guidance to the child

In determining which parent will maintain custody, the court will consider which parent is more likely to allow the child frequent contact with the other parent. There is no preference or presumption for or against joint legal custody, joint physical custody or sole custody. Complete discretion is given to the court. In all cases, the court may appoint a child custody evaluator to determine the best interest of the child. The evaluator will file a written confidential report of the evaluation 10 days before the hearing.

California's medical insurance guidelines: In a proceeding for child support, the court will consider the health insurance coverage part of the child support order if it is available to any of the parties at a reasonable cost through one of their employers. In any action instituted by a local child support agency for payment of child support, a completed state medical insurance form will be completed and sent by the local child support agency to the department of child support services.

How permanent are the provisions for California child support and custody? As in most states, court orders providing for support and custody of children are subject to change or modification due to changes in income and circumstances. Once a year, either spouse can require the other parent to complete an income and expense form to determine if a formal petition for a court order change should be filed. While all orders concerning the children are modifiable in the future, it is not advisable to not enter into an agreement based on the idea that it can always be changed or modified later.

Wage garnishment for child support payments: Almost every state, including California, has a provision for withholding child support directly from the earnings of the parent who has been ordered to provide support. In fact, in California, all child support orders must now include language for a mandatory income deduction order. The child support is then directly withheld from the earnings of the paying parent. It is withheld much like income tax is withheld. This way of paying and receiving child support is generally easier for both parties and considered a very dependable solution. Once the support is withheld, it is then sent by the employer to the state agency authorized to receive and disburse payments. Once it has been verified that the support was paid, it is then sent to the custodial parent.

If a non-custodial parent can show that they are providing more than 50 percent of the support for dependents not included in the court order from a second marriage, and is not in arrears, no more than 50% of their disposable income can be attached if they cannot pay the full court-ordered amount of both orders. That number goes to 55% if the non-custodial parent is in arrears, 60 percent for a person only providing support to dependents under the current order, and 65% for a person who is in arrears and paying only on the current order.

How does joint custody work? Joint or shared custody may be awarded if the court determines it's in ~~~~ interests or the child, and the parents have submitted an agreement requesting joint custody. Joint custody means joint legal and joint physical custody as defined below:

- joint legal custody - both parents share the right and responsibility to make the decisions relating to the health, education and welfare of the child
- joint physical custody - each of the parents have significant periods of physical custody of the child to assure the child frequent and continuing contact with both parents

While it is a 50-50 sharing of responsibilities and major decisions affecting the children, it rarely works out to be a 50-50 sharing of time with the children. Usually one parent is named as the primary joint custodian and the other parent is granted visitation.

How California determines child visitation: Generally, parents are free to visit with their children at all times that are mutually agreed to by both parents. However, when parents cannot agree, the standard visitation schedule is: every other weekend; four to six (4-6) weeks during the summer; alternating holidays.

COLORADO: HOW CHILD SUPPORT IS DETERMINED

Either parent may be ordered to provide child support. The factors the court considers include:

- the financial resources of the child
- the financial resources of the custodial parents
- the standard of living the child would have enjoyed if the marriage had not ended
- the physical, emotional and educational needs of the child
- the financial resources and needs of the non-custodial parent

Colorado has specific, standardized child support guidelines that outline the amounts to be paid. The court will follow these guidelines, which are assumed to be in the best interests of the child, unless the parents have agreed to an amount of child support considered fair and reasonable. Generally it's at least equal to the amount calculated by using the state guidelines.

At what age does child support payments end? If your child support order was entered on or after July, 1997, the support obligation stops when the child turns 19 unless:

- the parties agree otherwise by a stipulation signed after July 1997
- the child is mentally or physically disabled, and the court orders past age 19
- the child is in high school, or an equivalent program; in this case, support continues until a month after graduation but not beyond the age of 21

Custody guidelines: Joint or sole custody may be awarded by the Colorado courts based on the best interests of the child, without regard to the sex of the parents, and the following factors:

- the preference of the child if the child is sufficiently mature and capable of independent thinking
- the desire and ability of each parent to allow for an open, loving and frequent relationship between the child and the other parent

26

- the wishes of the parents regarding parenting time
- the child's adjustment to his or her home, school and community
- the mental and physical health of all involved
- any child abuse or spouse abuse by either parent
- the relationship of the child to the parents and siblings
- the ability of the parents to make joint decisions
- the ability as joint custodians to provide a positive and nourishing relationship with the child
- physical proximity of the parents
- whether joint custody would promote more frequent or continued contact between the child and both parents
- the ability of each party to place the need of the child ahead of his or her own needs

Colorado's medical insurance guidelines: Either or both parents must include the child under a medical insurance policy currently offered by their respective employers, or purchase or in some manner provide medical insurance for the child. The payment of a premium for medical insurance for the child will be added to the basic child support obligation and will be divided between the parents in proportion to their income.

How permanent are the provisions for Colorado child support and custody? The court will grant a modification of the initial court order if it finds that there has been a substantial and continuing change of circumstances or if it finds that the order does not contain a provision for medical support such as insurance coverage, payment for medical insurance deductibles and co-payments or un-reimbursed medical expenses. If there is less than a 10% change in the amount of support owed after applying the child support guidelines, the change is not considered a substantial and continuing change of circumstance and no modification will be granted.

Wage garnishment for child support payments: Colorado has a provision for withholding child support directly from the earnings of the parent obligated to provide support. It is withheld much like income tax is withheld from earnings payments. This way of paying and receiving child support is generally easier for both parties and considered a very dependable solution. The way it typically works is, once the support is withheld, it is then sent to the state agency authorized to receive and disburse payments. Once it has been verified that the support was paid, it is then sent to parent designated to receive the support.

Employers must honor out-of-state wage withholding orders as if the order were issued in Colorado. An employer that fails to comply with the terms of the wage withholding is liable for contempt of court charges. If a non-custodial parent can show that they are providing more than 50 percent of the support for dependents not included in the court order from a second marriage, and is not in arrears, no more than 50% of their disposable income can be attached if they cannot pay the full court-ordered amount of both orders. That number goes to 55% if the non-custodial parent is in arrears, 60 percent for a person only providing support to dependents under the current order, and 65% for a person who is in arrears and paying only on the current order.

How does joint custody work? Joint custody is a sharing of time with the child and a sharing of rights and responsibilities of the parents regarding major decisions. If the court finds that awarding joint custody is in the best interest of the child, then it will order it. Whether joint or sole custody is awarded, the court wants the parties to encourage continuing and frequent contact between the child and each parent.

How Colorado determines child visitation: Generally, parents are free to visit with their children at all times that are mutually agreed to by both parents. However, when parents cannot agree, the standard visitation schedule, now accepted in most states, is: every other weekend; four to six (4-6) weeks during the summer; alternating holidays.

CONNECTICUT: HOW CHILD SUPPORT IS DETERMINED

Either parent may be ordered to provide child support based on the following factors:

- the financial resources of the child
- the occupation and earning capacity of each parent
- the amount and sources of income for each parent
- the age and health of the child
- the estate and needs of the child
- the relative financial needs of the parents

Connecticut has **official child support guidelines** that outline the amounts to be paid that are based on a percentage of the income of the paying parent. These guidelines, which are assumed to be in the best interests of the child, will be followed unless the parents have agreed to an amount of child support considered fair and reasonable by the court – generally at least equal to the amount calculated by using the state guidelines.

The following percentages of net income are a general basis used in the Connecticut state child support guidelines. (The court may deviate from these guidelines only if the court believes it is in the best interest of the child to do so).

one child 20%; two children 25%; three children 30 %; four children 35%; five children 40%; six children 45%

At what age does child support payments end? If there is an unmarried child that's reached 18, is a full-time high school student and lives with one of the parents, the parents will maintain their respective support if the child needs it, until the child completes the twelfth grade or reaches 19 years of age, whichever comes first. If the child becomes emancipated, the obligation to pay support ends.

State's custody guidelines: Joint or sole custody may be awarded by the Connecticut courts based on the best interests of the child and the following factors (Connecticut family law presumes that joint custody is the preferred form of custody if both parents have agreed to it):

the reason for divorce if it's relevant to the best interests of the child; the wishes of the child if the child is capable of forming an intelligent choice and is of reasonable age; whether the party or parties satisfactorily completed the parenting education program as required by the court.

Connecticut's medical insurance guidelines: Generally, the decision as to which parent is going to provide medical insurance coverage for the child and how medical bills will be paid is set out in the marital settlement agreement of the divorcing parents. If it's not, in Connecticut, either parent may be ordered by the court to provide medical insurance for the child. But generally, if a reasonable medical insurance plan is available through a parent's employment, they are required to cover their child on it.

How permanent are the provisions for Connecticut child support and custody? As in most states, court orders providing for support and custody of children are subject to change or modification to reflect changes in income, and/or living arrangements of the children and the child's special needs.

28

Wage garnishment for child support payments: Almost every state, including Connecticut, has a provision for withholding child support directly from the earnings of the parent who has been ordered to provide support. It is withheld much like income tax is withheld from earnings payments.

Once the support is withheld, it is then sent to the state agency authorized to receive and disburse payments. Once it has been verified that the support was paid, it is then sent to the parent designated to receive the support. If a non-custodial parent can show that they are providing more than 50 percent of the support for dependents not included in the court order from a second marriage, and is not in arrears, no more than 50% of their disposable income can be attached if they cannot pay the full court-ordered amount of both orders. That number goes to 55% if the non-custodial parent is in arrears, 60 percent for a person only providing support to dependents under the current order, and 65% for a person who is in arrears and paying only on the current order.

How does joint custody work? There has been a nationwide movement encouraging parents to work together for the best interests of their children. Joint custody is now widely recognized by parents, courts and state legislatures as the preferred parenting plan for divorcing parents. Joint custody is presumed to be the form of custody that's in the best interests of the child, if both parents have agreed to it. Specifically, joint custody is a form of custody of minor children that requires both parents to share the responsibilities of the children, and for both parents to approve all major decisions related to the children.

While it is a 50-50 sharing of responsibilities and major decisions affecting the children, it rarely works out to be a 50-50 sharing of time with the children. Usually one parent is named as the residential custodian and the other parent is granted visitation. The residential custodian typically retains the decision making power to determine the child's primary residence and to designate things such as the child's primary physician unless there is an objection from the other joint custodian.

How Connecticut determines child visitation: Generally, parents are free to visit with their children at all times that are mutually agreed to by both parents. However, when parents cannot agree, the court will set visitation which is usually a combination of both parents' wishes.

DELAWARE: HOW CHILD SUPPORT IS DETERMINED

The Delaware courts assume each parent has an equal duty to support any children, and they look at the following factors when awarding child support:

- financial resources of the child
- standard of living the child would have enjoyed if the marriage hadn't ended
- age and health of the parents
- each parent's monthly net income
- age and health of the child
- the needs of the child and the primary support obligation of each child
- the relative financial means of the parents
- the number of dependents each parent supports
- the absolute minimum amount of income each parent must obtain to function at maximum productivity

The Delaware courts have created official child support guidelines designed to be in the best interests of the child. These guidelines are followed unless the parents have come to a child support agreement the courts find is fair and reasonable.

29

At what age does child support payments end? If there is an unmarried child that's reached 18, is a full-time high school student and lives with one of the parents, the parents will maintain their respective support if the child needs it, until the child completes the twelfth grade or reaches 19 years of age, whichever comes first.

Delaware's custody guidelines: Legal custody and residential arrangements are based on the best interest of the child. A decision will be made based on the following factors (In any case involving minor children, the court does not prefer one gender over the other when determining custody):

- the wishes of the child and the wishes of the parents
- the child's adjustment to school, home and community settings
- the mental and physical health of all involved
- the relationship of the child with all family members
- the compliance by both parents with the duties of supporting the child
- any evidence of domestic violence

Delaware's medical insurance guidelines: Generally, the decision as to which parent is going to provide medical insurance coverage for the child and how medical bills will be paid is set out in the marital settlement agreement. If a reasonable medical insurance plan is available through one of the parent's employment, he or she may be required to cover their child on it. If the non-custodial parent fails to pay any deductible or fails to pay the required portion of uncovered medical expenses, the IV-D agency may withhold the necessary amount from the obligor's income. The amount of the deductible or the additional medical expenses will be added to the child support obligation.

How permanent are the provisions for Delaware child support and custody? Court orders providing for support and custody of children are subject to change to reflect significant changes in income, and/or living arrangements of the children. While all orders concerning the children are modifiable in the future, we encourage you to not enter into an agreement based on the idea that it can always be changed or modified later.

Wage garnishment for child support payments: Delaware, like most states, has a provision for withholding child support directly from the earnings of the parent who has been ordered to provide support. It is withheld much like income tax is withheld from earnings payments. This way of paying and receiving child support is generally easier for both parties and considered a very dependable solution. Once the support is withheld, it is sent to the state agency authorized to receive and disburse payments. Once it has been verified that the support was paid, it is then sent to the parent designated to receive the support.

If a non-custodial parent can show that they are providing more than 50 percent of the support for dependents not included in the court order from a second marriage, and is not in arrears, no more than 50% of their disposable income can be attached if they cannot pay the full court-ordered amount of both orders. That number goes to 55% if the non-custodial parent is in arrears, 60 percent for a person only providing support to dependents under the current order, and 65% for a person who is in arrears and paying only on the current order.

How does joint custody work? Specifically, joint custody is a form of custody of minor children that requires both parents to share the responsibilities of the children, and for both parents to approve all major decisions related to the children.

While it is a 50-50 sharing of responsibilities and major decisions affecting the children, it rarely works out to be a 50-50 sharing of time with the children. Usually one parent is named as the primary joint custodian and the other parent is granted visitation. The primary joint custodian typically retains the decision making power to determine the child's primary residence and school and to designate things such as the child's primary physician. There is a presumption that a perpetrator of domestic violence will not be awarded joint or sole custody of the child.

How Delaware determines child visitation: Generally, parents are free to visit with their children at all times that are mutually agreed to by both parents. However, when parents cannot agree, the standard visitation schedule accepted most everywhere in the nation is: every other weekend; four to six (4-6) weeks during the summer; alternating holidays.

DISTRICT OF COLUMBIA: HOW CHILD SUPPORT IS DETERMINED

Either parent may be ordered to provide child support during and after the divorce process. There are official Child Support Guidelines that describe the amounts to be paid based on a percentage of the income of the paying parent. These guidelines are designed to be in the best interests of the child and will be followed unless the parents have an agreement approved by the court. Any other relevant factors that would make these guidelines unjust will be considered. The following percentages of the net income of the paying parent are what the D.C. child support guidelines are based on:

No of Children	Ages	Percentage of Income
1 child	0-6	20 - 23% depending on the level of income
1 child	7-12	22 - 25.3% depending on the level of income
1 child	13-21	23 - 26.45% depending on the level of income
2 children	0-6	26 - 29% depending on the level of income
2 children	7-12	28.6 - 31.9% depending on the level of income
2 children	13-21	29.9 - 33.5% depending on the level of income
3 children	0-6	30 - 33% depending on the level of income
3 children	7-12	33 - 36.3% depending on the level of income
3 children	13-21	34.5 - 37.95% depending on the level of income
4+ children	0-6	32 - 35% depending on the level of income
4+ children	7-12	35.2 - 38.5% depending on the level of income
4+ children	13-21	36.8 - 40.25% depending on level of income

At what age does child support payments end? When the child is age 21.

District of Columbia's custody guidelines: Joint or sole custody may be awarded during or after the divorce process by the D.C. courts. The decision will be made without regard to the parents' sex, sexual orientation, race, color, national origin or political affiliations. The court will consider the best interests of the child as determined by applying the following factors: (The courts presume that joint custody is best, unless determined otherwise. Also, the courts may order the parents to submit a written parenting plan for custody).

- the wishes of the child and the wishes of the parents
- the child's adjustment to school, home and community settings

- the mental and physical health of all involved
- the child's interaction with all significant family members
- the willingness of the parents to share custody and major decisions
- the prior involvement of each parent with the child
- issues/proximity of each parent as they relate to the practical consideration of the child's residential schedule
- sincerity of the parents' requests
- the age and the number of children involved
- the demands of the parents jobs
- resulting welfare status
- evidence of abuse by either parent
- financial capabilities
- benefits to the parties involved

District of Columbia's medical insurance guidelines: Generally, the decision as to which parent is going to provide medical insurance coverage for the child and how medical bills will be paid is set out in the marital settlement agreement. If a reasonable medical insurance plan is available through one of the parent's employment, they may be required to cover their child on it.

How permanent are the provisions for District of Columbia child support and custody? Court orders providing for support and custody of children are subject to change or modification to reflect changes in income, and/or living arrangements of the children. While all orders concerning the children are modifiable in the future, we encourage you to not enter into an agreement based on the idea that it can always be changed or modified later.

Wage garnishment for child support payments: Most all U.S. states, including the District of Columbia (D. C.), has a provision for withholding child support directly from the earnings of the parent who has been ordered to provide support. It is withheld much like income tax is withheld from earnings payments. This way of paying and receiving child support is generally easier for both parties and considered a very dependable solution. The way it typically works is, once the support is withheld, it is then sent to the state agency authorized to receive and disburse payments. Once it has been verified that the support was paid, it is then sent to the parent designated to receive the support.

If a non-custodial parent can show that they are providing more than 50 percent of the support for dependents not included in the court order from a second marriage, and is not in arrears, no more than 50% of their disposable income can be attached if they cannot pay the full court-ordered amount of both orders. That number goes to 55% if the non-custodial parent is in arrears, 60 percent for a person only providing support to dependents under the current order, and 65% for a person who is in arrears and paying only on the current order.

How does joint custody work? The current thinking or national trend is to encourage parents to work together for the best interests of their children. Joint custody is now widely recognized by parents, courts and state legislatures as the preferred parenting plan for divorcing parents. In D.C., joint custody is presumed to be in the best interest of the child, if both parents have agreed to it and it appears reasonable for the situation. But this presumption can be rebutted.

Specifically, joint custody is a form of custody of minor children that requires both parents to share the responsibilities of the children, and for both parents to approve all major decisions related to the children. While it is a 50-50 sharing of responsibilities and major decisions affecting the children, it rarely works out to be a 50-50 sharing of time with the children. Usually one parent is named as the primary joint custodian and the other parent is granted visitation. The primary joint custodian

32

typically retains the decision making power to determine the child's primary residence and school and to designate things such as the child's primary physician.

How District of Columbia determines child visitation: Generally, parents are free to visit with their children at all times that are mutually agreed to by both parents. However, when parents cannot agree, the standard visitation schedule accepted most everywhere in the nation is: every other weekend; four to six (4-6) weeks during the summer; alternating holidays.

FLORIDA: HOW CHILD SUPPORT IS DETERMINED

The courts may order either parent to pay an "equitable" amount of child support during or after the divorce process or in a situation between unmarried parents. This decision is based on the specific nature of the case. There are specific Florida child support guidelines, designed to be in the best interests of the child, that the courts use to determine the amount of child support. These guidelines are followed, unless there is an agreement by the parents as to an amount of child support considered fair and reasonable by the court — or there are additional relevant factors like:

- extraordinary medical, psychological, educational or dental expenses
- independent income of the child
- custodial parent receives both child support and spousal support
- seasonal variations in the parents' income
- recognizing older children usually have more expenses
- other relevant and extraordinary circumstances

At what age does child support payments end? If there is an unmarried child that's reached 18, is a full-time high school student and lives with one of the parents, the parents will maintain their respective support if the child needs it, until the child completes the twelfth grade or reaches 19 years of age, whichever comes first.

Florida's custody guidelines: Joint or sole custody may be awarded by the Florida courts, without preference to the sex of the parents. Both parents are given equal consideration. The decision will be made based on the best interests of the child and the following considerations:

- the moral character and prudence of the parents
- the capability and desire of each parent to meet the child's needs and ability to provide a stable home life
- the wishes of the child if of sufficient age
- the love and affection existing between the child and each parent
- the time the child has lived in a stable home and the desire for continuity
- the desire of each parent to allow for an open and loving relationship between the child and the other parent
- the child's adjustment to home, school and community environments
- the mental and physical health of all involved
- the relationship of the child with all family members
- the material needs of the child
- any evidence of domestic violence .

Florida's medical insurance guidelines: Generally, the decision as to which parent is going to provide medical insurance coverage for the child and how medical bills will be paid is set out in the marital settlement agreement. If a reasonable medical insurance plan is available through one of the parent's employment, they are required to cover their child on it.

How permanent are the provisions for Florida child support and custody? Court orders providing for support and custody of children are subject to change or modification to reflect significant changes in income, and/or living arrangements of the children. While all orders concerning the children are modifiable in the future, we encourage you to not enter into an agreement based on the idea that it can always be changed or modified later.

Wage garnishment for child support payments: Florida, like most states, has a provision for withholding child support directly from the earnings of the parent who has been ordered to provide support. It is withheld much like income tax is withheld from earnings payments. This way of paying and receiving child support is generally easier for both parties and considered a very dependable solution. The way it typically works is, once the support is withheld, it is then sent to the state agency authorized to receive and disburse payments. Once it has been verified that the support was paid, it is then sent to the parent designated to receive the support.

If a non-custodial parent can show that they are providing more than 50 percent of the support for dependents not included in the court order from a second marriage, and is not in arrears, no more than 50% of their disposable income can be attached if they cannot pay the full court-ordered amount of both orders. That number goes to 55% if the non-custodial parent is in arrears, 60 percent for a person only providing support to dependents under the current order, and 65% for a person who is in arrears and paying only on the current order.

How does joint custody work? The current thinking or national trend is to encourage parents to work together for the best interests of their children. Joint custody is now widely recognized by parents, courts and state legislatures as the preferred parenting plan for divorcing parents. In Florida, joint custody is referred to as "shared parental responsibility" and it requires both parents to share the responsibilities of the children, and for both parents to approve all major decisions related to the children.

While it is a 50-50 sharing of responsibilities and major decisions affecting the children, it rarely works out to be a 50-50 sharing of time with the children. Usually one parent is named as the primary joint custodian and the other parent is granted visitation. The primary joint custodian typically retains the decision making power to determine the child's primary residence and school and to designate things such as the child's primary physician.

How Florida determines child visitation: Generally, parents are free to visit with their children at all times that are mutually agreed to by both parents. However, when parents cannot agree, the standard visitation schedule accepted most everywhere in the nation is: every other weekend; four to six (4-6) weeks during the summer; alternating holidays.

GEORGIA: HOW CHILD SUPPORT IS DETERMINED

Both parents are liable for the support of their minor children. Therefore, the court may order child support from either parent, based on the child's needs and the parents' ability to pay. There are specific Georgia Child Support Guidelines, designed to be in the best interests of the child, that the courts use to determine the amount of child support.

34

These guidelines will be followed, unless there is an agreement by the parents as to an amount of child support considered fair and reasonable by the court, or there are any other extraordinary, relevant factors. The court may use its discretion to vary the final child support order by considering the following factors:

- ages of the children
- educational costs
- extraordinary medical expenses
- day care costs
- shared physical custody
- support obligation to another household
- income that should be imputed to a party due to the suppression of income
- extreme economic circumstances including an unusually high or low debt structure
- extraordinary travel expenses to exercise visitation or shared physical custody
- historical spending in the family for children which varies significantly from the percentage table
- in kind contribution of either parent
- income of the custodial parent

The following percentages of the gross income of the paying parent are what the Georgia child support guidelines are generally based on:

1 child 17 - 23%; 2 children 23 - 28%; 3 children 25 - 32%; 4 children 29 - 35%; 5 or more children 31 - 37%.

At what age does child support payments end? Generally, the obligation ends when the child reaches 18 years of age or the child graduates from high school, whichever occurs later. A child will also automatically be ineligible for child support if that child marries, is removed from disability status by a court order, or the child dies.

State's custody guidelines: The Georgia courts, based on the best interests of the child and the following considerations may award joint or sole custody: (When there is a history of domestic abuse, the Georgia courts presume joint custody should not be awarded to the abusive parent); the wishes of the child, if the child is of an appropriate age/maturity; the safety of the child; any history of domestic abuse.

Georgia's medical insurance guidelines: Particularly in recent cases, the determination of which parent will provide medical insurance and pay medical bills is included in the marital settlement agreement. However, in the absence of such an agreement, the court will determine which parent will provide medical insurance. Such a determination will be based on whether or not the parent has medical insurance reasonably available through his or her employment or union.

How permanent are the provisions for Georgia child support and custody? Court orders providing for support and custody of children are subject to change or modification to reflect significant changes in income, and/or living arrangements of the children. A modification requires a specific change in circumstances. While orders concerning the children may be modifiable in the future, we encourage you to not enter into an agreement based on the idea that it can always be changed or modified later.

Wage garnishment for child support payments: Georgia, like most states, has a provision for withholding child support directly from the earnings of the parent who has been ordered to provide support. It is withheld much like income tax is withheld from earnings payments. This way of paying and receiving child support is generally easier for both parties and considered a very dependable solution. The way it typically works is, once the support is withheld, it is then sent to the state agency authorized to receive and disburse payments. Once it has been verified that the support was paid, it is then sent to the parent designated to receive the support.

How does joint custody work? The current thinking or national trend is to encourage parents to work together for the best interests of their children. Joint custody is now widely recognized by parents, courts and state legislatures as the preferred parenting plan for divorcing parents.

While it is a 50-50 sharing of responsibilities and major decisions affecting the children, it rarely works out to be a 50-50 sharing of time with the children. Usually one parent is named as the primary joint custodian and the other parent is granted visitation. The primary joint custodian typically retains the decision making power to determine the child's primary residence and school and to designate things such as the child's primary physician. But remember, when there is a history of domestic abuse, the Georgia courts prefer not to award joint custody.

How Georgia determines child visitation: Generally, parents are free to visit with their children at all times that are mutually agreed to by both parents. However, when parents cannot agree, the standard visitation schedule accepted most everywhere in the nation is: every other weekend; four to six (4-6) weeks during the summer; alternating holidays.

HAWAII: HOW CHILD SUPPORT IS DETERMINED

Either parent may be ordered to provide child support. The factors the courts consider in determining the amount of child support or whether or not to modify an existing child support order are:

- all earnings, income and resources of both parents after tax deductions and social security
- earning potential, reasonable necessities and borrowing capacity of each parent
- the needs of the child for whom support is sought
- the amount of public assistance which would be paid for the child under the full standard of need as established by the public assistance department
- the existence of other dependents of the obligated parent
- providing incentives for both parents to work
- balancing the standard of living of both parents and child to avoid placing the child below the poverty level
- to avoid extreme and unfair changes in either parent's income depending on custody
- if parent purposely does not work, thirty (30) hours of weekly earnings at the minimum wage rate may be attributed to that parent's income (The above guidelines will be used unless there are exceptional circumstances. However, the guidelines are generally considered to be in the best interest of both parties).

At what age does child support payments end? Generally, the obligation ends when the child reaches 18 years of age.

State's custody guidelines: Based on the best interests and wishes of the child, the Hawaii courts may award joint or sole custody if the child is of an appropriate age to make such a choice. One of the requirements of awarding joint custody is the assurance that the child will have continued contact with both parents.

Hawaii's medical insurance guidelines: Generally, the decision as to which parent is going to provide medical insurance coverage for the child and how medical bills will be paid is set out in the marital settlement agreement. If a reasonable medical insurance plan is available through one of the parent's employment, they may be required to cover their child on it.

How permanent are the provisions for Hawaii child support and custody? Court orders providing for support and custody of children are subject to change or modification to reflect significant changes in income, and/or living arrangements of the children.

Wage garnishment for child support payments: Hawaii, like most states, has a provision for withholding child support directly from the earnings of the parent who has been ordered to provide support. It is withheld much like income tax is withheld from earnings payments. This way of paying and receiving child support is generally easier for both parties and considered a very dependable solution. Once the support is withheld, it is sent to the state agency authorized to receive and disburse payments. Once it has been verified that the support was paid, it is then sent to the parent designated to receive the support.

If a non-custodial parent can show that they are providing more than 50 percent of the support for dependents not included in the court order from a second marriage, and is not in arrears, no more than 50% of their disposable income can be attached if they cannot pay the full court-ordered amount of both orders. That number goes to 55% if the non-custodial parent is in arrears, 60 percent for a person only providing support to dependents under the current order, and 65% for a person who is in arrears and paying only on the current order.

How does joint custody work? The current thinking or national trend is to encourage parents to work together for the best interests of their children. Joint custody is now widely recognized by parents, courts and state legislatures as the preferred parenting plan for divorcing parents. Specifically, joint custody is a form of custody of minor children that requires both parents to share the responsibilities of the children, and for both parents to approve all major decisions related to the children.

While it is a 50-50 sharing of responsibilities and major decisions affecting the children, it rarely works out to be a 50-50 sharing of time with the children. Usually one parent is named as the primary joint custodian and the other parent is granted visitation. The primary joint custodian typically retains the decision making power to determine the child's primary residence and school and to designate things such as the child's primary physician.

How Hawaii determines child visitation: Generally, parents are free to visit with their children at all times that are mutually agreed to by both parents. However, when parents cannot agree, the standard visitation schedule accepted most everywhere in the nation is: every other weekend; four to six (4-6) weeks during the summer; alternating holidays.

IOWA: HOW CHILD SUPPORT IS DETERMINED

Either or both parents could receive a court order to provide child support for the child. The factors the courts consider are:

- the child's need for close contact with both parents
- the recognition of joint parental responsibilities for the child
- the specifics of each individual case

37

There are specific Iowa Child Support Guidelines, designed to be in the best interests of the child, that the courts use to determine the correct amount of child support. These will be followed, unless there is an agreement by the parents as to an amount of child support considered fair and reasonable by the court. This amount could also be adjust for fairness or special needs of the child. The following percentages of the net income of the paying parent are what the Iowa child support guidelines are based on:

1 child 20%; 2 children 25%; 3 children 30%; 4 children 35%; 5 children 40%; 6 children 45%.

At what age does child support payments end? Generally, the obligation ends when the child reaches 18 years of age or the child graduates from high school, whichever occurs later. A child will also automatically be ineligible for child support if that child marries, is removed from disability status by a court order, or the child dies.

State's custody guidelines: Usually parents are able to reach an agreement about the custody, child support and visitation concerning their children. If they cannot, then the courts will decide these issues for them. Joint or sole custody may be awarded based on the best interests of the child and in an effort to encourage the parents to share the rights and responsibilities of parenthood. Joint custody may be awarded if one of the parents requests it, and it's in the best interests of the child. The courts consider:

- the ability of the parents to make joint decisions
- the ability of the parents to encourage the sharing of love, affection and contact between the child and the other parent
- how close the parents live to one another and how this relates to the practical considerations of where the child will live
- the fitness and suitability of each parent
- the preference of the child, if of appropriate age
- the wishes of the parents
- whether both parents have actively taken care of the child during the marriage and since the separation
- whether the child will suffer psychologically, emotionally or developmentally due to lack of contact with both parents
- the safety of the child
- whether one or both parents agree to joint custody

Iowa's medical insurance guidelines: Generally, the decision as to which parent is going to provide medical insurance coverage for the child and how medical bills will be paid is set out in the marital settlement agreement. Usually, if a reasonable medical insurance plan is available through one of the parent's employment, they are required to cover their child on it.

How permanent are the provisions for Iowa child support and custody? Court orders providing for support and custody of children are subject to change or modification to reflect significant changes in income, and/or living arrangements of the children. While all orders concerning the children are modifiable in the future, we encourage you to not enter into an agreement based on the idea that it can always be changed or modified later.

Wage garnishment for child support payments: Iowa, like most states, has a provision for withholding child support directly from the earnings of the parent who has been ordered to provide support. It is withheld much like income tax is withheld from earnings payments. This way of paying and receiving child support is generally easier for both parties and considered a very dependable solution. The way it typically works is, once the support is withheld, it is then sent to the state agency authorized to receive and disburse payments. Once it has been verified that the support was paid, it is then sent to the parent designated to receive the support.

If a non-custodial parent can show that they are providing more than 50 percent of the support for dependents not included in the court order from a second marriage, and is not in arrears, no more than 50% of their disposable income can be attached if they cannot pay the full court-ordered amount of both orders. That number goes to 55% if the non-custodial parent is in arrears, 60 percent for a person only providing support to dependents under the current order, and 65% for a person who is in arrears and paying only on the current order.

How does joint custody work? The current trend is to encourage parents to work together for the best interests of their children. Joint custody is now widely recognized by parents, courts and state legislatures as the preferred parenting plan for divorcing parents. The specific considerations the Iowa court examines in determining an award of joint custody are listed above in the custody section. Specifically, joint custody is a form of custody of minor children that requires both parents to share the responsibilities of the children, and for both parents to approve all major decisions related to the children.

While joint custody is a 50-50 sharing of responsibilities and major decisions affecting the children, it rarely works out to be a 50-50 sharing of time with the children. Usually one parent is named as the primary joint custodian and the other parent is granted visitation. The primary joint custodian typically retains the decision making power to determine the child's primary residence and school and to designate things such as the child's primary physician.

How Iowa determines child visitation: Generally, parents are free to visit with their children at all times that are mutually agreed to by both parents. However, when parents cannot agree, the standard visitation schedule accepted most everywhere in the nation is: every other weekend; four to six (4-6) weeks during the summer; alternating holidays.

IDAHO: HOW CHILD SUPPORT IS DETERMINED

Child support in Idaho is set in compliance with Idaho's Child Support Guidelines. These guidelines are like laws. They call for a mathematical calculation based upon the gross income of both parents (or attributable income to either parent) which is applied to a sliding scale percentage based upon the number of children to be supported. It is not really a matter of negotiation

At what age does child support payments end? When the child turns 18 years of age. If the child is still in high school, payments will continue until the child graduates or turns 19, whichever occurs first.

Idaho's custody guidelines: The Idaho courts, based on the best interests of the child and the following factors may award joint or sole custody:

- the preference of the child
- the wishes of the parents
- the physical and mental health of all involved
- the relationship the child has with each family member
- the child's adjustment to home, school and community settings
- the need for continuity and stability in the child's life
- any domestic violence

39

Joint custody is allowed if the arrangements assure the child will have frequent contact with both parents. In fact, the Idaho courts assume joint custody is the preferred option, unless shown otherwise. If the child lives with a grandparent, the courts may offer that grandparent the same rights as a parent.

Idaho's medical insurance guidelines: The cost of medical insurance is an item governed by Idaho's Child Support Guidelines. Generally, the parent who can obtain the best, cheapest insurance coverage for the child must do so. The cost of such coverage and any uninsured portion of medical expenses is divided between the parents pro rata based upon their respective incomes. Then, this amount for medical expenses is either treated as a credit against or an addition to child support.

How **permanent are the provisions for Idaho child support and custody**? Child support and custody are always subject to modification upon a showing of a material change in circumstances.

Wage garnishment for child support payments: Idaho, like most states, has a provision for withholding child support directly from the earnings of the parent who has been ordered to provide support. In fact, all child support orders in Idaho contain provisions for enforcing the order by income withholding if the payments become over one month late. Income withholding works the same way income tax is withheld from earnings payments. This way of paying and receiving child support is generally easier for both parties and considered a very dependable solution. The way it typically works is, once the support is withheld, it is then sent to the state agency authorized to receive and disburse payments. Once it has been verified that the support was paid, it is then sent to the parent designated to receive the support.

If a non-custodial parent can show that they are providing more than 50 percent of the support for dependents not included in the court order from a second marriage, and is not in arrears, no more than 50% of their disposable income can be attached if they cannot pay the full court-ordered amount of both orders. That number goes to 55% if the non-custodial parent is in arrears, 60 percent for a person only providing support to dependents under the current order, and 65% for a person who is in arrears and paying only on the current order.

How does joint custody work? The current thinking or national trend is to encourage parents to work together for the best interests of their children. Joint custody is now widely recognized by parents, courts and state legislatures as the preferred parenting plan for divorcing parents. In fact, the Idaho courts assume joint custody is the preferred option, unless shown otherwise.

Specifically, joint custody is a form of custody of minor children that requires both parents to share the responsibilities of the children, and for both parents to approve all major decisions related to the children. Idaho presumes that joint custody is in the child's best interest. While it is a 50-50 sharing of responsibilities and major decisions affecting the children, it rarely works out to be a 50-50 sharing of time with the children. Usually one parent is named as the primary joint custodian and the other parent is granted visitation. The primary joint custodian typically retains the decision making power to determine the child's primary residence and school and to designate things such as the child's primary physician.

How Idaho determines child visitation: Visitation is either subject to a negotiated agreement of the parents or an order of the court in the event the parents are unable to agree. The court will consider all relevant facts and circumstances in establishing a visitation schedule. A standard visitation schedule accepted most everywhere in the nation is: every other weekend; four to six (4-6) weeks during the summer; alternating holidays.

ILLINOIS: HOW CHILD SUPPORT IS DETERMINED

Either or both parents could receive a court order to provide child support for the child, without regard to marital misconduct. The courts may also order one parent to make payments for a medical insurance premium for the child. The factors the courts consider are:

- the financial resources of the child
- the standard of living the child would have enjoyed if the marriage had not ended
- the physical and emotional health and educational needs of the child
- the financial resources, needs and obligations of each parent

There are **specific Illinois Child Support Guidelines**, designed to be in the best interests of the child, that the courts use to determine the correct amount of child support. These will be followed, unless there is an agreement by the parents as to an amount of child support considered fair and reasonable by the court. The following percentages of the net income of the paying parent are what the Illinois child support guidelines are based on:

- 1 child 20%; 2 children 25%; 3 children 32%; 4 children 40%; 5 children 45%; 6 or more children 50%

If child support obligations are not met, the Illinois driver's license of the person owing support may be revoked. If the court deviates from the above guidelines, the court's findings shall state the amount of support that would have been required under the guidelines, if determinable; and the court shall include the reason or reasons for deviation from the guidelines.

At what point does the obligation to pay child support end? Generally, the obligation ends when the **child reaches 18 years of age.**

State's custody guidelines: Joint or sole custody may be awarded based on the best interests of the child and the following factors:

- the preference of the child
- the wishes of the parents
- the physical and mental health of all involved
- the relationship the child has with each family member
- the child's adjustment to home, school and community settings
- the willingness of each parent to encourage a close and continuing relationship between the child and the other parent
- any history of violence by either parents

Marital misconduct that doesn't directly affect that parent's relationship with the child will not be considered. While the Illinois courts presume that the maximum involvement and cooperation of each parent is in the best interests of the child, that doesn't mean that joint custody is always presumed to be the best option.

Illinois's medical insurance guidelines: Generally, the decision as to which parent is going to provide medical insurance coverage for the child and how medical bills will be paid is set out in the marital settlement agreement. If it is not, then it will be addressed in the child support order. Usually, if a reasonable medical insurance plan is available through one of the parent's employment, they are required to cover their child on it.

How permanent are the provisions for Illinois child support and custody? Court orders providing for support and custody of children are subject to change or modification to reflect significant changes in income, and/or living arrangements of the children. While all orders concerning the children are

H1

modifiable in the future, it is inadvisable to enter into an agreement based on the idea that it can always be changed or modified later. Unless the parties have a written agreement stating otherwise, a motion to modify a custody judgment may be made no earlier than two years after the date of the prior judgment. The court may permit review of the order for modification before the expiration of two years if there is written evidence or reason to believe the child's present environment may endanger his or her physical, mental, moral or emotional health.

The court must find clear and convincing evidence that a change has occurred in the circumstances of the child or the parent having custody since the custody order, or it must find that there are circumstances that were unknown to the court at the time the prior order was issued. Modification will be based on the best interest of the child.

Wage garnishment for child support payments: Illinois, like most states, has a provision for withholding child support directly from the earnings of the parent who has been ordered to provide support. It is withheld much like income tax is withheld from earnings payments.

This way of paying and receiving child support is generally easier for both parties and considered a very dependable solution. The way it typically works is, once the support is withheld, it is then sent to the state agency authorized to receive and disburse payments. Once it has been verified that the support was paid, it is then sent to the parent designated to receive the support. If a parent's child support obligation is not met, that person's Illinois driver's license may be revoked.

How does joint custody work? The current trend is to encourage parents to work together for the best interests of their children. While the Illinois courts presume that the maximum involvement and cooperation of each parent with the child is best for the child, that doesn't mean that the courts presume joint custody is always the preferred option. Specifically, joint custody is a form of custody of minor children that requires both parents to share the responsibilities of the children, and for both parents to approve all major decisions related to the children. For an award of joint custody, the courts consider: the ability of the parents to cooperate effectively and consistently; the residential circumstances of each parent; any other relevant factors.

Also, for joint custody to be awarded, the courts require the parents to prepare a Joint Parenting Agreement which outlines each parent's rights and responsibilities for the care of the child and major educational, health care and religious training decisions. The residence of the child will be determined by either an agreement between the parents or a court order based on the above factors.

While joint custody is a 50-50 sharing of responsibilities and major decisions affecting the children, it rarely works out to be a 50-50 sharing of time with the children. Usually one parent is named as the primary joint custodian and the other parent is granted visitation.

How Illinois determines child visitation: Generally, parents are free to visit with their children at all times that are mutually agreed to by both parents. However, when parents cannot agree, the standard visitation schedule accepted most everywhere in the nation is: every other weekend; four to six (4-6) weeks during the summer; alternating holidays.

INDIANA: HOW CHILD SUPPORT IS DETERMINED

Either or both parents could receive a court order to provide child support for the child, without regard to marital fault. The child support court order may also include medical, hospital dental and educational support. The factors the courts consider are: the standard of living the child would have enjoyed if the marriage had not ended; the physical and emotional health and educational needs of the child ; the financial resources, needs and obligations of each parent.

There are **specific Indiana Child Support Guidelines**, designed to be in the best interests of the child, that the courts use to determine the correct amount of child support. These will be followed, unless there is an exception for deviation which is approved by the court. Indiana does not use net income to determine child support. Indiana uses gross income amounts. In addition, Indiana provides that child support is payable until the age of 21 unless the child is emancipated. It also provides for a sharing of post-secondary education expenses.

At what age does child support payments end? Generally, the obligation ends when the child reaches 18 years of age or the child graduates from high school, whichever occurs later.

Indiana's custody guidelines: Usually parents are able to reach an agreement about the custody, child support and visitation concerning their children. If they cannot, then the courts will decide these issues for them. Sole custody may be awarded based on the best interests of the child and the following factors:

- the age and sex of the child
- the preference of the child
- the wishes of the parents
- the child's adjustment to home, school and community settings
- the physical and mental health of all involved
- the relationship the child has with each family member
- whether there has been domestic violence

Indiana does not have a statutory provision for joint physical custody although the parties may agree to it. But the State does have a statutory provision for joint legal custody. This means that the parties share decision-making with regard to religion, education and medical care for the children. If the parents cannot communicate with one another, the court will not award joint legal custody. Even when joint legal custody is ordered, the custodial parent has the final decision-making power.

Indiana's medical insurance guidelines: Generally, the decision as to which parent is going to provide medical insurance coverage for the child and how medical bills will be paid is set out in the marital settlement agreement. If it is not, then the child support court order may include medical, hospital and dental support. Usually, if a reasonable medical insurance plan is available through one of the parent's employment, they are required to cover their child on it.

How permanent are the provisions for Indiana child support and custody? Court orders providing for support and custody of children are subject to change or modification to reflect significant changes in income, and/or living arrangements of the children. However, many local rules prohibit modification before one year has passed.

Wage garnishment for child support payments: Indiana, like most states, has a provision for withholding child support directly from the earnings of the parent who has been ordered to provide support. It is withheld much like income tax is withheld from earnings payments. This way of paying and receiving child support is generally easier for both parties and considered a very dependable solution. The way it typically works is, once the support is withheld, it is then sent to the state agency authorized to receive and disburse payments. Once it has been verified that the support was paid, it is then sent to the parent designated to receive the support.

How Indiana determines child visitation: Visitation guidelines may vary from county to county. Generally, parents are free to visit with their children at all times that are mutually agreed to by

43

both parents. However, when parents cannot agree, the standard visitation schedule accepted most everywhere in the nation is: every other weekend; four to six (4-6) weeks during the summer; alternating holidays.

KANSAS: HOW CHILD SUPPORT IS DETERMINED

Either or both parents could receive a court order to provide child support for the child. Marital misconduct will not be considered. The factors the courts consider are: the financial resources of the child; the health and educational needs of the child; the financial resources, needs and obligations of both parents.

Child support payments are paid through the court clerk or through the court trustee, unless the court orders otherwise. There are specific Kansas Supreme Court Child Support Guidelines, designed to be in the best interests of the child, that the courts use to determine the correct amount of child support. These will be followed, unless there is an agreement by the parents as to an amount of child support considered fair and reasonable by the court.

At what age does child support payments end? Generally, the obligation ends when the child reaches 18 years of age unless the child is still in high school - in which case the support ends upon the child's graduation from high school, or the child's 19th birthday, whichever occurs first.

State's custody guidelines: When parents have come to an agreement on their own concerning child custody, the courts will approve it, if it's in the best interests of the child. If they cannot, then the courts will decide these issues for them. Joint or sole custody may be awarded based on the best interests of the child. There is no preference given based on the sex of the parent, regardless of how old the child is. The court considers the
following factors:

- any time when the child was under the care of someone other than a parent, and those particular circumstances;
- the preference of the child;
- the wishes of the parents;
- the child's adjustment to home, school and community settings;
- the relationship the child has with each significant family member;
- the willingness of each parent to respect the bond between the child and the other parent;
- any spousal abuse.

Joint custody may be awarded if the court finds both parents are suitable. Also, the court may require the parents to submit a joint custody plan.

Kansas's medical insurance guidelines: Generally, the decision as to which parent is going to provide medical insurance coverage for the child and how medical bills will be paid is set out in the marital settlement agreement. If not, the courts will include orders for the inclusion of the child under a medical or medical/dental insurance policy for the child, or in some manner provide for the current and future medical needs of the child.

How permanent are the provisions for Kansas child support and custody? Court orders providing for support and custody of children are subject to change or modification to reflect significant changes in income, and/or living arrangements of the children. While all orders concerning the children are

44

modifiable in the future, we encourage you to not enter into an agreement based on the idea that it can always be changed or modified later.

Wage garnishment for child support payments: Kansas, like most states, has a provision for withholding child support directly from the earnings of the parent who has been ordered to provide support. It is withheld much like income tax is withheld from earnings payments. This way of paying and receiving child support is generally easier for both parties and considered a very dependable solution. The way it typically works is, once the support is withheld, it is then sent to the state agency authorized to receive and disburse payments. Once it has been verified that the support was paid, it is then sent to the parent designated to receive the support.

How does joint custody work? The current trend is to encourage parents to work together for the best interests of their children. Joint custody is now widely recognized by parents, courts and state legislatures as the preferred parenting plan for divorcing parents. In Kansas, joint custody may be awarded if the court finds both parents are suitable. Also, the court may require the parents to submit a joint custody plan. Specifically, joint custody is a form of custody of minor children that requires both parents to share the responsibilities of the children, and for both parents to approve all major decisions related to the children.

While joint custody is a 50-50 sharing of responsibilities and major decisions affecting the children, it rarely works out to be a 50-50 sharing of time with the children. Usually one parent is named as the primary joint custodian and the other parent is granted visitation. The primary joint custodian typically retains the decision making power to determine the child's primary residence and school and to designate things such as the child's primary physician.

How Kansas determines child visitation: Generally, parents are free to visit with their children at all times that are mutually agreed to by both parents. However, when parents cannot agree, the standard visitation schedule accepted most everywhere in the nation is: every other weekend; four to six (4-6) weeks during the summer; alternating holidays.

KENTUCKY: HOW CHILD SUPPORT IS DETERMINED

Either or both parents could receive a court order to provide a reasonable amount of child support. Marital misconduct will not be considered. The factors the courts consider are:

- the financial resources of the child
- the standard of living the child would have enjoyed if the marriage had not ended
- the health and educational needs of the child
- the financial resources, needs and obligations of both parents

There are specific Kentucky Child Support Guidelines, designed to be in the best interests of the child, that the courts use to determine the correct amount of child support. These will be followed, unless the courts decide otherwise based on these factors:

- the child's extraordinary needs
- either parent's extraordinary needs
- the independent financial resources of the child
- the combined parental income is in excess of the Kentucky child support guideline amounts

45

- an agreement between the parents for child support, that is if neither one is on public assistance
- any other extraordinary expense

The following percentages of the net income of the paying parent are what the Kentucky child support guidelines are generally based on, if there is not an agreement between the parents:

1 child 20%; 2 children 25%; 3 children 30%; 4 children; 5 children 40%; 6 children 45%.

At what age does child support payments end? Generally, the obligation ends when the child reaches 18 years of age unless the child is still in high school - in which case the support ends upon the child's graduation from high school, or the child's 19th birthday, whichever occurs first.

State's custody guidelines: Generally, the parents agree upon decisions about custody. If there is no agreement, then the courts will make these custody decisions. In Kentucky, joint or sole custody may be awarded based on the best interests of the child. The courts give equal consideration to both parents and consider the following factors:

- the preference of the child
- the wishes of the parents
- the child's adjustment to home, school and community settings
- the physical and emotional health of all involved
- the relationship the child has with each significant family member
- any domestic abuse

Any conduct of the parents, which does not affect their relationship with the child, will not be considered in the custody decision. If a parent fled the family home due to physical harm or threats of physical harm, then this abandonment will not be considered.

Kentucky's medical insurance guidelines: Generally, the decision as to which parent is going to provide medical insurance coverage for the child and how medical bills will be paid is set out in the marital settlement agreement. If not, the courts may order a parent to provide health care insurance coverage for the child.

How permanent are the provisions for Kentucky child support and custody? Court orders providing for support and custody of children are subject to change or modification to reflect significant changes in income, and/or living arrangements of the children. While all orders concerning the children are modifiable in the future, we encourage you to not enter into an agreement based on the idea that it can always be changed or modified later.

Wage garnishment for child support payments: Kentucky, like most states, has a provision for withholding child support directly from the earnings of the parent who has been ordered to provide support. It is withheld much like income tax is withheld from earnings payments. This way of paying and receiving child support is generally easier for both parties and considered a very dependable solution. The way it typically works is, once the support is withheld, it is then sent to the state agency authorized to receive and disburse payments. Once it has been verified that the support was paid, it is then sent to the parent designated to receive the support.

If a non-custodial parent can show that they are providing more than 50 percent of the support for dependents not included in the court order from a second marriage, and is not in arrears, no more than 50% of their disposable income can be attached if they cannot pay the full court-ordered amount of both orders. That number goes to 55% if the non-custodial parent is in arrears, 60 percent for a

46

person only providing support to dependents under the current order, and 65% for a person who is in arrears and paying only on the current order.

How does joint custody work? The current trend is to encourage parents to work together for the best interests of their children. Joint custody is now widely recognized by parents, courts and state legislatures as the preferred parenting plan for divorcing parents. Specifically, joint custody is a form of custody of minor children that requires both parents to share the responsibilities of the children, and for both parents to approve all major decisions related to the children.

While joint custody is a 50-50 sharing of responsibilities and major decisions affecting the children, it rarely works out to be a 50-50 sharing of time with the children. Usually one parent is named as the primary joint custodian and the other parent is granted visitation. The primary joint custodian typically retains the decision making power to determine the child's primary residence and school and to designate things such as the child's primary physician.

How Kentucky determines child visitation: Generally, the non-custodial parent is entitled to reasonable visitation pursuant to the Kentucky visitation guidelines. The court will deny reasonable visitation if, after a hearing, it is determined that visitation would seriously endanger the child's physical, mental, moral or emotional health.

Reasonable visitation means that a non-custodial parent is free to visit with their children at any time that is mutually agreed on by both the non-custodial and custodial parents. When parents are unable to agree, visitation is based on a standard visitation schedule that includes: every other weekend; four to six (4-6) weeks during the summer; alternating holidays.

LOUISIANA: HOW CHILD SUPPORT IS DETERMINED

Both parents are responsible for the support of any children from the marriage. The courts consider the needs of the child and the resources of each parent. There are specific Louisiana Child Support Guidelines, designed to be in the best interests of the child, that the courts use to determine the correct amount of child support. These will be followed, unless both parents agree to an amount other that calculated by the guidelines, or the courts decide the guidelines are unjust based on these factors:

- extraordinary medical expenses for the child or the parent responsible for child support
- disability of the parent responsible for support
- the need for immediate or temporary support
- an extraordinary community debt both parents share
- the combined income of the parents is less than that in the state guidelines
- having other dependents to support
- any other factors that would render the guidelines unjust

Louisiana **child support guidelines are defined by a schedule for support** which is based on the gross monthly income of both parents and the ratio of the paying parent's income to that of the receiving parent. The schedule does not just define a specific percentage of the net income of the paying parent as the support obligation. The support obligation is also based in part on the cost of the medical insurance premium, the cost of any daycare necessary for the parent to work and the cost of any private school tuition to which both parents had consented.

At what age does child support payments end? Generally, the obligation ends when the child reaches 18 years of age unless the child is still in high school - in which case the support ends upon the child's graduation from high school, or the child's 19th birthday, whichever occurs first.

Louisiana's custody guidelines: Generally, the parents agree upon decisions about custody. If there is no agreement, then the courts will make these custody decisions. In Louisiana, joint or sole custody may be awarded based on the best interests of the child. This is the order of the court's preference:

joint custody ; custody to either parent without considering race or sex; custody to the person(s) the child has been living with; custody to any other person the courts feel would provide an adequate and stable environment for the child.

Joint custody, the court's preference, will be awarded based on the following:

- the physical, emotional, religious and social needs of the child and the capability and desire of each parent to meet those needs
- the preference of the child, if of sufficient age
- the wishes of the parents
- the love and affection between the child and each parent
- the time the child has lived in a stable environment and the desire to maintain this, including the permanence of the custodial home
- the child's adjustment to home, school and community settings
- the willingness of each parent to allow for an open, loving and frequent relationship between the child and the other parent
- the physical and emotional health of all involved
- the distance between the parent's homes
- the moral fitness of each parent and any other relevant factors

Any conduct of the parents, which does not affect their relationship with the child, will not be considered in the custody decision. The parents should submit a plan for joint custody which designates the child's residence, child support payments and outlines the right to access and communication between each parent and the child. A parent not granted custody is allowed visitation, unless that parent has abused the child.

Louisiana's medical insurance guidelines: Generally, the decision as to which parent is going to provide medical insurance coverage for the child and how medical bills will be paid is set out in the marital settlement agreement. Usually, if a reasonable medical insurance plan is available through one of the parent's employment, they are required to cover their child on it. The parent paying this premium receives credit on the child support computation.

How permanent are the provisions for Louisiana child support and custody? Court orders providing for support and custody of children are subject to change or modification to reflect significant changes in income, and/or living arrangements of the children. While all orders concerning the children are modifiable in the future, we encourage you to not enter into an agreement based on the idea that it can always be changed or modified later.

Wage garnishment for child support payments: Louisiana, like most states, has a provision for withholding child support directly from the earnings of the parent who has been ordered to provide support. It is withheld much like income tax is withheld from earnings payments. This way of paying and receiving child support is generally easier for both parties and considered a very dependable solution. The way it typically works is, once the support is withheld, it is then sent to the state agency

48

authorized to receive and disburse payments. Once it has been verified that the support was paid, it is then sent to the parent designated to receive the support.

If a non-custodial parent can show that they are providing more than 50 percent of the support for dependents not included in the court order from a second marriage, and is not in arrears, no more than 50% of their disposable income can be attached if they cannot pay the full court-ordered amount of both orders. That number goes to 55% if the non-custodial parent is in arrears, 60 percent for a person only providing support to dependents under the current order, and 65% for a person who is in arrears and paying only on the current order.

How does joint custody work? The current trend is to encourage parents to work together for the best interests of their children. Joint custody is now widely recognized as the preferred parenting plan for divorcing parents. In Louisiana, joint custody is the courts' preferred option, if it proves to be in the best interests of the child. The factors the courts consider in deciding on joint custody are outlined above. Specifically, joint custody is a form of custody of minor children that requires both parents to share the responsibilities of the children, and for both parents to approve all major decisions related to the children.

While joint custody is a 50-50 sharing of responsibilities and major decisions affecting the children, it rarely works out to be a 50-50 sharing of time with the children. Usually one parent is named as the domiciliary parent and the other parent is granted visitation. The domiciliary parent typically retains the decision making power to determine all decisions other than major decisions. Major decisions can include the choice of school and significant medical treatment.

How Louisiana determines child visitation: Generally, parents are free to visit with their children at all times that are mutually agreed to by both parents. However, when parents cannot agree, the courts must impose a visitation schedule. If the parents have been awarded joint custody, some common visitation schedules are as follows:

- 50/50 custody - the child stays one week at one parent's house and one week at the other parent's house
- the child is at the domiciliary parent's house every day but three weekends out of the month he or she will spend at the other parent's house; the child spends 60% of holidays at the non-domiciliary parent's house; in the summer, the child is with the non-domiciliary parent and visits the domiciliary parent every other weekend
- the child spends every other weekend, one day during the week and a significant amount of time in the summer with the non-domiciliary parent; the child may spend the whole summer with the non-domiciliary parent and every other weekend with the domiciliary parent

In sole custody awards, a visitation schedule accepted almost everywhere in the nation is: every other weekend; four to six (4-6) weeks during the summer; alternating holidays.

MAINE: HOW CHILD SUPPORT IS DETERMINED

The courts may order either parent to provide child support, which could also include health insurance expenses for any minor child. There are specific Maine Child Support Guidelines, designed to be in the best interests of the child, that the courts use to determine the correct amount of child support. These will be followed, unless both parents agree to an amount other than that calculated by the guidelines, or the courts decide the guidelines would be unjust due to one or more of the following factors:

49

- the non-primary residential caretaker is providing residential care over 30% of the time
- there are more than 6 children requiring support
- the interrelation of the total child support with property division and spousal support, which are all being decided at the same time
- the financial resources of the child
- the financial resources and needs of each parent
- the standard of living the child would have enjoyed if the marriage had not failed
- the age and physical and emotional health of the child
- the educational needs of the child
- inflation as it relates to the cost of living
- income and financial contributions of a spouse or domestic associate of each parent
- other dependents of the parent providing support
- tax consequences of a support award
- health insurance premiums that are over 15% of the support award
- the substantial cost of any transportation for the child (the cost must exceed 15% of his/her total support to be considered substantial)

At what age does child support payments end? Generally, the obligation ends when the child reaches 18 years of age unless the child is still in high school - in which case the support ends upon the child's graduation from high school, or the child's 19th birthday, whichever occurs first. A child will also automatically be ineligible for child support if that child marries, or becomes a member of the armed services.

Maine's custody guidelines: Generally, the parents agree upon decisions about custody. If there is no agreement, then the courts will make these custody decisions. In Maine, the custody decisions are based on the best interests of the child, with no preference being given to the parents' sex or the child's age or sex. Three different types of custody may be awarded:

- parental rights and responsibilities for the child are divided between the parents either exclusively or proportionately; these responsibilities include the primary residence, parent-child contact, financial support, education, medical and dental care, religious upbringing, travel boundaries and expenses
- parental responsibilities are shared equally; most responsibilities are handled by joint decisions, and both parents retain equal rights and responsibilities
- one parent is granted sole parental rights and responsibilities for the child, except for child support

The courts consider the following factors:

- the age of the child
- the ability and desire of each parent to meet the child's needs
- the preference of the child, if of sufficient age
- time the child has lived in a stable, satisfactory environment and the desire of maintaining this stability
- each parent's desire and ability to promote an open and loving relationship between the child and the other parent
- the child's adjustment to home, school and community settings
- the relationship the child has with each significant family member

50

- the stability of the home environment that each parent is likely to provide
- a need for stability and continuity for the child
- parents' cooperation
- methods for resolving conflict
- the effect on the child of being raised by one parent rather than two
- any history of domestic violence and/or child abuse
- any other relevant factors that relate to the physical and/or psychological well-being of the child

Maine's medical insurance guidelines: Generally, the decision as to which parent is going to provide medical insurance coverage for the child and how medical bills will be paid is set out in the marital settlement agreement. However, if it has not been decided, the court may order medical and dental health insurance coverage to be paid by one of the parents. Usually, if a reasonable medical insurance plan is available through one of the parent's employment, they are required to cover their child on it.

How permanent are the provisions for Maine child support and custody? Court orders providing for support and custody of children are subject to change or modification to reflect significant changes in income, and/or living arrangements of the children. While all orders concerning the children are modifiable in the future, we encourage you to not enter into an agreement based on the idea that it can always be changed or modified later.

Wage garnishment for child support payments: Maine, like most states, has a provision for withholding child support directly from the earnings of the parent who has been ordered to provide support. It is withheld much like income tax is withheld from earnings payments.

This way of paying and receiving child support is generally easier for both parties and considered a very dependable solution. The way it typically works is, once the support is withheld, it is then sent to the state agency authorized to receive and disburse payments. Once it has been verified that the support was paid, it is then sent to the parent designated to receive the support. If a non-custodial parent can show that they are providing more than 50 percent of the support for dependents not included in the court order from a second marriage, and is not in arrears, no more than 50% of their disposable income can be attached if they cannot pay the full court-ordered amount of both orders. That number goes to 55% if the non-custodial parent is in arrears, 60 percent for a person only providing support to dependents under the current order, and 65% for a person who is in arrears and paying only on the current order.

How does joint custody work? The current trend is to encourage parents to work together for the best interests of their children. Joint custody is now widely recognized by parents, courts and state legislatures as the preferred parenting plan for divorcing parents. Specifically, joint custody is a form of custody of minor children that requires both parents to share the responsibilities of the children, and for both parents to approve all major decisions related to the children.

While joint custody is a 50-50 sharing of responsibilities and major decisions affecting the children, it rarely works out to be a 50-50 sharing of time with the children. Usually one parent is named as the primary joint custodian and the other parent is granted visitation. The primary joint custodian typically retains the decision making power to determine the child's primary residence and school and to designate things such as the child's primary physician.

How Maine determines child visitation: Generally, parents are free to visit with their children at all times that are mutually agreed to by both parents. However, when parents cannot agree, the standard visitation schedule accepted almost everywhere in the nation is: every other weekend; four to six (4-6) weeks during the summer; alternating holidays.

MARYLAND: HOW CHILD SUPPORT IS DETERMINED

The courts may order a parent to provide child support. There are specific Maryland Child Support Guidelines, designed to be in the best interests of the child, that the courts use to determine the correct amount of child support. These will be followed, unless both parents agree to an amount other than that calculated by the guidelines, or the courts decide the guidelines are unjust based on these factors:

the terms of any marriage settlement agreement; the presence in either parent's household of other children that also need to be supported by the parent.

The family home may be awarded to the parent with custody of the child to allow the child continuity in his or her home and community environment. The basic child support obligation is divided between the parents in proportion to their share of the combined adjusted actual income amount. The number of children there are to be supported is also factored in when figuring the child support obligation for the parents.

At what age does the obligation to pay child support end in Maryland? Generally, the obligation ends when the child reaches 18 years of age or the child graduates from high school, whichever occurs later. A child will also automatically be ineligible for child support if that child marries, is removed from disability status by a court order, or the child dies.

Maryland's custody guidelines: Generally, the parents agree upon decisions about custody. If there is no agreement, then the courts will make these custody decisions. In Maryland, joint or sole custody may be awarded to either or both parents, based on the best interests of the child. Custody may be denied if a parent seeking custody has abused the child. The courts will make an effort to allow the child to live in the environment and community that are most familiar to him or her. Generally the courts will allow the parent with custody of the child to use and possess the family home.

Maryland's medical insurance guidelines: Generally, the decision as to which parent is going to provide medical insurance coverage for the child and how medical bills will be paid is set out in the marital settlement agreement. Usually, if a reasonable medical insurance plan is available through one of the parent's employment, they are required to cover their child on it.

How permanent are the provisions for Maryland child support and custody? Court orders providing for support and custody of children are subject to change or modification to reflect significant changes in income, and/or living arrangements of the children. While all orders concerning the children are modifiable in the future, we encourage you to not enter into an agreement based on the idea that it can always be changed or modified later.

Wage garnishment for child support payments: Maryland, like most states, has a provision for withholding child support directly from the earnings of the parent who has been ordered to provide support. It is withheld much like income tax is withheld from earnings payments. This way of paying and receiving child support is generally easier for both parties and considered a very dependable solution. The way it typically works is, once the support is withheld, it is then sent to the state agency authorized to receive and disburse payments. Once it has been verified that the support was paid, it is then sent to the parent designated to receive the support.

52

If a non-custodial parent can show that they are providing more than 50 percent of the support for dependents not included in the court order from a second marriage, and is not in arrears, no more than 50% of their disposable income can be attached if they cannot pay the full court-ordered amount of both orders. That number goes to 55% if the non-custodial parent is in arrears, 60 percent for a person only providing support to dependents under the current order, and 65% for a person who is in arrears and paying only on the current order.

How does joint custody work? The current trend is to encourage parents to work together for the best interests of their children. Joint custody is now widely recognized by parents, courts and state legislatures as the preferred parenting plan for divorcing parents. Specifically, joint custody is a form of custody of minor children that requires both parents to share the responsibilities of the children, and for both parents to approve all major decisions related to the children.

While joint custody is a 50-50 sharing of responsibilities and major decisions affecting the children, it rarely works out to be a 50-50 sharing of time with the children. Usually one parent is named as the primary joint custodian and the other parent is granted visitation. The primary joint custodian typically retains the decision making power to determine the child's primary residence and school and to designate things such as the child's primary physician.

How Maryland determines child visitation: Generally, parents are free to visit with their children at all times that are mutually agreed to by both parents. However, when parents cannot agree, the standard visitation schedule accepted most everywhere in the nation is: every other weekend; four to six (4-6) weeks during the summer; alternating holidays.

MASSACHUSETTS: HOW CHILD SUPPORT IS DETERMINED

The courts may order either parent to provide child support, which could also include health insurance and education expenses, for any minor child. There are specific Massachusetts Child Support Guidelines, designed to be in the best interests of the child, that the courts use to determine the correct amount of child support. These will be followed unless both parents agree to an amount other than that calculated by the guidelines, or the courts decide the application of the guidelines is unjust for a particular case.

The following percentages of the net income of the paying parent are what the Massachusetts child support guidelines are generally based on. However the order may be increased or decreased by 2% depending on the circumstances of the particular case:

Gross Weekly Income	# of children	% of Income
$0 - $125	1 child	15% (at least $50/mo)
$125 - $200	1 child	25%
$201 - $500	1 child	27%
$0 - $125	2 children	18%
$125 - $200	2 children	28%
$201 - $500	2 children	30%
$0 - $125	3 children	21%

| $125 - $200 | 3 children | 31% |
| $201 - $500 | 3 children | 33% |

When there are more than three children, the courts will set an appropriate amount, though it will not be lower than the amount set for 3 children. Also the orders will be adjusted to reflect the cost for raising older children. When the children are 7 to 12 years of age, the basic order will be increased by 10% of the original order. When the children are ages 13 - 18, the basic order will be increased by 15% of the original order. If the custodial parent is working and earning more than $15,000 per year after deducting childcare expenses, then the order for child support will be reduced in an appropriate manner.

At what age does child support payments end? Generally, the obligation ends when the child reaches 18 years of age.

Massachusetts's custody guidelines: Parents may agree upon decisions about custody. If there is no agreement, then the courts will make these custody decisions. In Massachusetts, custody may be awarded to either parent, or to both parents or to a third party. If there is no marital misconduct, then the parent's rights to custody will be considered equally. The court considers the following: the child's overall happiness and welfare; whether or not the child's present or past living conditions adversely affect his or her physical, emotional or moral health.

Joint custody may be awarded if both parents agree, and the courts find it is in the best interests of the child. If the custody issue is contested, and either party seeks shared legal or physical custody; the parties jointly or individually must submit a shared custody plan, including provisions for the child's education, health care, visitation and procedures for resolving disputes between the parties regarding the child. Shared custody does not affect the amount of child support.

Massachusetts's medical insurance guidelines: Generally, health care coverage is provided for in the initial child support order. If one parent has access to an affordable health insurance plan through his or her place of employment, the court will require that the child be covered under that plan.

How permanent are the provisions for Massachusetts child support and custody? Court orders providing for custody of children are subject to change or modification to reflect significant changes in living arrangements of the children. Support orders may be modified also, but require a proven change in circumstances or written findings by the court that the application of the state guidelines was unjust in the particular case While all orders concerning the children are modifiable in the future, we encourage you to not enter into an agreement based on the idea that it can always be changed or modified later.

Wage garnishment for child support payments: Massachusetts, like most states, has a provision for withholding child support directly from the earnings of the parent who has been ordered to provide support. It is withheld much like income tax is withheld from earnings payments. This way of paying and receiving child support is generally easier for both parties and considered a very dependable solution. Once the support is withheld, it is sent to the agency authorized to receive and disburse payments. Once the payment has been recorded, it is sent to the parent designated to receive the support.

If a non-custodial parent can show that they are providing more than 50 percent of the support for dependents not included in the court order from a second marriage, and is not in arrears, no more than 50% of their disposable income can be attached if they cannot pay the full court-ordered amount of both orders. That number goes to 55% if the non-custodial parent is in arrears, 60 percent for a person only providing support to dependents under the current order, and 65% for a person who is in arrears and paying only on the current order.

54

How does joint custody work? The current trend is to encourage parents to work together for the best interests of their children. Joint custody is now widely recognized by parents, courts and state legislatures. However, there is no presumption either in favor or against shared legal or physical custody in Massachusetts.

When the parents have reached an agreement providing for the child's custody, the court may enter the order unless the court makes specific findings indicating that the arrangement would not be in the best interest of the child. Specifically, joint custody is a form of custody of minor children that requires both parents to share the responsibilities of the children, and for both parents to approve all major decisions related to the children. Massachusetts recognizes two types of shared custody:

1. shared physical custody - the child shall have periods of residence with and under the supervision of each parent
2. shared legal custody - a sharing of the major decisions regarding the child (i.e. medical care, education and religion)

How Massachusetts determines child visitation: Generally, parents are free to visit with their children at all times that are mutually agreed to by both parents. However, when parents cannot agree, the standard visitation schedule accepted almost everywhere in the nation is: every other weekend; four to six (4-6) weeks during the summer; alternating holidays.

MICHIGAN: HOW CHILD SUPPORT IS DETERMINED

A child is entitled to support from his or her natural or adoptive parents. Support includes the payment of medical, dental, childcare and education expenses. There are specific Michigan Child Support Guidelines, designed to be in the best interests of the child, that the courts use to determine the correct amount of child support. These will be followed unless both parents agree to an amount other than that calculated by the guidelines, or the courts decide the guidelines are unjust for that particular case. In either case, the court must set forth in the writing the following:

- the support amount determined by the application of the Michigan Child Support Guidelines' child support formula
- how the support order entered by the court varies from the amount determined with the child support formula
- the value of the property or other support awarded in lieu of the payment of support
- the reasons the court found the application of the child support formula to be unjust (if applicable) [The Michigan Child Support Guidelines are generally based upon the needs of the child and the actual resources of each parent].

At what age does child support payments end? Generally, the obligation ends when the child reaches 18 years of age or the child graduates from high school, whichever occurs later.

Michigan's custody guidelines: Generally, the parents agree upon decisions about custody. If there is no agreement, then the courts will make these custody decisions. In Michigan, custody may be awarded to either parent, or to both parents, and is based on the best interest of the child as set forth by these elements:

- the moral fitness of each parent

- the needs of the child, including physical, emotional, mental, religious and social needs
- the ability and desire of each parent to meet the child's needs
- the child's preference, if the child is of sufficient age
- the love, affection and emotional ties between the child and each parent
- the length of time the child has lived in a stable and satisfactory environment the desire to maintain this
- the ability and desire of each parent to promote an open, loving and frequent relationship between the child and the other parent
- the child's adjustment to home, school and community settings
- the mental and physical health of all involved
- the permanence of the proposed custodial homes as it pertains to the family unit
- any history or evidence of domestic abuse
- any other relevant factors

If joint custody is a consideration, the courts will consider the above factors, as well as the following: the cooperation of the parents in making joint decisions for the child; whether the parents agree on joint custody

If the parents agree to joint custody, the court will order joint custody unless, based on clear and convincing evidence, the court determines that joint custody is not in the best interest of the child. If joint custody is awarded, both parents share in the decision making process for the child's welfare. Child support responsibilities remain, even if joint custody is awarded. Each parent continues to be responsible for the child support based on the needs of the child and the parent's resources. An award of joint custody, by itself, is not a ground for modification or the child support order.

Michigan's medical insurance guidelines: Generally, the decision as to which parent is going to provide medical insurance coverage for the child and how medical bills will be paid is set out in the marital settlement agreement. However, if it has not been decided, the court may order health care, dental care and child care to be paid by one or both of the parents. Usually, if a reasonable medical insurance plan is available through one of the parent's employment, they are required to cover their child on it. If a parent is self-employed and maintains health coverage, the court will require that the parent maintain dependent health care coverage for the benefit of the minor children and adult children, if available at a reasonable cost.

How permanent are the provisions for Michigan child support and custody? Court orders providing for support and custody of children are subject to change or modification to reflect significant changes in income, and/or living arrangements of the children. While all orders concerning the children are modifiable in the future, it is not advisable to enter into an agreement based on the idea that it can always be changed or modified later.

Wage garnishment for child support payments: Michigan, like most states, has a provision for withholding child support directly from the earnings of the parent who has been ordered to provide support. It is withheld much like income tax is withheld from earnings payments. This way of paying and receiving child support is generally easier for both parties and considered a very dependable solution. The way it typically works is, once the support is withheld, it is then sent to the state agency authorized to receive and disburse payments. Once it has been verified that the support was paid, it is then sent to the parent designated to receive the support.

How does joint custody work? The current trend is to encourage parents to work together for the best interests of their children. Joint custody is now widely recognized by parents, courts and state legislatures as the preferred parenting plan for divorcing parents. Specifically, joint custody is a form of custody of minor children that requires both parents to share the responsibilities of the children, and for both parents to approve all major decisions related to the children.

While joint custody is a 50-50 sharing of responsibilities and major decisions affecting the children, it rarely works out to be a 50-50 sharing of time with the children. Usually one parent is named as the primary joint custodian and the other parent is granted parenting time. The primary joint custodian typically retains the decision making power to determine the child's primary residence and school and to designate things such as the child's primary physician.

How Michigan determines child visitation: Generally, parents are free to visit with their children at all times that are mutually agreed to by both parents. However, when parents cannot agree, the standard visitation schedule accepted almost everywhere in the nation is: every other weekend; four to six (4-6) weeks during the summer; alternating holidays.

MINNESOTA: HOW CHILD SUPPORT IS DETERMINED

The courts may order either parent to provide child support. Marital fault will not be considered. The factors the courts will consider are:

- the financial resources of the child and the custodial parents
- the standard of living the child would have enjoyed if the marriage had not failed
- the health and educational needs of the child
- the amount of public aid received by the child
- any tax consequences of the support payments
- any debt the parents have

The court is obligated to require that all child support payments be sent directly to the public agency responsible for child support enforcement if: the parent entitled to the child support payment is receiving or has applied for public assistance; the parent has applied for child support and maintenance collection services.

In addition, if either parent is receiving public assistance or has applied for public assistance, he or she must notify the public authority of all proceedings for divorce, separation, or determination of parentage or the custody of a child. Such notice must contain the full name of the parties, social security numbers and birth dates. Once the notice is received, the court will set child support for an amount in compliance with Minnesota Child Support Guidelines.

There are **specific Minnesota Child Support Guidelines** designed to be in the best interests of the child that the courts use to determine the correct amount of child support. These will be followed, unless both parents agree to an amount other than that calculated by the guidelines, or the courts decide that the guidelines are unjust. The court must comply with Minnesota Child Support Guidelines by multiplying the obligor parent's net income by the percentage indicated in the following chart:

Net Monthly Income	Number of children						
	1	2	3	4	5	6	7
$551 - $600	16%	19%	22%	25%	28%	30%	32%

$601 - $650	17%	21%	24%	27%	29%	32%	34%
$651 - $700	18%	22%	25%	28%	31%	34%	36%
$701 - $750	19%	23%	27%	30%	33%	36%	38%
$751 - $800	20%	24%	28%	31%	35%	38%	40%
$801 - $850	21%	25%	29%	33%	36%	40%	42%
$851 - $900	22%	27%	31%	34%	38%	41%	44%
$901 - $950	23%	28%	32%	36%	40%	43%	46%
$951 - $1,000	24%	29%	34%	38%	41%	45%	48%
$1,001 - $5,000	25%	30%	35%	39%	43%	47%	50%

When calculating monthly child support, net monthly income is determined as total monthly income minus: federal income tax, state income tax, social security, reasonable pension deduction, union dues, cost of dependent health insurance coverage, cost of individual or group health/hospitalization or an amount of actual medical expenses.

At what age does child support payments end? Generally, the obligation ends when the child reaches 18 years of age or the child graduates from high school, whichever occurs later. A child will also automatically be ineligible for child support if that child marries, or is removed from disability status by a court order.

Minnesota's custody guidelines: Generally, the parents agree upon decisions about custody. If there is no agreement, then the courts will make these custody decisions. Joint or sole custody may be awarded based on the best interests of the child and the following considerations:

- the child's cultural background
- the physical and mental health of all involved
- the ability and desire of each parent to provide love, affection and guidance to the child
- the ability and desire of the parents to continue raising the child in any particular culture, religion or creed
- the child's preference, if the child is of sufficient age
- the length of time the child has lived in a stable and satisfactory environment the desire to maintain this
- the wishes of the parents
- the child's adjustment to home, school and community settings
- the relationship the child has with each significant family member
- the conduct, as it relates to the child, of the proposed guardian
- the stability of the home environment each parent could offer
- the need for stability and continuity in the child's life
- the effect of any of domestic abuse on the child
- the child's primary care taker and any other relevant factors

If both parents request joint custody, then the courts presume joint custody is the best option for the child, unless there is any history of abuse. If there is history of abuse, joint custody is not considered to be the best option. Joint custody will be based on the above factors, plus: the ability of the parents to cooperate in the rearing of the children; dispute resolution methods used in any major decision in the rearing of a child; whether it would be detrimental to the child if one parent were to have sole authority over the child's upbringing; whether domestic abuse has occurred between the parents.

Minnesota's medical insurance guidelines: Generally, the decision as to which parent is going to provide medical insurance coverage for the child and how medical bills will be paid is set out in the marital settlement agreement.

How permanent are the provisions for Minnesota child support and custody? Court orders providing for support and custody of children are subject to change or modification to reflect significant changes in income, and/or living arrangements of the children. While all orders concerning the children are modifiable in the future, we encourage you to not enter into an agreement based on the idea that it can always be changed or modified later.

Wage garnishment for child support payments: Minnesota has a provision for withholding child support directly from the earnings of the parent who has been ordered to provide support. It is withheld much like income tax is withheld from earnings payments.

This way of paying and receiving child support is generally easier for both parties and considered a very dependable solution. The way it typically works is, once the support is withheld, it is then sent to the state agency authorized to receive and disburse payments. Once it has been verified that the support was paid, it is then sent to the parent designated to receive the support.

How does joint custody work? The current trend is to encourage parents to work together for the best interests of their children. Joint custody is now widely recognized by parents, courts and state legislatures as the preferred parenting plan for divorcing parents. In Minnesota , if the parents request joint custody, then the courts assume it is in the best interests of the child, unless there is a history of abuse. Specifically, joint custody is a form of custody of minor children that requires both parents to share the responsibilities of the children, and for both parents to approve all major decisions related to the children. While joint custody is a 50-50 sharing of responsibilities and major decisions affecting the children, it rarely works out to be a 50-50 sharing of time with the children.

How Minnesota determines child visitation: Generally, parents are free to visit with their children at all times that are mutually agreed to by both parents. However, when parents cannot agree, the standard visitation schedule accepted almost everywhere in the nation is: every other weekend; four to six (4-6) weeks during the summer; alternating holidays.

MISSISSIPPI: HOW CHILD SUPPORT IS DETERMINED

The courts may order either or both parents to provide child support, based on what they determine is just and equitable. When both parents have income or estates, each parent may be ordered by the court to provide support in proportion to his or her financial circumstances.

There are **specific Mississippi Child Support Guidelines**, designed to be in the best interests of the child, that the courts use to determine the correct amount of child support. These will be followed, unless both parents agree to an amount other than that calculated by the guidelines, or the courts decide that the guidelines are unjust. The guidelines are based on the following percentages of the net income of the parent responsible for support:

- 1 child 14%; 2 children 20%; 3 children 22%; 4 children 24%; 5 or more children 26%.

59

At what age does child support payments end? Generally, the obligation ends when the child reaches 21 years of age.

Mississippi's custody guidelines: Generally, the parents agree upon decisions about custody. If there is no agreement, then the courts will make these custody decisions. In Mississippi, joint or sole custody may be awarded, based on the best interests of the child. The may order one of the following custody awards:

- joint physical and legal custody to both parents
- physical custody to both parents and legal custody to one parent
- legal custody to both parents and physical custody to one parent
- custody to a third party if the parents are considered unfit

If both parents request joint custody, and the divorce was based on irreconcilable differences, then the courts presume joint custody is in the best interests of the child. If both parents are fit and the child is 12 years of age or older, then the child may choose the parent he or she wishes to live with. If child abuse has been alleged, then the courts will order an investigation.

Mississippi's medical insurance guidelines: Generally, the decision as to which parent is going to provide medical insurance coverage for the child and how medical bills will be paid is set out in the marital settlement agreement. If these decisions have not been addressed, then the Mississippi courts may order a parent to provide health insurance coverage for the child, if this coverage is available at a reasonable cost through an employer or organization.

How permanent are the provisions for Mississippi child support and custody? Court orders providing for support and custody of children are subject to change or modification to reflect significant changes in income, and/or living arrangements of the children. While all orders concerning the children are modifiable in the future, we encourage you to not enter into an agreement based on the idea that it can always be changed or modified later.

Wage garnishment for child support payments: Most states, including Mississippi, have a provision for withholding child support directly from the earnings of the parent who has been ordered to provide support. It is withheld much like income tax is withheld from earnings payments. This way of paying and receiving child support is generally easier for both parties and considered a very dependable solution. The way it typically works is, once the support is withheld, it is then sent to the state agency authorized to receive and disburse payments. Once it has been verified that the support was paid, it is then sent to the parent designated to receive the support.

How does joint custody work? The current trend is to encourage parents to work together for the best interests of their children. Joint custody is now widely recognized by parents, courts and state legislatures as the preferred parenting plan for divorcing parents. Specifically, joint custody is a form of custody of minor children that requires both parents to share the responsibilities of the children, and for both parents to approve all major decisions related to the children.

While joint custody is a 50-50 sharing of responsibilities and major decisions affecting the children, it rarely works out to be a 50-50 sharing of time with the children. Usually one parent is named as the primary joint custodian and the other parent is granted visitation. The primary joint custodian typically retains the decision making power to determine the child's primary residence and school and to designate things such as the child's primary physician.

How Mississippi determines child visitation: Generally, parents are free to visit with their children at all times that are mutually agreed to by both parents. However, when parents cannot agree, the standard visitation schedule accepted almost everywhere in the nation is: every other weekend; four to six (4-6) weeks during the summer; alternating holidays.

MISSOURI: HOW CHILD SUPPORT IS DETERMINED

Under most circumstances, both parents have a duty to support their children. In determining the amount of child support, the courts consider the following factors:

- the financial needs and resources of the child
- the financial resources and needs of the parents
- the standard of living the child would have enjoyed had the marriage not ended
- the physical and emotional condition of the child and the child's educational needs
- the child's physical and legal custody arrangements, including the amount of time the child spends with each parent and the reasonable expenses associated with the custody or visitation arrangements
- the reasonable work-related child care expenses of each parent

There are specific **Missouri Child Support Guidelines**, designed to be in the best interests of the child, that the courts use to determine the correct amount of child support. These will be followed unless both parents agree to an amount other than that calculated by the guidelines, or the courts decide the guidelines are unjust or inappropriate due to the particular circumstances of a case. In determining monthly child support, the court will use the "income shares model" for its calculations. The "income shares model" is designed to allow the child the same amount of financial support as the parents would have contributed had the household remained intact. Such a model is for the basic child support obligation, thereby excluding parental expenditures for child care and the child's share of health insurance premiums and extraordinary medical expenses. Child support will also be adjusted in accordance with the percentage of overnight periods that the child spends with the non-custodial parent.

At what age does child support payments end? Generally, the obligation ends when the child reaches 18 years of age or the child graduates from high school, whichever occurs later. A child will also automatically be ineligible for child support if that child marries, is removed from disability status by a court order, or the child dies.

Missouri's custody guidelines: The parents may agree upon decisions about custody. If there is no agreement, then the courts will make these custody decisions. In Missouri, joint or sole custody may be awarded, based on the best interests of the child. In doing so, the court will consider all relevant factors, including:

- both parents' proposed parenting skills and proposed custody schedule when submitted to the court
- the child's need to maintain frequent, continuing and meaningful relationships with both parents
- each parent's ability and willingness to perform his or her parental role
- the interaction and interrelationship of the child with parents, siblings and any other person who may significantly affect the child's best interests
- which parent is more likely to allow the child frequent, continuing and meaningful contact with the other parent

- the child's adjustment to the child's home, school and community
- the intention of either parent to relocate the principal residence of the child
- the child's preference regarding who will be his or her custodian
- the mental and physical health of all individuals involved, including any history of abuse of any individuals

If the court finds that a pattern of domestic violence has occurred, and the court also finds that awarding custody to the abusive parent is in the best interest of the child; the court must enter written findings of fact and conclusions of law. In all custody cases involving domestic violence, custody and visitation rights will be ordered in a manner that best protects the child and the parent or other family or household member who is the victim of domestic violence from any further harm.

In making the custody decision, no preference is given based on a parent's age, sex or financial status, or the child's age or sex. The courts do have a preference of joint custody. In all instances a parenting plan is required to be included in a decree of dissolution. If a history of abuse toward the child is proven, that parent may lose certain custody rights at least temporarily. A parent who is not granted custody is entitled to reasonable visitation.

Missouri's medical insurance guidelines: Generally, the decision as to which parent is going to provide medical insurance coverage for the child and how medical bills will be paid is set out in the marital settlement agreement. If these decisions have not been addressed, then the Missouri courts my order a parent to provide health insurance coverage for the child, if this coverage is available at a reasonable cost through an employer, union or other organization.

How permanent are the provisions for Missouri child support and custody? Court orders providing for support and custody of children are subject to change or modification in the event of substantial and continuing changes in circumstances such as significant changes in income and/or living arrangements of the children and/or the parents. While all orders concerning the children are modifiable in the future, we encourage you to not enter into an agreement based on the idea that it can always be changed or modified later.

Wage garnishment for child support payments: Most states, including Missouri, have a provision for withholding child support directly from the earnings of the parent who has been ordered to provide support. It is withheld much like income tax is withheld from earnings payments. This way of paying and receiving child support is generally easier for both parties and considered a very dependable solution. The way it typically works is, once the support is withheld, it is then sent to the state agency authorized to receive and disburse payments. Once it has been verified that the support was paid, it is then sent to the parent designated to receive the support.

If a non-custodial parent can show that they are providing more than 50 percent of the support for dependents not included in the court order from a second marriage, and is not in arrears, no more than 50% of their disposable income can be attached if they cannot pay the full court-ordered amount of both orders. That number goes to 55% if the non-custodial parent is in arrears, 60 percent for a person only providing support to dependents under the current order, and 65% for a person who is in arrears and paying only on the current order.

How does joint custody work? The current trend is to encourage parents to work together for the best interests of their children. Joint legal and physical custody are now widely recognized by parents, courts and state legislatures as the preferred parenting plan for divorcing parents. The Missouri courts encourage both joint legal and physical custody. Specifically, joint legal custody is a form of custody of minor children that requires both parents to share the responsibilities for the health, education and welfare of the children, and for both parents to approve all major decisions related to the children. While joint legal custody is a 50-50 sharing of responsibilities and major decisions affecting the children, it rarely works out to be a 50-50 sharing of time with the children. Usually, one parent is

62

named as the sole physical custodian, and the other parent is granted visitation. However, as indicated above, there is a preference for "joint physical custody" even if it is not on a 50-50.

How Missouri determines child visitation: Generally, parents are free to visit with their children at all times that are mutually agreed to by both parents. However, when parents cannot agree, the standard visitation schedule accepted almost everywhere in the nation is: every other weekend; four to six (4-6) weeks during the summer; alternating holidays. every other weekend; four to six (4-6) weeks during the summer; alternating holidays.

MONTANA: HOW CHILD SUPPORT IS DETERMINED

The courts may order either parent to provide child support based on the following factors:

- the financial resources of the child
- the standard of living the child would have enjoyed if the marriage had not ended
- the physical and emotional conditions as well as the educational and medical needs of the child
- the financial resources, needs and obligations of both parents
- the child's age
- the cost of day care if needed
- the parenting plan for the child, ordered by the court or decided on by the parents
- the needs of any other person that either of the parents has an obligation to support
- the needs of any person, other than the child, whom either parent is legally obligated to support

In addition to the regular child support award, the courts may order: a portion of one of the parent's property to be set aside in a trust fund for the child; a parent to provide health insurance coverage for the child, if it's available at a reasonable cost There are specific Montana Child Support Guidelines, designed to be in the best interests of the child. The court must determine or modify child support based upon the standards set forth above, including cases where the order is issued by default. The guidelines will also be used in those cases in which the parties have entered a support agreement. The amount determined under the guidelines is presumed to be reasonable unless the court finds by clear and convincing evidence that using the guidelines is unjust to the child or to any of the parties involved.

At what age does child support payments end? Generally, the obligation ends when the child reaches 18 years of age or the child graduates from high school, whichever occurs later.

Montana's custody guidelines: Parenting Plans are what the courts refer to as the custody arrangements. Joint or sole parenting plans may be entered, without regard to the sex of the parents and based on the best interests of the child. In determining the child's best interest, the court will consider:

- the wishes of the child and the wishes of the parents
- the child's adjustment to school, home and community settings
- the mental and physical health of all involved
- any history of domestic abuse or a threat of abuse by a parent against the other parent or a child
- any chemical dependency or substance abuse

63

- the relationship between the child and each significant family member
- the degree of stability and continuity in the child's care
- the developmental needs of the child
- whether a parent as failed to pay the costs associated with the child's birth
- whether the child has a continuing and frequent relationship with both parents
- whether a parent has knowingly failed to financially pay birth-related costs (that the parent is able to pay) which are considered to be in the child's best interest
- any adverse effects on the child caused by a parent trying to continuously have the parenting (custody) plan amended, and trying to amend a final plan without ever making an effort to comply with it. (Parents will be required to submit a parenting plan.)

Montana's medical insurance guidelines: Each temporary or final support order must include a medical support order. The court may require that health insurance be provided as part of the child support judgment. If the health care insurance becomes unavailable to the providing party through loss or change of employment or otherwise, the party must, in absence of an agreement, obtain comparable insurance or request that the court modify the requirement. All temporary child support orders must contain a provision requiring the party insuring the child to continue providing insurance coverage, pending the final resolution of the case.

How permanent are the provisions for Montana child support and custody? A court may order a modification: upon a showing of a substantial change in circumstances; upon written consent of the parties; upon application to the health and human services (it must be at least 12 months since the establishment of the order or since the most recent modification)

Wage garnishment for child support payments: Most states, including Montana, have a provision for withholding child support directly from the earnings of the parent who has been ordered to provide support. This way of paying and receiving child support is generally easier for both parties and considered a very dependable solution. The way it typically works is, once the support is withheld, it is then sent to the state agency authorized to receive and disburse payments. Once the support payment has been recorded, it is then sent to the parent designated to receive the support.

If a non-custodial parent can show that they are providing more than 50 percent of the support for dependents not included in the court order from a second marriage, and is not in arrears, no more than 50% of their disposable income can be attached if they cannot pay the full court-ordered amount of both orders. That number goes to 55% if the non-custodial parent is in arrears, 60 percent for a person only providing support to dependents under the current order, and 65% for a person who is in arrears and paying only on the current order.

How does joint custody work? Joint custody or joint parenting is now widely recognized by parents, courts and state legislatures. Specifically, joint parenting is a form of custody of minor children that requires both parents to share the responsibilities of the children, and for both parents to approve all major decisions related to the children.

While joint parenting is a 50-50 sharing of responsibilities and major decisions affecting the children, it rarely works out to be a 50-50 sharing of time with the children. Usually one parent is named as the primary joint custodian and the other parent is granted visitation. The primary joint custodian typically retains the decision making power to determine the child's primary residence and school and to designate things such as the child's primary physician. The objectives of a final parenting plan are to:

- protect the best interest of the child

64

- provide for the child's physical care
- provide for the child's changing needs
- maintain the child's emotional stability
- set forth authority and responsibilities of the parent
- encourage parents to meet their responsibilities

How Montana determines child visitation: Generally, parents are free to visit with their children at all times that are mutually agreed to by both parents. However, when parents cannot agree, the standard visitation schedule accepted almost everywhere in the nation is: every other weekend; four to six (4-6) weeks during the summer; alternating holidays. (More specific visitation arrangements must be included as part of the parenting plan).

NORTH CAROLINA: HOW CHILD SUPPORT IS DETERMINED

Both parents are considered to be responsible for the support of a minor child. Therefore either parent may be ordered to pay child support. The factors the courts consider are:

- the reasonable needs of the child
- the earnings, conditions and standard of living the child enjoys
- the child care and home making contributions of each parent
- any joint or shared custody arrangements
- the parent's ability to pay
- the parent's own special needs
- any other support provided to the child, such as work related day care, medical expenses, health insurance coverage, etc.
- any prior obligations of a parent to pay child support or alimony
- any other relevant factors

Payments ordered for the support of a minor child will be paid on a monthly basis. There are official North Carolina Child Support guidelines, designed to be in the best interests of the child, that the courts use to help determine the correct amount of child support. These guidelines will be followed, unless the parents agree to an amount other than that calculated by the guidelines, or the courts decide the guidelines are unjust for a particular case.

At what age does child support payments end? Generally, the obligation ends when the child reaches 18 years of age. If the child is already otherwise emancipated, payments will stop at the time of emancipation. If the child is still in primary or secondary school when he or she reaches the age of 18, support payments will continue until that child graduates, ceases to attend school on a regular basis, fails to make satisfactory academic progress towards graduation or reaches the age of 20 - whichever of these comes first. Based on its discretion, the court may order payments to cease at age 18, regardless of graduation date or any other factors.

North Carolina's custody guidelines: The parents may agree upon decisions about parenting and custody. If there is no agreement, then the courts will make these decisions. Joint or sole custody may be awarded, based on the best interests and the welfare of the child. There is no presumption by the courts that either parent is better suited to have custody. The courts will consider all relevant factors, including any history of domestic violence and the safety of the child. Beyond that, there are no specific factors for consideration outlined in the statute.

65

North Carolina's medical insurance guidelines: Generally, the decision as to which parent is going to provide medical insurance coverage for the child and how medical bills will be paid is set out in the marital settlement agreement. If it is not, the courts may order a parent to provide medical insurance coverage for the child.

How permanent are the provisions for North Carolina child support and custody? Court orders providing for support and custody of children are subject to change or modification to reflect significant changes in income, and/or living arrangements of the children. While all orders concerning the children are modifiable in the future, we encourage you to not enter into an agreement based on the idea that it can always be changed or modified later.

Wage garnishment for child support payments: Most states, including North Carolina, have a provision for withholding child support directly from the earnings of the parent who has been ordered to provide support. This often becomes the preferred method of payment when child support payments become delinquent. The payments are withheld much like income tax is withheld from earnings payments. This way of paying and receiving child support is generally easier for both parties and considered a very dependable solution. The way it typically works is, once the support is withheld, it is then sent to the state agency authorized to receive and disburse payments. Once it has been verified that the support was paid, it is then sent to the parent designated to receive the support.

If a non-custodial parent can show that they are providing more than 50 percent of the support for dependents not included in the court order from a second marriage, and is not in arrears, no more than 50% of their disposable income can be attached if they cannot pay the full court-ordered amount of both orders. That number goes to 55% if the non-custodial parent is in arrears, 60 percent for a person only providing support to dependents under the current order, and 65% for a person who is in arrears and paying only on the current order.

How does joint custody work? Joint custody is now widely recognized by parents, courts and state legislatures as the preferred parenting plan. Specifically, joint custody is a form of custody of minor children that requires both parents to share the responsibilities of the children, and for both parents to take part in all major decisions related to the children.

While joint custody is a 50-50 sharing of responsibilities and major decisions affecting the children, it rarely works out to be a 50-50 sharing of time with the children. Often one parent is named as the primary joint custodian and the other parent is granted visitation which is sometimes referred to as secondary custody. The primary joint custodian typically retains the decision making power to determine the child's primary residence and school and to designate things such as the child's primary physician.

How North Carolina determines child visitation: Generally, parents are free to visit with their children at all times that are mutually agreed to by both parents. However, when parents cannot agree to exactly when visitation will occur, a typical visitation schedule accepted almost everywhere in the nation is: every other weekend; four to six (4-6) weeks during the summer; alternating holidays.

NORTH DAKOTA: HOW CHILD SUPPORT IS DETERMINED

Either parent may be ordered to pay child support. In determining the right amount of child support, the courts consider what is needed to give the child sufficient financial support, and an education that is appropriate for the child's circumstances and aptitudes. There are official North Dakota Child Support guidelines, designed to be in the best interests of the child, that the courts use to help determine the correct amount of child support. The courts may also order an additional add-on amount for childcare.

At what age does child support payments end? Generally, the obligation ends when the child reaches 18 years of age.

North Dakota's custody guidelines: Custody in North Dakota is based on the best interest of the child. The best interest and welfare of the child is determined by the court's consideration of the following factors:

- the love, affection and other emotional ties existing between the parents and the child
- the capacity and disposition of the parents to give the child love, affection and guidance and to continue the education of the child
- the disposition of the parents to provide the child with food, clothing, medical care (or remedial care permitted in lieu of medical care) and material needs
- the length of time the child has lived in a stable satisfactory environment and the desirability of maintaining continuity
- the permanence, as a family unit, of the existing or proposed custodial home
- the moral fitness of the parents
- the home, school and community record of the child
- the reasonable preference of the child if the court deems the child to be of sufficient intelligence, understanding and experience to express a preference
- evidence of domestic violence
- the interaction and interrelationship (or the potential interaction and interrelationship) of the child with any person who resides in, is present in or frequents the household of a parent
- the making of false allegations about harm to a child by one parent against the other
- any other factors considered by the court to be relevant to a particular child custody dispute

North Dakota's medical insurance guidelines: Generally, the decision as to which parent is going to provide medical insurance coverage for the child and how medical bills will be paid is set out in the marital settlement agreement. Usually, if a reasonable medical insurance plan is available through one of the parent's employment, they are required to cover their child on it. The availability of health insurance at a reasonable cost to a child who is the subject of a child support order constitutes a material change of circumstances. The need to provide the child's health care coverage through health insurance or other means also constitutes a material change of circumstance.

How permanent are the provisions for North Dakota child support and custody? Court orders providing for support and custody of children are subject to change or modification based upon a material change of circumstance. While all orders concerning the children are modifiable in the future, we encourage you to not enter into an agreement based on the idea that it can always be changed or modified later.

Wage garnishment for child support payments: Most states have a provision for withholding child support directly from the earnings of the parent who has been ordered to provide support. The payments are withheld much like income tax is withheld from earnings payments.

This way of paying and receiving child support is generally easier for both parties and considered a very dependable solution. The way it typically works is, once the support is withheld, it is then sent to the state agency authorized to receive and disburse payments. Once it has been verified that the support was paid, it is then sent to the parent designated to receive the support.

67

How does joint custody work? Under joint custody, each parent has the following custody and visitation rights and duties:

- the right to access and obtain copies of the child's educational, medical, dental, religious, insurance and other records or information
- the right to attend educational conferences concerning the child
- the right to reasonable access to the child by written, telephonic and electronic means
- the duty to inform the other parent as soon as reasonable possible of serious accident or serious illness for which the child receives health care treatment
- the duty to keep the other parent informed of the name and address of the school the child attends

How North Dakota determines child visitation: In a divorce ruling, the court may give direction for the custody, care and education of the children of the marriage. The court may modify this ruling at any time. After making an award of custody, the court will, upon request of the non-custodial parent, grant rights of visitation. The rights of visitation will be awarded to enable the child and the non-custodial parent to maintain a parent-child relationship that will be beneficial to the child.

If, after a hearing, the court finds that visitation is likely to endanger the child's physical or emotional health, the court will not grant visitation rights to the non-custodial parent. If the court finds that the non-custodial parent has committed an act of domestic violence which has resulted in bodily injury or has involved the use of a dangerous weapon, the court will allow only supervised visitation. If the court finds that a parent has sexually abused the child, the court shall prohibit all visitation and contact between the child and the abusive parent. If the court finds that the abusive parent has successfully completed a treatment program for sexual abusers and that supervised visitation is in the child's best interest, the court will allow supervised visitation.

NEBRASKA: HOW CHILD SUPPORT IS DETERMINED

The courts consider the earning power of each parent in determining a fair child support order. There are official Nebraska Child Support Guidelines, designed to be in the best interests of the child, that the courts also use to help determine the correct amount of child support. These will be followed unless both parents agree to an amount other than that calculated by the guidelines and the court agrees with the parents, or the courts decide the guidelines are unjust due to the particular circumstances of a case.

The following percentages are rough averages of the percent of net income to be paid by the obligated parent. These are what the guidelines are generally based on. Percentages vary depending on the income levels of the parents:

1 child 20%; 2 children 25%; 3 children 30%; 4 children 35%; 5 children 40%; 6 children 45%.

At what age does child support payments end? Generally, the obligation ends when the child reaches 19 years of age.

Nebraska's custody guidelines: Generally, the parents agree upon decisions about parenting and custody. Many courts require parents to try to work out a parenting plan through mediation. If there is no agreement, then the courts will make these decisions. While it is not the preferred arrangement, joint custody may be awarded if both parents agree to it. In Nebraska, joint or sole custody may be awarded, without regard to the sex of the parents, based on the best interests of the child and the following factors:

- the preference of the child, if the child is of an appropriate age
- the general health, welfare and social behavior of the child
- any credible evidence of domestic abuse
- the child's relationship to each parent prior to the divorce proceedings

Nebraska's medical insurance guidelines: Most often, the parent paying child support is ordered to provide medical insurance. The decision as to which parent has the obligation to cover medical insurance and how medical bills will be paid is set out in the marital settlement agreement. Usually, if a reasonable medical insurance plan is available through one of the parent's employment, they are required to cover their child on it.

How permanent are the provisions for Nebraska child support and custody? Court orders providing for support and custody of children are subject to change or modification to reflect significant changes in income, and/or living arrangements of the children or their needs. While all orders concerning the children are modifiable in the future, we encourage you to not enter into an agreement based on the idea that it can always be changed or modified later.

Wage garnishment for child support payments: Most states, including Nebraska, have a provision for withholding child support directly from the earnings of the parent who has been ordered to provide support. It is withheld much like income tax is withheld from earnings payments. This way of paying and receiving child support is generally easier for both parties and considered a very dependable solution. The way it typically works is, once the support is withheld, it is then sent to the state agency authorized to receive and disburse payments. Once it has been verified that the support was paid, it is then sent to the parent designated to receive the support.

The court cannot set a level of support that reduces the non-custodial parent's take home pay, after child support, to less than $687 per month. If a non-custodial parent can show that they are providing more than 50 percent of the support for dependents not included in the court order from a second marriage, and is not in arrears, no more than 50% of their disposable income can be attached if they cannot pay the full court-ordered amount of both orders. That number goes to 55% if the non-custodial parent is in arrears, 60 percent for a person only providing support to dependents under the current order, and 65% for a person who is in arrears and paying only on the current order.

How does joint custody work? The State law states that joint custody should be ordered only in the "most rare" cases. Formal joint custody gives both parents equal rights to make decisions about the child just as they both had when they were married. For joint custody to work, the parents have to be able to work together cooperatively to decide the important and day-to-day issues in their child's life.

Usually, it is expected that the child will spend amount of time with each parent. When this happens, child support is figure differently. While Nebraska law does not favor true joint custody, it does strongly encourage parents to work out a realistic, detailed and personalized parenting plan through mediation. The plan should include how decisions will be made, who makes which decisions, how information is shared and how the child's time is divided.

How Nebraska determines child visitation: Generally, parents are free to visit with their children at all times that are mutually agreed to by both parents. However, when parents cannot agree, the standard visitation schedule accepted almost everywhere in the nation is: every other weekend; four to six (4-6) weeks during the summer; alternating holidays.

69

NEW HAMPSHIRE: HOW CHILD SUPPORT IS DETERMINED

Reasonable provisions for the support and education of a child may be ordered to be paid a parent. There are official New Hampshire Child Support guidelines, designed to be in the best interests of the child, that the courts use to help determine the correct amount of child support. The guidelines are based on the net income of the parent paying the child support and the number of children owed child support:

> one child - 25% of net income; two children - 33% of net income; three children - 40% of net income; four or more children - 45% of net income

These guidelines will be followed, unless both parents agree to an amount that's at least equal to that calculated by the guidelines, or the courts decide the guidelines are unjust due to the following considerations of the particular case:

- any extraordinary medical, dental or educational expenses for the child
- a significantly higher or lower income of either parent compared to the income assumptions in the guidelines
- any economic consequences caused by any stepparents or stepchildren
- any extraordinary expenses associated with the actual physical custody
- any economic consequences to either parent of selling the family home
- state and federal tax consequences
- any split or shared custody arrangements
- any other significant factors

At what age does child support payments end? Generally, the obligation ends when the child reaches 18 years of age. Obligation also ends when the child gets married or begins military service.

New Hampshire's custody guidelines: Generally, the parents agree upon decisions about parenting and custody. If there is no agreement, then the courts will make these decisions. Joint custody – the sharing of responsibility for all parental decisions and rights, except physical custody – is presumed to be in the best interests of the child, unless there is any evidence of child abuse by one of the parents. The courts consider the following factors in custody decisions: the preference of the child; the education of the child; any findings or recommendations of an objective mediator; any other relevant factors.

The courts will give no preference to a parent based on the sex of the parent. If a parent with primary joint custody rights interferes with the visitation schedule the other parent, the courts may choose to change the custody order.

New Hampshire's medical insurance guidelines: Generally, the decision as to which parent is going to provide medical insurance coverage for the child and how medical bills will be paid is set out in the marital settlement agreement. Usually, if a reasonable medical insurance plan is available through the non-custodial parent's employment, they are required to cover their child on it.

How permanent are the provisions for New Hampshire child support and custody? Court orders providing for support and custody of children are subject to change or modification to reflect significant changes in income, and/or living arrangements of the children. While all orders concerning the children are modifiable in the future, we encourage you to not enter into an agreement based on the idea that it can always be changed or modified later.

Wage garnishment for child support payments: Most states, including New Hampshire, have a provision for withholding child support directly from the earnings of the parent who has been ordered to provide support. It is withheld much like income tax is withheld from earnings payments. This way of paying and receiving child support is generally easier for both parties and considered a very dependable solution. The way it typically works is, once the support is withheld, it is then sent to the state agency authorized to receive and disburse payments. Once it has been verified that the support was paid, it is then sent to the parent designated to receive the support.

If a non-custodial parent can show that they are providing more than 50 percent of the support for dependents not included in the court order from a second marriage, and is not in arrears, no more than 50% of their disposable income can be attached if they cannot pay the full court-ordered amount of both orders. That number goes to 55% if the non-custodial parent is in arrears, 60 percent for a person only providing support to dependents under the current order, and 65% for a person who is in arrears and paying only on the current order.

How does joint custody work? Joint custody is now widely recognized by parents, courts and state legislatures as the preferred parenting plan. In fact, in New Hampshire, joint custody is presumed to be best for the child, unless there is evidence of child abuse by one of the parents. Specifically, joint custody is a form of custody of minor children that requires both parents to share the responsibilities of the children, and for both parents to approve all major decisions related to the children.

While joint custody is a 50-50 sharing of responsibilities and major decisions affecting the children, it rarely works out to be a 50-50 sharing of time with the children. Usually one parent is named as the primary joint custodian and the other parent is granted visitation. The primary joint custodian typically retains the decision making power to determine the child's primary residence and school and to designate things such as the child's primary physician.

How New Hampshire determines child visitation: Generally, parents are free to visit with their children at all times that are mutually agreed to by both parents. However, when parents cannot agree, the standard visitation schedule accepted almost everywhere in the nation is: every other weekend; four to six (4-6) weeks during the summer; alternating holidays.

NEW JERSEY: HOW CHILD SUPPORT IS DETERMINED

Provisions for the support, care and education of a child may be ordered to be paid by a parent. The factors the courts consider are:

- the needs of the child
- the standard or living and the financial circumstances of both parents
- the financial resources, needs and obligations of both parents
- the earning power of each parent
- the child's need and capacity for education, including college work
- the age and health of the parents and the child
- any income and assets and earning ability of the child
- whether either parent has a responsibility to support others
- any debts and liabilities of the parents or the child
- any other relevant factors

There are **official New Jersey Child Support guidelines**, designed to be in the best interests of the child, that the courts use to help determine the correct amount of child support. These will be followed, unless both parents agree to an amount other than that calculated by the guidelines, or the courts decide the guidelines are unjust due to specific circumstances of the case.

At what age does child support payments end? Generally, the obligation ends when the child reaches 18 years of age.

New Jersey's custody guidelines: Generally, the parents agree upon decisions about parenting and custody. If there is no agreement, then the courts will make these decisions. Joint or sole custody may be awarded, without any preference given based on the sex of the parent. The courts consider the best interest of the child based on the following:

- the parents' ability to agree and communicate in matters relating to the child
- the parents' ability to accept the custody arrangement
- any history of failing to allow parenting time without good cause (i.e. abuse)
- the interaction and relationship of the child with his or her parents and siblings
- domestic violence
- child's safety and the odds of either parent being abused by the other
- the child's preference as soon as the child is of sufficient age to make an intelligent and informed decision
- the continuity and quality of the child's education
- fitness of the parents
- stability of the home environment and the needs of the child
- proximity of the parents' homes
- parents' employment responsibilities and the extent and quality of the time spent with the child prior to the separation
- the age and number of children in each household

New Jersey's medical insurance guidelines: Generally, the decision as to which parent is going to provide medical insurance coverage for the child and how medical bills will be paid is set out in the marital settlement agreement. Usually, if a reasonable medical insurance plan is available through one of the parent's employment, they are required to cover their child on it.

How permanent are the provisions for New Jersey child support and custody? Court orders providing for support and custody of children are subject to change or modification to reflect significant changes in income, and/or living arrangements of the children. While all orders concerning the children are modifiable in the future, we encourage you to not enter into an agreement based on the idea that it can always be changed or modified later.

Wage garnishment for child support payments: Most states, including New Jersey, have a provision for withholding child support directly from the earnings of the parent who has been ordered to provide support. It is withheld much like income tax is withheld from earnings payments.

This way of paying and receiving child support is generally easier for both parties and considered a very dependable solution. The way it typically works is, once the support is withheld, it is then sent to the state agency authorized to receive and disburse payments. Once it has been verified that the support was paid, it is then sent to the parent designated to receive the support. The parent receiving child support is given a choice of whether or not it shall be paid through the state agency. For this privilege, the parent will generally pay a nominal fee and become a IV-D services recipient.

How does joint custody work? To understand joint custody, you must first know that there are two types of custody - physical custody and legal custody. Physical custody refers to where the child resides. In joint physical custody (now called shared custody) of minor children, both parents share the responsibilities of the children, and both parents approve all major decisions related to the children. The children must reside with each parent more than 28% of the time in order to fall into this category Joint physical custody, on the other hand, is a 50-50 sharing of responsibilities and major decisions affecting the children, it rarely works out to be a 50-50 sharing of time with the children. Usually, one parent is named as the parent of primary residence and the other parent (called the parent of alternate residence) is granted parenting time. The parent of primary residence typically retains the decision making power to determine the child's primary residence and school and to designate things such as the child's primary physician.

Legal custody does not involve where the child resides. In joint legal custody, the child may live with one parent, but both parents receive the health, education and welfare reports, and both have input but not veto power in major decisions such as college or non-elective surgery. When the parents cannot agree, the court decides for them.

How New Jersey determines child visitation: Generally, parents are free to have parenting time with their children at times that are mutually agreed to by both parents. However, when parents cannot agree, the standard parenting time schedule accepted almost everywhere in the nation is: every other weekend; four to six (4-6) weeks during the summer; alternating holidays.

When a parent lives in another state and has infrequent parenting time on a regular basis, they often receive a large share of the parenting time during the summer and on school vacations during the year (i.e., winter break, spring break, February vacation, summer recess).

NEW MEXICA: HOW CHILD SUPPORT IS DETERMINED

Child support may be ordered to be paid by either or both parents, depending on the financial resources of the parents. There are official New Mexico Child Support guidelines, designed to be in the best interests of the child, that the courts use to help determine the correct amount of child support. There are separate worksheets for determining the correct amount of child support to be paid by parents with visitation and parents with shared responsibility. These state child support guidelines will be followed, unless both parents agree to an amount other than that calculated by the guidelines, or the courts decide the guidelines are unjust due to specific circumstances of the case, including:

- any extraordinary uninsured medical, dental or counseling expenses for the child
- any extraordinary educational expenses for the child
- any transportation expenses or communication expenses for the child's long distance visitation or time sharing with the other parent
- a substantial hardship for either parent or the child

At what age does child support payments end? Generally, the obligation ends when the child reaches 18 years of age. A child will also automatically be ineligible for child support if that child marries, or is removed from disability status by a court order.

New Mexico's custody guidelines: Generally, the parents agree upon decisions about parenting and custody. If there is no agreement, then the courts will make these decisions. Joint or sole custody may be awarded, based on the best interests of the child and without any preference given to the sex of the parents. In New Mexico, it is presumed that joint custody is best for the child, unless it is shown otherwise. The factors the courts consider in all custody cases include:

the wishes of the child and the wishes of the parents; the relationship the child has with each significant family member; the child's adjustment to home, school and community settings; the physical and mental health of all involved. When specifically considering joint custody, the courts also look at:

- the ability of the parents to cooperate and make joint decisions
- the distance between the parent's residences
- whether joint custody will promote a more frequent and continuing relationship between the child and each parent
- the love, affection and emotional ties between the child and the parents
- the ability of each parent to provide food, clothing, medical care and material needs for the child and how well they manage these tasks
- whether each parent is willing to accept all the responsibilities of parenting and the flexibility to share custody responsibilities
- whether each parent can allow the other to provide childcare without intruding
- whether the parenting plan submitted by the couple is suitable for an award of joint custody

New Mexico's medical insurance guidelines: Generally, the decision as to which parent is going to provide medical insurance coverage for the child and how medical bills will be paid is set out in the marital settlement agreement. Usually, if a reasonable medical insurance plan is available through one of the parent's employment, they are required to cover their child on it.

How permanent are the provisions for New Mexico child support and custody? Court orders providing for support and custody of children are subject to change or modification to reflect significant changes in income, and/or living arrangements of the children. While all orders concerning the children are modifiable in the future, we encourage you to not enter into an agreement based on the idea that it can always be changed or modified later.

Wage garnishment for child support payments: Most states, including New Mexico, have a provision for withholding child support directly from the earnings of the parent who has been ordered to provide support. It is withheld much like income tax is withheld from earnings payments. This way of paying and receiving child support is generally easier for both parties and considered a very dependable solution. The way it typically works is, once the support is withheld, it is then sent to the state agency authorized to receive and disburse payments. Once it has been verified that the support was paid, it is then sent to the parent designated to receive the support.

How does joint custody work? Joint custody is now widely recognized by parents, courts and state legislatures as the preferred parenting plan. Joint custody or shared responsibility is defined as each parent having the child in their home at least 35% of the time during the year. More generally, it is a form of custody of minor children that requires both parents to share the responsibilities of the children, and for both parents to approve all major decisions related to the children.

Joint custody, on the other hand, is a 50-50 sharing of responsibilities and major decisions affecting the children, it rarely works out to be a 50-50 sharing of time with the children. Often one parent is named as the primary joint custodian and the other parent is granted visitation. The primary joint custodian typically retains the decision making power to determine the child's primary residence and school and to designate things such as the child's primary physician.

74

How New Mexico determines child visitation: Generally, parents are free to visit with their children at all times that are mutually agreed to by both parents. In joint custody cases, each parent has the child in their home at least 35% of the time per year. However, when parents cannot agree to exactly when visitation will occur, the standard visitation schedule accepted almost everywhere in the nation is: every other weekend; four to six (4-6) weeks during the summer; alternating holidays.

OREGON: HOW CHILD SUPPORT IS DETERMINED

Either or both parents may be ordered to provide child support. In determining child support the courts will consider:

- all earnings, income and resources of each parent, including real and personal property
- the earnings history and potential of each parent
- the reasonable necessities of each parent
- the ability of each parent to borrow
- the educational, physical and emotional needs of the child for whom the support is sought
- the amount of assistance which would be paid to the child under the full standard of the states IV-A plan
- pre-existing support orders and current dependents
- any social security or veterans' benefits paid to the child as a result of the parent's disability or retirement

According to Oregon's guidelines, the child is entitled to benefit from the income of both parents to the same extent that he or she would have if the family had remained intact. Both parents should share in the costs of supporting the child in the same proportion as each parent's income bears to the combined income of both parents. Child support in Oregon must also be determined to insure, as a minimum, that the child being supported benefits from the income and resources of the absent parent on a fair basis in comparison with any other minor children of the absent parent.

There are **official Oregon Child Support guidelines**, designed to be in the best interests of the child, that the courts use to help determine the correct amount of child support. These guidelines will be followed, unless the parents have agreed to a child support amount approved by the court, or the court finds these guidelines unjust for a particular case. The formula used in the guidelines to determine each parent's support obligation is based on the combined income of both parents and then determines each parent's pro rated share of the base support amount.

At what age does child support payments end? Generally, the obligation ends when the child reaches 18 years of age or 21 years of age if the child is in school half-time or more.

Oregon's custody guidelines: In determining the custody of a minor child, primary consideration is given to the best interests and welfare of the child. The court will award joint or sole custody based on the best interests of the child after considering factors including but not limited to:

- the emotional ties between the child and other family members
- the interest of the parties in the child and their attitudes toward the child
- the desirability of continuing an existing relationship
- the abuse of one parent by the other
- the preference for the primary caregiver of the child if the caregiver is deemed fit by the court

- the willingness and ability of each parent to facilitate and encourage a close and continuing relationship between the other parent and the child; however, the court may not consider such willingness and ability if one parent shows that the other parent has sexually assaulted or engaged in a pattern of abusive behavior against the parent or a child (The court will not award sole or joint custody of a child to a parent who has committed abuse against the other parent or a child. No preference in custody shall be given based solely on gender).

Oregon's medical insurance guidelines: All child support orders and any modifications of those orders, require that the obligor shall name the subject child as the beneficiary on any health insurance plan that is available (under the terms of an applicable contract) to the obligor at a reasonable cost.

Health insurance is considered reasonable in cost if coverage for the child is employment related insurance or other group health insurance which is available at a monthly cost not to exceed the amount of the monthly child support obligation. The obligor cannot be ordered to pay the other parent for out-of-pocket child health care costs totaling more than what would be the obligor's share of the insurance if the insurance were reasonable in cost. If health insurance is not available to an obligor at the time a child support order is entered, the order shall include a provision requiring the obligor to provide health insurance in the future when health insurance becomes available to the obligor.

How permanent are the provisions for Oregon child support and custody? Court orders providing for support and custody of children are subject to change or modification based upon a substantial change in circumstance. While all orders concerning the children are modifiable in the future, we encourage you to not enter into an agreement based on the idea that it can always be changed or modified later.

Wage garnishment for child support payments: Most states, including Oregon, have a provision for withholding child support directly from the earnings of the parent who has been ordered to provide support. In some cases, the courts will order the support to be withheld. The payments are withheld much like income tax is withheld from earnings payments. This way of paying and receiving child support is generally easier for both parties and considered a very dependable solution. The way it typically works is, once the support is withheld, it is then sent to the state agency authorized to receive and disburse payments. Once it has been verified that the support was paid, it is then sent to the parent designated to receive the support.

If a non-custodial parent can show that they are providing more than 50 percent of the support for dependents not included in the court order from a second marriage, and is not in arrears, no more than 50% of their disposable income can be attached if they cannot pay the full court-ordered amount of both orders. That number goes to 55% if the non-custodial parent is in arrears, 60 percent for a person only providing support to dependents under the current order, and 65% for a person who is in arrears and paying only on the current order.

How does joint custody work? Joint custody is an arrangement by which parents share rights and responsibilities for major decisions concerning the child, including but not limited to the child's residence, education, health care and religious training. An order providing for joint custody may specify one home as the primary residence of the child and designate one parent to have sole power to make decisions about specific matters while both parents retain equal rights and responsibilities for other decisions. The court will not order joint custody unless both parents agree to the terms and conditions of the order. When parents have agreed to joint custody in an order or decree, the court may not overrule that agreement by ordering sole custody to one parent. Modification of a joint custody order requires the showing of changed circumstances and the showing that the modification is in the best interests of the child.

How Oregon determines child visitation: Generally, parents are free to visit with their children at all times that are mutually agreed to by both parents. However, when parents cannot agree to exactly when visitation will occur, the standard visitation schedule accepted almost everywhere in the nation is: every other weekend; four to six (4-6) weeks during the summer; alternating holidays.

NEVADA: HOW CHILD SUPPORT IS DETERMINED

Temporary and permanent child support may be ordered to be paid by either parent. (Temporary support is for the divorce proceeding time period only.) There are official Nevada Child Support guidelines, designed to be in the best interests of the child, that the courts use to help determine the correct amount of child support. These guidelines will be followed, unless both parents agree to an amount that's at least equal to that calculated by the guidelines, or the courts decide the guidelines are unjust due to the following considerations:

- the cost of health insurance
- the cost of child care
- any special educational needs of the child
- the age of the child
- any responsibility of either parent to support other individuals
- the value of the services the parents contribute
- any public aid paid to the child
- any pregnancy expenses
- any travel expenses related to the child visiting the parents
- the amount of time the child spends with each parent
- the relative income of each parent
- any other necessary expenses

The following percentages of the gross monthly income of the parent paying child support are what the guidelines are generally based on: 1 child 18%; 2 children 25%; 3 children 29%; 4 children 31%; for each additional child, an additional 2% of the parent's gross monthly is added, but the total will not exceed more than $500 per child per month.

At what age does child support payments end? Generally, the obligation ends when the child reaches 18 years of age unless the child is still in high school - in which case the support ends upon the child's graduation from high school, or the child's 19th birthday, whichever occurs first. A child will also automatically be ineligible for child support if that child is removed from disability status by a court order.

Nevada's custody guidelines: Generally, the parents agree upon decisions about parenting and custody. If there is no agreement, then the courts will make these decisions. In Nevada, joint or sole custody may be awarded, without regard to the sex of the parents, based on the best interests of the child and the following factors: the preference of the child, if the child is of an appropriate age; the wishes of the parents; whether either parent has committed domestic violence; any other relevant factors.

The courts presume joint custody is the preferred option if both parents agree to joint custody, either by signing an agreement or stating so in open court. There is also a presumption that it's in the best interests of the child to not have custody awarded to a parent with any history of domestic violence.

77

Nevada's medical insurance guidelines: Generally, the decision as to which parent is going to provide medical insurance coverage for the child and how medical bills may be paid is set out in the marital settlement agreement.

How permanent are the provisions for Nevada child support and custody? The court may, at any time, modify or vacate its order even if the divorce was obtained by default without an appearance in the action by one of the parties. Any order for joint custody may be modified or terminated by the court upon the petition of one or both parents or on the court's own motion if it is shown that the best interest of the child requires the modification or termination. The court shall state, in its decision, the reasons for the court order of modification or termination if either parent opposes it. While all orders concerning the children may be modifiable in the future, it is not advisable to not enter into an agreement based on the idea that it can be modified later.

Wage garnishment for child support payments: Most states, including Nevada, have a provision for withholding child support directly from the earnings of the parent who has been ordered to provide support. It is withheld much like income tax is withheld from earnings payments. This way of paying and receiving child support is generally easier for both parties and considered a very dependable solution. The way it typically works is, once the support is withheld, it is then sent to the state agency authorized to receive and disburse payments. Once it has been verified that the support was paid, it is then sent to the parent designated to receive the support.

How does joint custody work? Joint custody is now widely recognized by parents, courts and state legislatures. The Nevada legislature recognizes the importance of encouraging family preservation after separation and divorce and the vital necessity for maintaining both paternal and maternal influences. The court's preference is joint custody if the parents have agreed to joint custody in open court. However, if the child is a product of sexual assault, the assault creates a presumption that joint custody with the sexual assault perpetrator is not in the best interest of the child. The same holds true if the parent has been convicted of first degree murder.

While joint custody is a 50-50 sharing of responsibilities and major decisions affecting the children, it rarely works out to be a 50-50 sharing of time with the children. Usually one parent is named as the primary joint custodian and the other parent is granted visitation. The primary joint custodian typically retains the decision making power to determine the child's primary residence and school and to designate things such as the child's primary physician.

How Nevada determines child visitation: Generally, parents are free to visit with their children at all times that are mutually agreed to by both parents. However, when parents cannot agree, the standard visitation schedule accepted almost everywhere in the nation is: every other weekend; four to six (4-6) weeks during the summer; alternating holidays.

NEW YORK: HOW CHILD SUPPORT IS DETERMINED

Either or both parents may be ordered to pay for the support, maintenance and education of the child. The courts may also order a parent to provide health insurance coverage for the child. There are official New York Child Support guidelines, designed to be in the best interests of the child, that the courts use to help determine the correct amount of child support. These guidelines are based on the belief that both parents will share the responsibility for the support of their children. The state child support guidelines will be followed, unless the parents agree to an amount other than that calculated by the guidelines, or the courts decide the guidelines are unjust based on the following considerations:

- the financial resources of the child;

78

- the health of the child and any special needs or aptitudes of the child;
- financial resources, needs and obligations of both parents;
- the tax consequences to both parents;
- the non-monetary contributions the parents make toward the care and well-being of the child;
- the educational needs of either parent;
- whether one parents income is substantially less than the others;
- any needs of other children belonging to the non-custodial parent;
- any extraordinary expenses the non-custodial parent spends in order to visit the child;
- any other relevant factor.

The child support guidelines are based on the presumption that the non-custodial parent should pay a certain percentage of their income each month to cover all expenses with the exception of the following: additional expenses of child care; uncovered medical expenses; educational expenses.

These are usually prorated in proportion to each parent's income. The custodial parent is expected to pay for everything else. The state guidelines are generally based on the percentage of the non-custodial parent's net income after taxes, as follows:

One child 17%; Two children 25%; Three children 29%; Four children 31%; Five children 35%.

At what age does child support payments end? Generally, the obligation ends when the child reaches 21 years of age. A child over the age of 21 will also automatically be ineligible for child support if that child is removed from disability status by a court order.

New York's custody guidelines: Generally, the parents agree upon decisions about parenting and custody. If there is no agreement, then the courts will make these decisions. Joint or sole custody may be awarded, based on the best interests of the child and without any preference given to either parent. There are no specific factors for consideration listed in the statute.

New York's medical insurance guidelines: Generally, the decision as to which parent is going to provide medical insurance coverage for the child and how medical bills will be paid is set out in the marital settlement agreement. If it is not, the courts may order a parent to provide medical insurance coverage for the child. Usually, if a reasonable medical insurance plan is available through one of the parent's employment, they are required to cover their child on it.

How permanent are the provisions for New York child support and custody? Court orders providing for support and custody of children are subject to change or modification to reflect significant changes in income, and/or living arrangements of the children. While all orders concerning the children are modifiable in the future, we encourage you to not enter into an agreement based on the idea that it can always be changed or modified later.

Wage garnishment for child support payments: Most states, including New York, have a provision for withholding child support directly from the earnings of the parent who has been ordered to provide support. It is withheld much like income tax is withheld from earnings payments. This way of paying and receiving child support is generally easier for both parties and considered a very dependable solution. The way it typically works is, once the support is withheld, it is then sent to the state agency authorized to receive and disburse payments. Once it has been verified that the support was paid, it is then sent to the parent designated to receive the support.

How does joint custody work? Joint custody is now widely recognized by parents, courts and state legislatures as the preferred parenting plan. Joint custody can be broken down in to two areas – legal custody and physical custody. Legal custody has to do with who has the legal rights to make major decisions affecting the child. There can be joint legal custody or sole legal custody, based on the parents' determination as to who should be making these decisions.

Physical custody refers to where the child should live. There are three options here: joint physical custody, sole physical custody and split physical custody. Sole physical custody usually means that the child lives predominantly with one parent and spends less then 26% of the over nights in a calendar year with the other parent. Split physical custody usually means the child essentially has two homes and lives at each close to an equal amount of time, generally a 50-50 sharing of time. But it can also be a 50-50 split of the children. If there are two children, split custody could mean that each parent has physical custody of one child.

How New York determines child visitation: Generally, parents are free to visit with their children at all times that are mutually agreed to by both parents. However, when parents cannot agree to exactly when visitation will occur, the standard visitation schedule accepted almost everywhere in the nation is: every other weekend; four to six (4-6) weeks during the summer; alternating holidays.

OHIO: HOW CHILD SUPPORT IS DETERMINED

Either or both parents may be ordered to pay child support. Marital misconduct will not be considered. Health care insurance may be ordered to be provided for the child and the spouse.

There are official Ohio Child Support Guidelines, designed to be in the best interests of the child, that the courts use to help determine the correct amount of child support. These guidelines are based on a pro rated share for each parent of the combined net income of both parents. These guidelines will be followed, unless the parents have agreed to a child support amount on their own, or the court finds these guidelines unjust for a particular case. Special factors for adjusting the guidelines include:

- special or unusual needs of the child
- obligations for other minor or handicapped children
- other court-ordered payments
- extended visitation or extraordinary expenses for visitation
- mandatory wage deductions
- a great difference in income in the two parent's households
- benefits that either parent receives from remarrying or from sharing living expenses with others
- taxes
- significant contributions from a parent toward the child's expenses
- the financial resources and earning power of the child
- the standard or living of each parent and the standard of living the child would have enjoyed if the marriage had continued
- the age and the physical, emotional and general needs of the child
- the medical and educational needs of the child
- comparing the earning power, financial resources, assets, needs and obligations of each parent
- the educational aptitude of the child and any educational opportunities
- the responsibility of each parent for the support of others
- the value of services contributed by the custodial parent
- other relevant factors

At what age does child support payments end? Generally, the obligation ends when the child reaches 18 years of age or the child graduates from high school, whichever occurs later. A child will also automatically be ineligible for child support if that child marries, or is removed from disability status by a court order.

Ohio's custody guidelines: Generally, the parents agree upon decisions about parenting and custody. Joint custody arrangements have become commonplace. If there is no agreement between the parents, then the courts will make these decisions. Custody is referred to as "parental rights and responsibilities." Joint custody is referred to as "shared parenting."

Shared parenting or sole parental rights and responsibilities may be awarded based on the best interests of the child. Both parents are considered to have equal rights to custody. The factors the courts consider are:

- the child's preference
- the child's adjustment to home, school and community settings
- the mental and physical health of all involved
- the child's relationship with each significant family member
- whether one parent has willfully denied visitation to the other parent
- any history of abuse or domestic violence by a parent or anyone who will reside in the household
- whether either parent lives or intends to move outside Ohio
- the ability of the parents to make joint decisions
- the health and safety of the child
- the distance between the two parents' households, as it relates to shared parenting
- the child's available time to spend with parents and siblings and each parent's available time
- any failure to pay child support
- other relevant factors

For shared parenting to be awarded, both parents must request it and they must submit a shared parenting plan. The financial status of a parent is not considered in allocating parental rights and responsibilities.

Ohio's medical insurance guidelines: Generally, the decision as to which parent is going to provide medical insurance coverage for the child and how medical bills will be paid is set out in the marital settlement agreement. If it is not, the courts may order a parent to provide health insurance coverage for the child.

How permanent are the provisions for Ohio child support and custody? Court orders providing for support and custody of children are subject to change or modification to reflect significant changes in income, and/or living arrangements of the children. While all orders concerning the children are modifiable in the future, we encourage you to not enter into an agreement based on the idea that it can always be changed or modified later.

Wage garnishment for child support payments: Most states, including Ohio, have a provision for withholding child support directly from the earnings of the parent who has been ordered to provide support. The payments are withheld much like income tax is withheld from earnings payments. This way of paying and receiving child support is generally easier for both parties and considered a very dependable solution. The way it typically works is, once the support is withheld, it is then sent to an agency authorized to receive and disburse payments. Once it has been verified that the support was paid, it is then sent to the parent designated to receive the support.

If a non-custodial parent can show that they are providing more than 50 percent of the support for dependents not included in the court order from a second marriage, and is not in arrears, no more than 50% of their disposable income can be attached if they cannot pay the full court-ordered amount of both orders. That number goes to 55% if the non-custodial parent is in arrears, 60 percent for a person only providing support to dependents under the current order, and 65% for a person who is in arrears and paying only on the current order.

How does joint custody work? Joint custody is now widely recognized by parents, courts and state legislatures as the preferred parenting plan. In Ohio, joint custody is called shared parenting. Specifically, shared parenting is a form of custody of minor children that requires both parents to share the responsibilities of the children, and for both parents to approve all major decisions related to the children.

While shared parenting is a 50-50 sharing of responsibilities and major decisions affecting the children, it rarely works out to be a 50-50 sharing of time with the children. Often one parent is named as the primary joint custodian and the other parent is granted visitation. The primary joint custodian typically retains the decision making power to determine the child's primary residence and school and to designate things such as the child's primary physician.

How Ohio determines child visitation: Generally, parents are free to visit with their children at all times that are mutually agreed to by both parents. However, when parents cannot agree to exactly when visitation will occur, the standard visitation schedule accepted most everywhere in the nation is: every other weekend; four to six (4-6) weeks during the summer; alternating holidays.

OKLAHOMA: HOW CHILD SUPPORT IS DETERMINED

Both parents are expected to contribute to the support of their children. The parent awarded custody of the child must provide for the education and support of the child to the best of their abilities. The courts may order a portion of the non-custodial parent's property to be set aside for the custodial parent to use for the child. The courts will consider:

- the income and the means of each parent
- the property and assets of each parent

There are official Oklahoma Child Support guidelines, designed to be in the best interests of the child, that the courts use to help determine the correct amount of child support. These guidelines will be followed, unless the parents have agreed to a child support amount on their own, or the court finds these guidelines unjust for a particular case. Child support computation forms are available from the clerk of the court. The guidelines are based on the combined gross income of both parties. If a party is self-employed, his or her gross income is calculated as ordinary receipts minus ordinary and necessary expenses required for business operations.

At what age does child support payments end? When the child reaches the age of 18 or graduates from high school, whichever occurs last. If the child marries, child support is no longer required.

Oklahoma's custody guidelines: The court will base its custody decree on its evaluation of the best interests of the physical, mental and moral welfare of the child. The court has the discretion to grant either joint or sole custody. One or both parents may submit a written request and plan for joint custody, detailing facts such as the physical living arrangements for the child, child support obligation, medical and dental care for the child, school placement and visitation rights. An affidavit signed by the parents promising to abide by such a plan will be also submitted to the court.

The court may alter the plan submitted by the parents or entirely deny joint custody if it finds that joint custody is not in the best interest of the child. The parents may modify the plan for joint custody at any time, but a copy of the modification must be filed with the court. The court will evaluate all modifications based on the best interest of the child and will approve or disapprove the modifications. The court may also terminate the plan for joint custody if it determines that it is not in the best interest of the child upon the request of either party. When awarding custody to either party, the court will consider, among other factors, which parent is more likely to allow the child or children frequent and continuing contact with the non-custodial parent. In addition, the court cannot base its decision upon the gender of either party.

Oklahoma's medical insurance guidelines: Generally, the decision as to which parent is going to provide medical insurance coverage for the child and how medical bills will be paid is set out in the marital settlement agreement. If it is not, the courts may order a parent to provide medical insurance coverage for the child. Usually, if a reasonable medical insurance plan is available through one of the parent's employment, they are required to cover their child on it.

How permanent are the provisions for Oklahoma child support and custody? Court orders providing for support and custody of children are subject to change or modification to reflect significant changes in income, and/or living arrangements of the children. While all orders concerning the children are modifiable in the future, we encourage you to not enter into an agreement based on the idea that it can always be changed or modified later.

Wage garnishment for child support payments: Most states, including Oklahoma, have a provision for withholding child support directly from the earnings of the parent who has been ordered to provide support. The payments are withheld much like income tax is withheld from earnings payments. This way of paying and receiving child support is generally easier for both parties and considered a very dependable solution. The way it typically works is, once the support is withheld, it is then sent to the state agency authorized to receive and disburse payments. Once it has been verified that the support was paid, it is then sent to the parent designated to receive the support.

If a non-custodial parent can show that they are providing more than 50 percent of the support for dependents not included in the court order from a second marriage, and is not in arrears, no more than 50% of their disposable income can be attached if they cannot pay the full court-ordered amount of both orders. That number goes to 55% if the non-custodial parent is in arrears, 60 percent for a person only providing support to dependents under the current order, and 65% for a person who is in arrears and paying only on the current order.

How does joint custody work? Joint custody has become commonplace in much of the nation. However, in Oklahoma, the courts have no preference toward joint or sole custody. Specifically, joint custody is a form of custody of minor children that requires both parents to share the responsibilities of the children, and for both parents to approve all major decisions related to the children. While joint custody is a 50-50 sharing of responsibilities and major decisions affecting the children, it rarely works out to be a 50-50 sharing of time with the children. Often one parent is named as the primary joint custodian and the other parent is granted visitation. The primary joint custodian typically retains the decision making power to determine the child's primary residence and school and to designate things such as the child's primary physician.

How Oklahoma determines child visitation: Generally, parents are free to visit with their children at all times that are mutually agreed to by both parents. However, when parents cannot agree to exactly when visitation will occur, the standard visitation schedule accepted most everywhere in the nation is: every other weekend; four to six (4-6) weeks during the summer; alternating holidays.

83

TENNESSEE: HOW CHILD SUPPORT IS DETERMINED

Either or both parents may be ordered to pay child support. The factors the courts consider include:

- the financial resources of the child
- the standard of living the child would have enjoyed if the marriage had continued
- the child's physical and emotional health and educational needs
- the financial resources, needs and obligations of each parent
- the non-custodial parent's earning power
- the age and health of the child
- all contributions by each parent to the child's welfare
- any pension or retirement benefits the parent's have
- the amount of visitation the non-custodial parent receives and any other relevant factors

There are official Tennessee Child Support guidelines, designed to be in the best interests of the child, that the courts use to help determine the correct amount of child support. These guidelines will be followed, unless the parents have agreed to a child support amount that's at least equal to the amount in the guidelines, or the courts find them inappropriate or unjust for a particular case. The state guidelines are generally based on a percentage of the net income of the parent ordered to pay child support, as follows:

One child 21%; Two children 32%; Three children 41%; Four children 46%; Five or more children 50%

At what age does child support payments end? Generally, the obligation ends when the child reaches 18 years of age or the child graduates from high school, whichever occurs later.

Tennessee's custody guidelines: The parents may agree upon decisions about parenting and custody. If there is no agreement between the parents, then the courts will make these decisions. In suits requiring the court to make a child custody decision, the court will examine the best interest of the child based on the following factors:

- the love, affection and emotional ties existing between the parents and the child
- the disposition of the parents to provide the child with food, clothing, medical care, education and other necessary care
- the degree to which a parent has been the primary caregiver
- the importance of continuity in the child's life and the length of time the child has lived in a stable, satisfactory environment
- the stability of the family unit of the parents
- the mental and physical health of the parents
- the home, school and community record of the child
- the reasonable preference of the child if twelve years of age or older
- evidence of physical or emotional abuse to the child, to the other parent or to any other person
- the character and behavior of any other person who resides in or frequents the home of either parent

84

- each parent's past, and potential future, performance of parenting responsibilities, including their willingness and ability to facilitate and encourage a close and continuing relationship between the child and the other parent

Joint or sole custody may be awarded based on the best interests of the child and by considering the child's reasonable preference, especially for children twelve years of age and older. In Tennessee, the courts have a presumption that joint custody is in the best interests of the child when the parents have agreed to this, either in writing or in open court. Neither parent is presumed to be better suited for custody. However, if the child is of a tender age, the sex of the parent may be considered in the custody decision.

Tennessee's medical insurance guidelines: Generally, the decision as to which parent is going to provide medical insurance coverage for the child and how medical bills will be paid is set out in the marital settlement agreement. If it is not, the courts may order a parent to provide health insurance coverage for the child. Also, the Tennessee courts may order the parent responsible for child support to maintain a life insurance policy benefiting the child.

How permanent are the provisions for Tennessee child support and custody? Court orders providing for support and custody of children are subject to change or modification to reflect significant changes in income, and/or living arrangements of the children. While all orders concerning the children are modifiable in the future, we encourage you to not enter into an agreement based on the idea that it can always be changed or modified later.

Wage garnishment for child support payments: Most states, including Tennessee, have a provision for withholding child support directly from the earnings of the parent who has been ordered to provide support. The payments are withheld much like income tax is withheld from earnings payments. This way of paying and receiving child support is generally easier for both parties and considered a very dependable solution. The way it typically works is, once the support is withheld, it is then sent to the state agency authorized to receive and disburse payments. Once it has been verified that the support was paid, it is then sent to the parent designated to receive the support.

How does joint custody work? Joint custody is now widely recognized by parents, courts and state legislatures as the preferred parenting plan. Specifically, joint custody is a form of custody of minor children that requires both parents to share the responsibilities of the children, and for both parents to approve all major decisions related to the children.

While joint custody is a 50-50 sharing of responsibilities and major decisions affecting the children, it rarely works out to be a 50-50 sharing of time with the children. Often one parent is named as the primary joint custodian and the other parent is granted visitation. The primary joint custodian typically retains the decision making power to determine the child's primary residence and school and to designate things such as the child's primary physician.

How Tennessee determines child visitation: Generally, parents are free to visit with their children at all times that are mutually agreed to by both parents. However, when parents cannot agree to exactly when visitation will occur, the standard visitation schedule accepted most everywhere in the nation is: every other weekend; four to six (4-6) weeks during the summer; alternating holidays.

PENNSYLVANIA: HOW CHILD SUPPORT IS DETERMINED

Either or both parents may be ordered to provide child support, based on their ability to pay. The courts will consider:

85

- the net income, assets and earning power of the parents
- any unusual needs of the child or the parents
- any extraordinary expenses

There are official Pennsylvania Child Support guidelines, designed to be in the best interests of the child, that the courts use to help determine the correct amount of child support. These guidelines will be followed, unless the parents have agreed to a child support amount approved by the court, or the court finds these guidelines unjust for a particular case. The formula used in the guidelines to determine each parent's support obligation is based on the combined income of both parents, and then determines each parent's pro rated share of the base support amount.

At what age does child support payments end? Generally, the obligation ends when the child reaches 18 years of age or the child graduates from high school, whichever occurs later. A child will also automatically be ineligible for child support is removed from disability status by a court order.

Pennsylvania's custody guidelines: Generally, the parents agree upon decisions about parenting and custody. If there is no agreement between the parents, then the courts will make these decisions. Joint or sole custody may be awarded based on the best interests of the child, and the following considerations: which parent is more likely to promote frequent physical contact between the child and the other parent; whether either parent has a history of violent, abusive or harassing behavior

In considering custody, the recommendations of a counselor may be used by the courts. Both parents may be required to attend counseling sessions regarding the child's custody. When joint custody is a possibility, the courts may require the parents to submit a joint parenting plan.

Pennsylvania's medical insurance guidelines: If health care is available at a reasonable cost to the non-custodial parent through employment or other group coverage, the court will require that the non-custodial parent provide coverage to the children. The same applies to the custodial parent. Unless the non-custodial parent is already providing health care to the children, the custodial parent must provide coverage if it is available to them at a reasonable cost through employment or other group coverage.

If custody is shared, and health care coverage is available to both parents, the court will require that one or both parents provide coverage of the children. In determining which of the parents will provide health coverage in this case, the court will consider financial ability of the parties and the extent of coverage available to each parent. If neither the non-custodial parent nor the custodial parent have access to employment related benefits, the court will order that one or both parents obtain health care coverage for the children which is available at a reasonable cost. For any uninsured expenses, the court will divide the deductible between both parents. The court will also likely assign to each parent a percentage of all uninsured expenses that have accumulated prior to the filing of the divorce. Within thirty days of the order requiring health care coverage or after any change in employment or coverage, the parent responsible for providing health care coverage must provide proof of coverage by submitting:

- the name of the health care provider
- the identification number
- insurance cards
- the address to which claims should be sent
- a description of all restrictions on usage
- a copy of the benefit booklet or coverage
- a description of all deductibles and co-payments

86

- copies of claim forms

How permanent are the provisions for Pennsylvania child support and custody? Court orders providing for support and custody of children are subject to change or modification to reflect significant changes in income, and/or living arrangements of the children. While all orders concerning the children are modifiable in the future, we encourage you to not enter into an agreement based on the idea that it can always be changed or modified later.

Wage garnishment for child support payments: Most states have a provision for withholding child support directly from the earnings of the parent who has been ordered to provide support. The payments are withheld much like income tax is withheld from earnings payments. This way of paying and receiving child support is generally easier for both parties and considered a very dependable solution. The way it typically works is, once the support is withheld, it is then sent to the state agency authorized to receive and disburse payments. Once it has been verified that the support was paid, it is then sent to the parent designated to receive the support.

How does joint custody work? Joint legal custody has become commonplace in much of the nation. Specifically, joint legal custody is a form of custody of minor children that requires both parents to share the responsibilities of the children, and for both parents to approve all major decisions related to the children.

While joint legal custody is a 50-50 sharing of responsibilities and major decisions affecting the children, it is rarely in conjunction with a joint physical custody order (a 50-50 sharing of time with the children). Often one parent is named as the primary physical custodian and the other parent is granted visitation or partial physical custody rights.

How Pennsylvania determines child visitation: Generally, parents are free to spend time with their children at all times that are mutually agreed to by both parents. However, when parents cannot agree to exactly when visitation will occur, a standard partial custody schedule accepted most everywhere in the nation is: every other weekend; four to six (4-6) weeks during the summer; alternating holidays.

RHODE ISLAND: HOW CHILD SUPPORT IS DETERMINED

Either parent may be ordered to provide child support in any proceeding for divorce, divorce from bed and board (legal separation) or any miscellaneous petition without filing for divorce or child support. Generally, the court will award child support based on the court guidelines. However, if the court finds that the guidelines are not fair for a particular case, the court will base its decision on the following factors:

- the financial resources of the child
- the financial resources of the custodial parent
- the standard of living the child would have enjoyed if the marriage had continued
- the physical, emotional and educational needs of the child
- the financial resources of the non-custodial parent

There are official Rhode Island Child Support guidelines, designed to be in the best interests of the child, the courts use to help determine the correct amount of child support.

At what age does child support payments end? Generally, the obligation ends when the child reaches 18 years of age. The court has the discretion to order child support and educational expenses for children attending high school when the child is 18 or for 90 days after graduation. Child support will not be awarded for a child 19 years or older. If the child suffers from disabilities that require care and expense, the court may award support until he or she reaches 21 years of age.

Rhode Island's custody guidelines: Generally, the parents agree upon decisions about parenting and custody. If there is no agreement between the parents, then the courts will make these decisions. Custody decisions are based on the best interests of the child. Reasonable visitation will be granted to a non-custodial parent, unless the courts feel it would be harmful to the child. There are no specific considerations outlined in the statute. Also, there is no specific provision for joint custody in Rhode Island.

The non-custodial parent has a reasonable right of visitation unless good cause exists to deny visitation. Past and present domestic violence affecting the best interest of the child will be considered by the court in devising a visitation schedule. The receipt of public assistance by either parent is not a factor in visitation. As a custodial parent, it is important to abide by the court ordered visitation schedule. If a motion for contempt is filed against the custodial parent for failure to comply with the court order, the court will issue a more definite schedule. If the custodial parent fails to comply with the visitation order a second time, the court may consider changing custody to the non-custodial parent. The non-custodial parent is also subject to a contempt motion for failure to comply with the court ordered visitation schedule. In this case, the court may sanction the non-custodial parent for the contempt.

Rhode Island's medical insurance guidelines: Generally, the decision as to which parent is going to provide medical insurance coverage for the child and how medical bills will be paid is set out in the marital settlement agreement. Usually, if a reasonable medical insurance plan is available through one of the parent's employment, they are required to cover their child on it.

How permanent are the provisions for Rhode Island child support and custody? Court orders providing for support and custody of children are subject to change or modification to reflect significant changes in income, and/or living arrangements of the children. While all orders concerning the children are modifiable in the future, it is not advisable for you to enter into an agreement based on the idea that it can always be changed or modified later.

Wage garnishment for child support payments: Most states, including Rhode Island, have a provision for withholding child support directly from the earnings of the parent who has been ordered to provide support. The payments are withheld much like income tax is withheld from earnings payments. This way of paying and receiving child support is generally easier for both parties and considered a very dependable solution. The way it typically works is, once the support is withheld, it is then sent to the state agency authorized to receive and disburse payments. Once it has been verified that the support was paid, it is then sent to the parent designated to receive the support.

By statute, all child support orders issued, enforced or modified after January 1, 1994 are subject to immediate wage withholding unless the court finds there is: good cause to not impose wage withholding, or a written agreement by both parties involved which provides for an alternative arrangement for the timely payment of support due under the support order.

How does joint custody work? Joint custody has become commonplace in much of the nation. Specifically, joint custody is a form of custody of minor children that requires both parents to share the responsibilities of the children, and for both parents to approve all major decisions related to the children.

While joint custody is a 50-50 sharing of responsibilities and major decisions affecting the children, it rarely works out to be a 50-50 sharing of time with the children. One parent will have physical possession of the child which amounts to the day-to-day care and control of the child. Joint custody also allows the non-possessory parent to have access to educational, medical, religious and other miscellaneous records without the express permission of the possessory parent.

How Rhode Island determines child visitation: Generally, parents are free to visit with their children at all times that are mutually agreed to by both parents. The guiding principle of visitation schedules is still the best interest of the child. A visitation schedule imposed by the court will depend on a number of factors, including but not limited to: the age of the child; geographical proximity between the child and the non-possessory parent; the work schedules of both parents

SOUTH CAROLINA: HOW CHILD SUPPORT IS DETERMINED

Both parents have a joint responsibility to provide child support. There are official South Carolina Child Support guidelines, based on notarized financial declaration and designed to be in the best interests of the child, that the courts use to help determine the correct amount of child support. These guidelines will be followed, unless one of the following factors would make them unjust:

- educational expenses for the child or for a spouse
- the equitable distribution of property
- any consumer debts
- if the family has more than 6 children
- extraordinary medical or dental expenses for the child or either parent that isn't reimbursed
- mandatory retirement deductions of either parent
- support obligations for other dependents
- other court ordered payments
- any available income of the child
- a substantial disparity in income of the parents, making it impractical for the non-custodial parent to pay the guideline amount
- the effect of alimony on the circumstances
- any agreements between the spouses, if found to be in the best interests of the child

At what age does child support payments end? Generally, the obligation ends when the child reaches 18 years of age or the child graduates from high school, whichever occurs later. A child will also automatically be ineligible for child support if that child is removed from disability status by a court order.

South Carolina's custody guidelines: Generally, the parents agree upon decisions about parenting and custody. If there is no agreement between the parents, then the courts will make these decisions. In all child custody cases, the mother and father are held responsible for the welfare and education of the minor children in question. The non-custodial parent and the custodial parent have the same right to access of educational records and medical records as well as the same right to participate in the child's school activities. Access remains equal unless otherwise mandated by a court order. Joint or sole custody may be awarded based on the following factors:

- which parent is primary caretaker
- the mental and physical fitness of both parents
- the religious faith of the parents and the child
- immoral conduct of either parent if it affects the child
- the child's welfare

89

- the child's preference
- and the best spiritual and other interests of the child

South Carolina's medical insurance guidelines: Generally, the decision as to which parent is going to provide medical insurance coverage for the child and how medical bills will be paid is set out in the marital settlement agreement. Usually, if a reasonable medical insurance plan is available through one of the parent's employment, they are required to cover their child on it. In order to be enforceable, a court order mandating medical insurance coverage must include the following:

- the name, social security number and last known mailing address of the parent as well as the name, social security number, date of birth and mailing address of each child covered by the order
- a description of the type of coverage that will be provided by the plan
- the period to which the order applies
- each plan to which the order applies

How permanent are the provisions for South Carolina child support and custody? Court orders providing for support and custody of children are subject to change or modification to reflect a "substantial change" in circumstances or financial ability of either party and/or living arrangements of the children. While all orders concerning the children are modifiable in the future, we encourage you to not enter into an agreement based on the idea that it can always be changed or modified later.

Wage garnishment for child support payments: Most states, including South Carolina, have a provision for withholding child support directly from the earnings of the parent who has been ordered to provide support. In some cases, the courts may require withholding income in order to guarantee the child support payments are made. The payments are withheld much like income tax is withheld from earnings payments. This way of paying and receiving child support is generally easier for both parties and considered a very dependable solution. The way it typically works is, once the support is withheld, it is then sent to the state agency authorized to receive and disburse payments. Once it has been verified that the support was paid, it is then sent to the parent designated to receive the support.

If a non-custodial parent can show that they are providing more than 50 percent of the support for dependents not included in the court order from a second marriage, and is not in arrears, no more than 50% of their disposable income can be attached if they cannot pay the full court-ordered amount of both orders. That number goes to 55% if the non-custodial parent is in arrears, 60 percent for a person only providing support to dependents under the current order, and 65% for a person who is in arrears and paying only on the current order.

How does joint custody work? Joint custody is now widely recognized by parents, courts and state legislatures as the preferred parenting plan in much of the nation. Specifically, joint custody is a form of custody of minor children that requires both parents to share the responsibilities of the children, and for both parents to approve all major decisions related to the children.

While joint custody is a 50-50 sharing of responsibilities and major decisions affecting the children, it rarely works out to be a 50-50 sharing of time with the children. Often one parent is named as the primary joint custodian and the other parent is granted visitation. The primary joint custodian typically retains the decision making power to determine the child's primary residence and school and to designate things such as the child's primary physician.

How South Carolina determines child visitation: Generally, parents are free to visit with their children at all times that are mutually agreed to by both parents. However, when parents cannot agree to exactly when visitation will occur, the standard visitation schedule accepted almost everywhere in the nation is: every other weekend; four to six (4-6) weeks during the summer; alternating holidays; Father's Day with the father , Mother's Day with the mother .

SOUTH DAKOTA: HOW CHILD SUPPORT IS DETERMINED

Either or both parents may be ordered to pay child support. There are official South Dakota Child Support guidelines, designed to be in the best interests of the child, that the courts use to help determine the correct amount of child support. These guidelines will be followed, unless one of the following factors convinces the courts to adjust them:

- the financial condition of either parent that would make the guidelines unjust
- any income tax consequences
- any special needs of the child
- any income from others besides the parents
- the effect of the custody and visitation decisions
- an agreement between the parents that provides other forms of support that benefit the child
- a voluntary reduction in the income of either parent
- any other obligations of financial support for subsequent children

At what age does child support payments end? Generally, the obligation ends when the child reaches 18 years of age unless the child is still in high school - in which case the support ends upon the child's graduation from high school, or the child's 19th birthday, whichever occurs first. A child will also automatically be ineligible for child support if that child marries, is removed from disability status by a court order, or the child dies.

South Dakota's custody guidelines: Generally, the parents agree upon decisions about parenting and custody. If the parents cannot reach an agreement, then the courts will make these decisions. Under state statute, the courts may order the parties to mediate child custody and visitation disputes.

Joint legal, joint physical or sole custody may be awarded based on the best interests of the child and the discretion of the court. No preference is given to either parent based on their sex. Marital fault is not considered, unless it is relevant to whether that person is a fit parent to have custody. The courts may consider the wishes of the child. In joint custody decisions, the courts consider the requests of the parents and the best interests of the child.

South Dakota's medical insurance guidelines: Generally, the decision as to which parent is going to provide medical insurance coverage for the child and how medical bills will be paid is set out in the marital settlement agreement. Usually, if a reasonable medical insurance plan is available through one of the parent's employment, they are required to cover their child on it. Under state statute, the custodial parent pays the first $250 of any uncovered medical expenses, and the remainder is split between the parents based on their percentage of support under the guidelines.

How permanent are the provisions for South Dakota child support and custody? Court orders providing for support and custody of children are subject to change or modification to reflect significant changes in income, and/or living arrangements of the children. While all orders concerning the children are modifiable in the future, we encourage you to not enter into an agreement based on the idea that it can always be changed or modified later.

Wage garnishment for child support payments: Most states, including South Dakota, have a provision for withholding child support directly from the earnings of the parent who has been ordered to provide support. The payments are withheld much like income tax is withheld from earnings payments. This way of paying and receiving child support is generally easier for both parties and considered a very dependable solution. The way it typically works is, once the support is withheld, it is then sent to the state agency authorized to receive and disburse payments. Once it has been verified that the support was paid, it is then sent to the parent designated to receive the support. The payment of child support through the state agency is now mandatory in every case in South Dakota.

If a non-custodial parent can show that they are providing more than 50 percent of the support for dependents not included in the court order from a second marriage, and is not in arrears, no more than 50% of their disposable income can be attached if they cannot pay the full court-ordered amount of both orders. That number goes to 55% if the non-custodial parent is in arrears, 60 percent for a person only providing support to dependents under the current order, and 65% for a person who is in arrears and paying only on the current order.

How does joint custody work? Joint custody is now widely recognized by parents, courts and state legislatures as the preferred parenting plan in much of the nation. Specifically, joint custody is a form of custody of minor children that requires both parents to share the responsibilities of the children and for both parents to approve all major decisions related to the children such as the health, education and welfare of the children.

While joint legal custody envisions a 50-50 sharing of responsibilities on major decisions affecting the children, it does not work out to be a 50-50 sharing of time with the children. Often one parent is named as the primary joint custodian and the other parent is granted visitation. The primary physical custodian typically retains the decision making power to determine the child's primary residence and school and to designate things such as the child's primary physician. Joint physical custody envisions an equal custody arrangement where the child would spend roughly equal time with each parent. This arrangement requires a good level of communication and cooperation between parents.

How South Dakota determines child visitation: Generally, parents are free to visit with their children at all times that are mutually agreed to by both parents. However, when parents cannot agree to exactly when visitation will occur, the standard visitation schedule accepted almost everywhere in the nation is: every other weekend; six to eight (6-8) weeks during the summer; lternating holidays, including: New Year's, Easter, Memorial Day, 4th of July, Labor Day, Thanksgiving, Christmas Eve and Christmas Day; fathers get Father's Day and the father's birthday, mothers get Mother's Day and the mother's birthday.

WASHINGTON: HOW CHILD SUPPORT IS DETERMINED

Either parent may be ordered to pay child support. Marital misconduct is not considered. The courts will consider all relevant factors. The courts may also require either parent to provide health insurance for the child. There are official Washington Child Support guidelines, designed to be in the best interests of the child, that the courts use to help set child support amounts. The guidelines will be followed, unless the parents have agreed to a child support amount approved by the courts, or the courts determine the guidelines are unjust for a particular case.

At what age does child support payments end? Generally, the obligation ends when the child reaches 18 years of age or the child graduates from high school, whichever occurs later. A child will also automatically be ineligible for child support if that child marries, is removed from disability status by a court order, or the child dies. When considering whether or not to order support for postsecondary

92

educational expenses, the court shall determine whether or not the child is in fact dependent and is relying upon the parents for the reasonable necessities of life. The court will exercise its discretion when determining whether or not and for how long to award postsecondary educational support based upon the following factors:

- the age of the child
- the child's needs
- the expectations of the parties for their children when the parents were together
- the child's prospects, desires, aptitudes, abilities and/or disabilities
- the nature of the postsecondary education being sought
- the parents' level of education
- the parents' standard of living
- the parents' current and future resources
- the amount and type of support that the child would have received if the parents had stayed together

Washington's custody guidelines: Generally, the parents agree upon decisions about parenting and custody. If there is no agreement, then the courts will make these decisions. Joint or sole custody may be awarded based on the best interests of the child, but joint or "shared" custody is presumed to be in the best interest of the child. Every petition for divorce in Washington in which a minor child is involved must include a proposed parenting plan. Parents are encouraged to make an agreement concerning the parenting plan. The parenting plan objectives are to protect the best interests of the child, and to:

- provide for physical care for the child
- maintain the child's emotional stability
- provide for the child's changing needs, minimizing the need for future modifications
- designate the authority and responsibility of each parent
- minimize the child's exposure to negative conflict
- encourage the parents to reach agreements regarding the child

The parenting plan should provide for: dispute resolution; a residential schedule for the child; how the decision-making authority relating to the child is allocated

If the parents have not made agreements, the courts will determine the decision-making authority of the parents and the residential provisions for the child. Equal-time alternating residential care will only be ordered if:

- there is no history of domestic or substance abuse, abandonment or neglect
- the parents have agreed to joint residential custody
- there is a history of shared parenting and cooperation
- the parents are available to each other, especially in terms of location
- this arrangement is considered best for the child

Washington's medical insurance guidelines: Health insurance coverage for the child will be provided by one or both of the parents if the coverage for the child is available through employment or is union related, and the cost of the coverage does not exceed 25% of the obligated parent's basic child support obligation. When the child has special needs, health insurance coverage will be provided by one or both of the parents even if the cost of the coverage exceeds the obligated parent's basic child support obligation. The obligated parent must maintain health insurance coverage for the child, if available, until further notice from the court or until health insurance is no longer available through the parent's employer or union.

A parent who is required to provide health insurance coverage is liable for any covered health care costs for which that parent receives direct payment from an insurer. The obligated parent must also provide proof that coverage is available or not available within 20 days of the order or within 20 days of the date the coverage becomes available. The proof of coverage must be sent to the custodial parent or to the Washington State Support Registry, depending on where the parent has been ordered to send payments. If the proof of health insurance coverage availability is not provided within 20 days, the custodial parent or the Department of Social and Health Services may seek direct enforcement of the coverage through the obligated parent's employer or union without further notice to the obligated parent.

How permanent are the provisions for Washington child support and custody? Court orders providing for support and custody of children are subject to change or modification to reflect changes in income, and/or living arrangements of the children. While all orders concerning the children are modifiable in the future, we encourage you to not enter into an agreement based on the idea that it can always be changed or modified later.

Washington law permits a party to seek current information on income and taxes from the other party. The parents must turn over this information to the statewide Child Support Schedule. Ideally, the parents would compare this information and agree on whether or not an adjustment is proper. If they can agree, they may obtain the adjustment in an written agreed order. If one parent refuses to cooperate with the adjustment, a court hearing may be required to review financial information and rule on an adjustment. The court may order adjustments to the residential aspects of a parenting plan upon the showing of a substantial change in circumstance of either parent or the child. This kind of a change can be difficult to prove. The court may approve a minor modification in a parenting plan without proof of a substantial change in circumstances if the proposed modification does not change the primary residence of the child or if the modification is based on a change of residence or an involuntary change in work schedule by a parent which makes the residential schedule in the parenting plan impractical to follow. A minor modification may not result in a change that exceeds of 24 full days or 90 overnights pre-year.

In order to approve a modification, the court must find that the decree of dissolution or parenting plan does not provide reasonable time with the non-primary residential parent at the time the petition for modification is filed. The court must also find that it is in the best interest of the child to increase residential time with the non-primary residential parent. Additionally, any minor modification will not be the sole basis for adjusting or modifying child support.

Wage garnishment for child support payments: Most states, including Washington, have a provision for withholding child support directly from the earnings of the parent who has been ordered to provide support. The payments are withheld much like income tax is withheld from earnings payments. This way of paying and receiving child support is generally easier for both parties and considered a very dependable solution. The way it typically works is, once the support is withheld, it is then sent to the state agency authorized to receive and disburse payments. Once it has been verified that the support was paid, it is then sent to the parent designated to receive the support.

If a non-custodial parent can show that they are providing more than 50 percent of the support for dependents not included in the court order from a second marriage, and is not in arrears, no more than 50% of their disposable income can be attached if they cannot pay the full court-ordered amount of both orders. That number goes to 55% if the non-custodial parent is in arrears, 60 percent for a person only providing support to dependents under the current order, and 65% for a person who is in arrears and paying only on the current order.

94

How does joint custody work? Joint custody is now widely recognized by parents, courts and state legislatures as the preferred parenting plan in much of the nation. The courts decide on both joint and sole decision-making authority of the parents, and parental residential care, which could include equal-time alternating residential care. They have considerations in making decisions in both areas. So it's possible to have a 50-50 sharing of responsibilities and major decisions affecting the children, and not a 50-50 sharing of time or residential care with the children. It's also possible to have both a 50-50 sharing of responsibilities and a 50-50 sharing of time or shared residential care with the children.

How Washington determines child visitation: Generally, parents are free to visit with their children at all times that are mutually agreed to by both parents. When the courts have not awarded the parents with the equal-time alternating residential care provision, and the parents cannot agree to exactly when visitation will occur, the standard visitation schedule accepted most everywhere in the nation is: every other weekend; four to six (4-6) weeks during the summer; alternating holidays; two mid-week overnights per month (if the parents live reasonably close together).

TEXAS: HOW CHILD SUPPORT IS DETERMINED

What does the court consider when determining the amount of child support? Support amounts are based on income and ability to pay according to state guidelines. Texas considers the financial support of children to be a joint responsibility of both parents. However, in determining the amount of child support to be paid by the non-custodial parent to the custodial parent, only the non-custodial parent's income is considered.

Support will be paid as a flat percentage of the non-custodial parent's income (less allowable deductions) for each child. The courts presume that the custodial parent will spend at least an equal percentage of their income directly for supporting the children.

How do your individual salaries affect support payments? Even though Texas considers the financial responsibility for raising children to be a shared responsibility, only the non-custodial parent's income is considered in calculating child support. The income/salary of the custodial parent generally does not come into question unless there is evidence that simply following the guidelines is not in the best interest of the child.

Does it make a difference if your spouse or you have a second family, stepchildren, or other children? The court will take into consideration any child support or alimony payments being made by a parent when the amount of support is being calculated for the current divorce. If one parent is making support payments that are not court-ordered, but can prove are being made, that will be considered in the support amount determination.

Texas uses a complex set of guidelines and formulas to determine how support should be paid when a non-custodial parent has children in multiple households. It is based on adding a total support obligation for all children as if they lived in one household. The procedure then considers the number of children involved in the current proceeding, and applies credits for support to children who are not part of the current proceeding. There is much more involved in this particular aspect of determining support.

Without the aid of counsel or a state caseworker, these amounts are very difficult to calculate. The resources or needs of either parent's new spouse or dependants may not be used to increase or decrease the child support obligation. The exception to this is award of additional court-ordered support payments. If the non-custodial parent remarries, has a second family, then divorces again, they can seek a modification based on court-ordered support for the second family.

Support payments, alimony or similar obligations in place prior to the second divorce/support proceeding are considered in modifications. The court cannot set a level of support that totals more than 50 to 65 percent of the non-custodial parent's earnings, when support payments are calculated from all court orders. As a result, a custodial parent (or parents) may only receive a pro-rated share of their support, if the non-custodial parent has multiple support orders.

At what age does child support payments end? Generally, the obligation ends when the child reaches 18 years of age or the child graduates from high school, whichever occurs later. However, a court can order the obligation to continue for an indefinite period if the child is disabled. A child will automatically be ineligible for child support if that child marries, is removed from disability status by a court order, or the child dies.

Texas's custody guidelines: Actually, parents are encouraged to agree on parenting and custody issues. If there is no agreement between the parents, or their agreement is not found to be in the child's best interest, then the courts will make these decisions. Custody is often called managing conservatorship. Joint or sole managing conservatorship may be awarded based on the best interests of the child and in some cases, considering the child's preference. The sex of the parents is not considered. Other factors the courts consider include: the age, circumstances, needs and best interests of the child; the parents' circumstances; any evidence of abuse; any other relevant factors.

The courts now encourage joint legal custody whenever practical, based on their own considerations. The courts will not award joint custody if there is any credible evidence of spousal or child abuse. The courts will award joint custody if the parents have a written parenting agreement that:

- designates which parent has the exclusive right to establish the county of primary residence of the child
- establishes the geographic area of residence for the child
- states the rights and duties of each parent regarding the child's care, support and education
- includes ways to minimize disruption of the child's schooling, routine and association with friends
- was entered into voluntarily and knowingly
- is in the best interests of the child

Texas's medical insurance guidelines: In any divorce proceeding where children are involved, the court will assign a health benefit plan to be maintained, usually through either parent's employment. If there is no health plan reasonable available, the court may order other remedies for providing health care/insurance. Medical insurance premiums are assumed to be the responsibility of the non-custodial parent. Medical insurance premiums are considered an addition to the amount of support that is otherwise calculated by using the support guidelines.

Most often, the non-custodial parent will maintain a policy available through their employer. If that is not possible and the custodial parent has a policy available through their employer, the custodial parent will enroll the child, and the non-custodial parent will be ordered to pay the premium. If the custodial parent does not have a policy available, the court may order the non-custodial parent to purchase a policy. If the non-custodial parent cannot afford a private policy, they may be ordered to apply for coverage through Texas Healthy Kids Corporation.

If that coverage is not available, as a last resort, the non-custodial parent will be ordered to pay an additional amount of support for medical expenses. Extraordinary and/or non-reimbursed medical expenses may be cause for the court to deviate from the standard support guidelines, but generally are treated as an expense that is allocated between the parents according to their financial circumstances. Day care costs are considered after the basic support obligation is determined. The cost of day care incurred by either parent in order to obtain or maintain employment, can be treated as a reason to deviate from the standard support guidelines.

How permanent are the provisions for Texas child support and custody? Court orders providing for support and custody of children are subject to change or modification to reflect significant changes in income, and/or living arrangements of the children. While all orders concerning the children are modifiable in the future, we encourage you to not enter into an agreement based on the idea that it can always be changed or modified later.

Wage garnishment for child support payments: Most states, including Texas, have a provision for withholding child support directly from the earnings of the parent who has been ordered to provide support. The payments are withheld much like income tax is withheld from earnings payments. This way of paying and receiving child support is generally easier for both parties and considered a very dependable solution. The way it typically works is, once the support is withheld, it is then sent to the state agency authorized to receive and disburse payments. Once it has been verified that the support was paid, it is then sent to the parent designated to receive the support.

How does joint custody work? Joint custody is now widely recognized by parents, courts and state legislatures as the preferred parenting plan. Specifically, joint custody is a form of custody of minor children that requires both parents to share the responsibilities of the children, and for both parents to approve all major decisions related to the children.

While joint custody is a 50-50 sharing of responsibilities and major decisions affecting the children, it rarely works out to be a 50-50 sharing of time with the children. Often one parent is named as the primary joint custodian and the other parent is granted visitation. The primary joint custodian typically retains the decision making power to determine the child's primary residence and school and to designate things such as the child's primary physician.

How Texas determines child visitation and custody: When disputes arise over support payments, courts view visitation and support as separate issues. The level of support you receive depends on your custody arrangement. If you have primary physical custody, you will receive an amount based on that.

If you and your child's other parent share custody, the level of support will be based on the shared custody arrangement. The Texas statutes dealing with custody — referred to as "conservatorship" can be found at http://www.capitol.state.tx.us/statutes/fa/fa015300toc.html. In the past, if a non-custodial parent refused to pay support, there was not much the other parent could do — except refuse visitation. The courts now recognize that visitation and support payments are two separate issues. If you are the custodial parent, and your support is late or nonexistent, understand you still must allow visitation. Refusing to allow visitation, based on not receiving child support, could put you at risk for a contempt of court citation. A contempt charge also could be leveled against a non-custodial parent who stops paying support based on the claim that they have not been allowed visitation.

Generally, parents are free to visit with their children at all times that are mutually agreed to by both parents. However, when parents cannot agree to exactly when visitation will occur, the standard visitation schedule accepted most everywhere in the nation is: every other weekend; four to six (4-6) weeks during the summer; alternating holidays.

UTAH: HOW CHILD SUPPORT IS DETERMINED

97

Either or both parents may be ordered to pay child support payments, including medical and dental expenses and health insurance. The courts will also order the parents to share day care and childcare expenses while the custodial parent is working or undergoing any training. There are official Utah Child Support guidelines, designed to be reasonable and in the best interests of the child, that the courts use to help determine the correct amount of child support. The guidelines will be followed, unless the parents have agreed to a different child support amount, or the courts determine the guidelines are unjust for a particular case. Factors for deviating from the guidelines include: the standard of living and the situation of the parties; the relative wealth and income of the parents; the earning power of each parent; the needs of the parents and the child; the ages of all involved; any responsibility of either parent to support others.

The state guidelines are generally based on a percentage of the total gross income of both parents, the number of children to be supported and the percentage each parent contributes to the total gross income.

At what age does child support payments end? Generally, the obligation ends when the child reaches 18 years of age or the child graduates from high school, whichever occurs later. A child will also automatically be ineligible for child support if that child marries, is removed from disability status by a court order, or the child dies.

Utah's custody guidelines: Generally, the parents agree upon decisions about parenting and custody. If there is no agreement between the parents, then the courts will make these decisions. Joint or sole custody may be awarded based on the best interests of the child and the following factors:

- which parent is the primary care giver
- the past conduct and the moral standards of the parents
- the welfare of the child
- the child's preference if they are at least 12 years of age
- which parent is likely to act in the best interests of the child
- which parent is likely to allow frequent and on-going contact between the child and the other parent

If the other spouse has abandoned a spouse, the court is likely to give the abandoned spouse custody of any children. If there is an allegation of child abuse by either parent, an investigation will be ordered. The courts will not discriminate against a parent with a disability when considering child custody. Joint custody may be ordered if:

- it appears to be in the best interests of the child
- both parents agree to joint custody
- both parents appear capable of implementing and managing joint custody
- upon consideration of certain factors, such as each parents' ability to give first priority to the child's welfare and their ability to make joint decisions benefiting the child, the parents appear prepared and mature enough for joint custody

Utah's medical insurance guidelines: Generally, the decision as to which parent is going to provide medical insurance coverage for the child and how medical bills will be paid is set out in the marital settlement agreement. If it is not, the courts may order a parent to pay medical and dental expenses and provide health insurance coverage for the child. Usually, if a reasonable medical insurance plan is available through one of the parent's employment, they are required to cover their child on it. Both parents are required to share, equally, any uninsured expenses.

How permanent are the provisions for Utah child support and custody? Court orders providing for support and custody of children are subject to change or modification to reflect significant changes in income, and/or living arrangements of the children. While all orders concerning the children are modifiable in the future, we encourage you to not enter into an agreement based on the idea that it can always be changed or modified later.

Wage garnishment for child support payments: Most states, including Utah, have a provision for withholding child support directly from the earnings of the parent who has been ordered to provide support. The payments are withheld much like income tax is withheld from earnings payments. This way of paying and receiving child support is generally easier for both parties and considered a very dependable solution. The way it typically works is, once the support is withheld, it is then sent to the state agency authorized to receive and disburse payments. Once it has been verified that the support was paid, it is then sent to the parent designated to receive the support.

If a non-custodial parent can show that they are providing more than 50 percent of the support for dependents not included in the court order from a second marriage, and is not in arrears, no more than 50% of their disposable income can be attached if they cannot pay the full court-ordered amount of both orders. That number goes to 55% if the non-custodial parent is in arrears, 60 percent for a person only providing support to dependents under the current order, and 65% for a person who is in arrears and paying only on the current order.

How does joint custody work? Joint custody is now widely recognized by parents, courts and state legislatures as the preferred parenting plan in much of the nation. Specifically, joint custody is a form of custody of minor children that requires both parents to share the responsibilities of the children, and for both parents to approve all major decisions related to the children.

While joint custody is a 50-50 sharing of responsibilities and major decisions affecting the children, it rarely works out to be a 50-50 sharing of time with the children. Often one parent is named as the primary joint custodian and the other parent is granted visitation. The primary joint custodian typically retains the decision making power to determine the child's primary residence and school and to designate things such as the child's primary physician.

How Utah determines child visitation: Generally, parents are free to visit with their children at all times that are mutually agreed to by both parents. However, when parents cannot agree to exactly when visitation will occur, the standard visitation schedule accepted most everywhere in the nation is: every other weekend; four to six (4-6) weeks during the summer; alternating holidays; one week night a week (5:30 - 8:30 PM).

VERMONT: HOW CHILD SUPPORT IS DETERMINED

Either or both parents may be ordered to pay child support, and health insurance coverage for the child, based on the following factors:

- the financial resources of the child
- the financial resources of the custodial parent
- the standard of living the child would have enjoyed if the marital relationship had not ended
- the physical and emotional health and the educational needs of the child
- the financial resources, needs and obligations of the non-custodial parent
- inflation as it relates to the cost of living

99

- the cost of any educational needs for a parent if the costs are incurred for the purpose of increasing the earning capacity of the parent
- extraordinary travel and other travel related expenses incurred in exercising the right to parent child contact
- any other relevant factors

There are official Vermont Child Support guidelines, designed to be reasonable and in the best interests of the child, that the courts use to help determine the correct amount of child support. The guidelines will be followed, unless the parents have agreed to a different child support amount, or the courts determine the guidelines are unjust for a particular case.

At what age does child support payments end? Generally, the obligation ends when the child reaches 18 years of age or the child graduates from high school, whichever occurs later. A child will also automatically be ineligible for child support if that child marries, is no longer disabled as determined by the court, or the child dies.

Vermont's custody guidelines: Generally, the parents are permitted to agree upon decisions about parenting and custody. If there is no agreement between the parents, then the courts will make these decisions. Joint or sole custody may be awarded based on the best interests of the child and all relevant factors, including:

- the relationship of the child with each parent and the ability and disposition of each parent to provide the child with love, affection and guidance
- the ability and disposition of each parent to assure that the child receives adequate food, clothing, medical care, other material needs and a safe environment
- the ability and willingness of each parent to meet the child's present and future developmental needs
- the quality of the child's adjustment to the child's present housing, school and community and the potential effect of any change
- the ability and willingness of each parent to foster a positive relationship and frequent and continuing contact with the other parent, including physical contact, except when physical contact will result in harm to the child or a parent
- the quality of the child's relationship with the primary care provider, if appropriate given the child's age and development
- the relationship of the child with any other person who may significantly affect the child
- the ability and willingness of the parents to communicate, cooperate with each other and make joint decisions concerning the children when parental rights and responsibilities are to be shared or divided
- evidence of abuse and the impact of the abuse on the child and on the relationship between the child and the abusive parent

Vermont's medical insurance guidelines: Generally, the decision as to which parent is going to provide medical insurance coverage for the child and how medical bills will be paid is set out in the marital settlement agreement. If it is not, the courts may order a parent to provide health insurance coverage for the child. Usually, if a reasonable medical insurance plan is available through one of the parent's employment, they are required to cover their child on it.

How permanent are the provisions for Vermont child support and custody? Court orders for child support may be modified, and if modified, the new terms will apply to all future payments. If the party applying for the modification can demonstrate a "real, substantial and unanticipated change of circumstances," the court may modify the existing order.

However, if the court order has not been modified or reviewed for at least three years, the court may not require a showing of "real, substantial and unanticipated change of circumstances" to order a modification. In addition, a child support order that was entered prior to the adoption of the child support guidelines and varies at least ten percent from the amount required to be paid according to the guidelines, will be considered a real, substantial and unanticipated change of circumstances. Therefore, this justifies a court ordered modification.

Wage garnishment for child support payments: Most states, including Vermont, have a provision for withholding child support directly from the earnings of the parent who has been ordered to provide support. The payments are withheld much like income tax is withheld from earnings payments. This way of paying and receiving child support is generally easier for both parties and considered a very dependable solution. The way it typically works is, once the support is withheld, it is then sent to the state agency authorized to receive and disburse payments. Once it has been verified that the support was paid, it is then sent to the parent designated to receive the support.

If a non-custodial parent can show that they are providing more than 50 percent of the support for dependents not included in the court order from a second marriage, and is not in arrears, no more than 50% of their disposable income can be attached if they cannot pay the full court-ordered amount of both orders. That number goes to 55% if the non-custodial parent is in arrears, 60 percent for a person only providing support to dependents under the current order, and 65% for a person who is in arrears and paying only on the current order.

How does joint custody work? Rather than joint custody in Vermont, there is the possibility of a sharing of parental rights and responsibilities. In an action to determine child custody and support, the court will make a determination regarding the parental rights and responsibilities owed to any minor child of the parties. Depending on the best interest of the child, the court may order the parties to divide or share the parental rights and responsibilities.

If the parties cannot agree to divide or share responsibilities, the court will award parental rights and responsibilities to one parent. The court must order what is in the best interest of the child after evaluating all relevant evidence, statutory factors and the attributes of each parent. The court must provide a proper, complete and balanced analysis of the child's best interest.

How Vermont determines child visitation: Generally, parents are free to visit with their children at all times that are mutually agreed to by both parents. However, when parents cannot agree to exactly when visitation will occur, the standard visitation schedule accepted most everywhere in the nation is: every other weekend; four to six (4-6) weeks during the summer; alternating holidays.

Visitation may have a significant effect on the total amount of child support obligation owed to the child. If visitation exceeds the standard schedule and custody is shared, child support will be determined by the shared cost guidelines adopted by the human services agency. The parent who exercises physical custody for a greater period of time over the other parent will be considered the custodial parent. Physical custody is defined as keeping the child overnight.

VIRGINIA: HOW CHILD SUPPORT IS DETERMINED

Either or both parents may be ordered to pay child support, based on the following factors:

101

- the financial resources of the child
- the standard of living the child would have enjoyed if the marriage had not ended
- the physical, emotional and educational needs of the child
- the earning power of each parent
- the age and health of the child
- how the marital property was divided
- both the monetary and non-monetary contributions each parent makes to the family's well being
- the education of the parents and their ability to secure education and training
- tax consequences
- any special medical, dental or child care expenses
- the financial resources, needs and obligations of each parent
- any other relevant factors

There are official Virginia Child Support guidelines, designed to be in the best interests of the child, that the courts use to help determine the correct amount of child support. The guidelines will be followed unless the parents have agreed to a child support amount that at least equals the amount in the guidelines, or the courts determine the guidelines are unjust for a particular case based upon the relevant evidence pertaining to the following factors:

- actual monetary support for other children, other family members or former family members
- arrangements regarding custody of the children
- attributed income to a party who is voluntarily unemployed or voluntarily under-employed, as long as income may not be attributed to the custodial parent when a child is not in school and child care services are not available, and the cost of such child care services are not included in the computation
- debts of either party arising during the marriage for the benefit of the child
- debts incurred for production of income
- direct payments ordered by the court for health care coverage, maintaining life insurance coverage, education expenses or other court-ordered direct payments for the benefit of the child costs related to the provision of health care coverage
- extraordinary capital gains such as capital gains resulting from the sale of the marital house
- age, physical and mental condition of the child or children, including extraordinary medical or dental expenses and child care expenses
- independent financial resources (if any) of the child or children
- standard of living for the family established during the marriage
- earning capacity, obligations, needs and financial resources of each parent
- education and training of the parties and the ability and opportunity for the parties to secure such training and education
- contributions, monetary and non-monetary, of each party to the well-being of the family
- provisions made with regard to the marital property
- tax consequences to the parties regarding claims for dependent children and child care expenses
- a written agreement between the parties which includes the amount of child support
- a stipulated decree, which includes the amount of child support agreed to by both parties or by counsel for the parties

- such other factors, including tax consequences to each party as they are necessary to consider the equities for the parents and children

At what age does child support payments end? Generally, the obligation ends when the child reaches 18 years of age or the child graduates from high school, whichever occurs later. A child will also automatically be ineligible for child support if that child marries, is removed from disability status by a court order, or the child dies.

Virginia's custody guidelines: Generally, the parents agree upon decisions about parenting and custody. If there is no agreement between the parents, then the courts will make these decisions. Joint or sole custody may be awarded based on the best interests of the child and all relevant factors, including:

- the age of the child
- the child's wishes
- the child's needs, including material needs
- the love and affection that exists between the child and each parent
- the mental and physical health of all involved
- the role each parent has played in caring for the child
- any history of domestic abuse .

Virginia's medical insurance guidelines: The court has the authority to order a party to provide health care coverage for the dependent children if it is available at a reasonable cost.

How permanent are the provisions for Virginia child support and custody? Court orders providing for support and custody of children are subject to change or modification to reflect a material change in circumstance. The court may, upon petition of either of the parents, on its own motion or upon petition of public welfare, revise and alter court orders providing for support and custody of children as the circumstances of the parents and the benefit of the children may require.

The intentional withholding of visitation of a child from the other parent without just cause may constitute a material change of circumstances justifying a change of custody in the discretion of the court.

Wage garnishment for child support payments: Most states, including Virginia, have a provision for withholding child support directly from the earnings of the parent who has been ordered to provide support. The payments are withheld much like income tax is withheld from earnings payments. This way of paying and receiving child support is generally easier for both parties and considered a very dependable solution. The way it typically works is, once the support is withheld, it is then sent to the state agency authorized to receive and disburse payments. Once it has been verified that the support was paid, it is then sent to the parent designated to receive the support.

If a non-custodial parent can show that they are providing more than 50 percent of the support for dependents not included in the court order from a second marriage, and is not in arrears, no more than 50% of their disposable income can be attached if they cannot pay the full court-ordered amount of both orders. That number goes to 55% if the non-custodial parent is in arrears, 60 percent for a person only providing support to dependents under the current order, and 65% for a person who is in arrears and paying only on the current order.

How does joint custody work? Joint custody can be one of the following:

1. joint legal custody where both parents retain joint responsibility for the care and control of the child and joint authority to make decisions concerning the child, even though the child's primary residence may be with only one parent
2. joint physical custody where both parents share physical and custodial care of the child
3. any combination of of joint legal and joint physical custody which the court deems to be in the best interest of the child

How Virginia determines child visitation: Generally, parents are free to visit with their children at all times that are mutually agreed to by both parents. However, when parents cannot agree to exactly when visitation will occur, the standard visitation schedule accepted most everywhere in the nation is: every other weekend; four to six (4-6) weeks during the summer; alternating holidays.

WEST VIRGINIA: HOW CHILD SUPPORT IS DETERMINED

Either parent may be ordered to make periodic child support payments and provide health insurance coverage for the child. All relevant factors will be considered. There are official West Virginia Child Support guidelines, designed to be in the best interests of the child, that the courts use to help determine the correct amount of child support. The guidelines will be followed, unless the parents have agreed to a child support amount approved by the courts, or the courts determine the guidelines are unjust for a particular case.

At what age does child support payments end? Generally, the obligation ends when the child reaches 18 years of age or the child graduates from high school, whichever occurs later. A child will also automatically be ineligible for child support if that child marries, is removed from disability status by a court order, or the child dies. Upon finding good cause, a court may order that child support payments continue beyond the age of 18 if the child is unmarried, residing with a parent and is enrolled as a full-time student in a secondary or vocational program and making substantial progress towards a diploma. In this case, payments will not extend past the date that the child reaches the age of 20.

West Virginia's custody guidelines: Either parent may be granted custody of the child. There is a presumption in favor of the parent who has been the primary caretaker for the child. The statute has no specific considerations listed. Also, West Virginia does not have a statutory provision for joint custody.

West Virginia's medical insurance guidelines: Generally, the decision as to which parent is going to provide medical insurance coverage for the child and how medical bills will be paid is set out in the marital settlement agreement. If it is not, then the courts may require either parent to provide health insurance coverage for the child. Usually, if a reasonable medical insurance plan is available through one of the parent's employment, they are required to cover their child on it.

How permanent are the provisions for West Virginia child support and custody? Court orders providing for support and custody of children are subject to change or modification to reflect a substantial change in circumstances. While all orders concerning the children are modifiable in the future, we encourage you to not enter into an agreement based on the idea that it can always be changed or modified later.

Wage garnishment for child support payments: Most states, including West Virginia, have a provision for withholding child support directly from the earnings of the parent who has been ordered to provide support. In fact, in West Virginia, every divorce decree involving children has a provision for the withholding of child support. The payments are withheld much like income tax is withheld from earnings payments. This way of paying and receiving child support is generally easier for both parties and considered a very dependable solution. The way it typically works is, once the support is withheld, it is then sent to the state agency authorized to receive and disburse payments. Once it has been verified that the support was paid, it is then sent to the parent designated to receive the support.

If a non-custodial parent can show that they are providing more than 50 percent of the support for dependents not included in the court order from a second marriage, and is not in arrears, no more than 50% of their disposable income can be attached if they cannot pay the full court-ordered amount of both orders. That number goes to 55% if the non-custodial parent is in arrears, 60 percent for a person only providing support to dependents under the current order, and 65% for a person who is in arrears and paying only on the current order.

How does joint custody work? While joint custody is now widely recognized by parents, courts and state legislatures as the preferred parenting plan in much of the nation, West Virginia does not have a statutory provision for joint custody. Usually, joint custody is a 50-50 sharing of parental responsibility for all decisions relating to the child, but it isn't always a 50-50 sharing of time with the child. One parent is usually named the primary joint custodian and the other is allowed visitation, though they do share the decision-making authority.

How West Virginia determines child visitation: Generally, parents are free to visit with their children at all times that are mutually agreed to by both parents. When the courts have not awarded the parents with the equal-time alternating residential care provision, and the parents cannot agree to exactly when visitation will occur, the standard visitation schedule accepted most everywhere in the nation is: every other weekend; four to six (4-6) weeks during the summer ; alternating holidays.

WISCONSIN: HOW CHILD SUPPORT IS DETERMINED

Either parent may be ordered to pay child support, health care expenses and health insurance coverage for the child. The courts consider the best interests of the child and the following factors:

- the financial resources of the child
- the standard of living the child would have enjoyed if the marriage had continued
- the physical, mental and emotional and educational needs of the child
- the parent's financial resources, income, earning power, needs and obligations
- the age and health of the child
- the best interest of the child
- maintenance received by either party
- the desirability of the parent with custody to remain in the home as a full time parent
- the cost of day care if the parent with custody works outside the home, or the value of the child care provided by the parent
- tax consequences
- any joint custody arrangements
- any extraordinary travel expenses incurred by exercising a the right of physical placement
- the needs of any person, other than the child, whom either party is obliged to support
- any other relevant factors

The courts may order a parent to seek employment. Also, they courts may order alimony and child support payments to be combined into one "family support" payment. There are official Wisconsin Child Support guidelines, designed to be in the best interests of the child, that the courts use to help determine the correct amount of child support. The guidelines will be followed, unless the parents have agreed to a child support amount approved by the courts, or the courts determine the guidelines are unjust for a particular case.

The state guidelines are generally based on a percentage of the net income of the parent ordered to pay child support, as follows: one child 17%; two children 25%; three children 29%.

At what age does child support payments end? Generally, the obligation ends when the child reaches 18 years of age or the child graduates from high school, whichever occurs later. A child will also automatically be ineligible for child support if that child marries, is removed from disability status by a court order, or the child dies.

Wisconsin's custody guidelines: Generally, the parents agree upon decisions about parenting and custody. If there is no agreement, then the courts will make these decisions. Joint or sole custody may be awarded. The courts use the terms "legal custody and physical placement." These decisions will be made based on the best interests of the child and the following factors:

- the preference of the child
- the parents' wishes
- the child's adjustment to home, school, religion and community settings
- the mental and physical health of all involved
- the relationship the child has with each significant family member
- any findings or recommendations by a neutral mediator
- whether child care is available or not
- any history of domestic abuse
- any history of drug or alcohol abuse
- whether one parent is likely to interfere in an unreasonable manner with the child's relationship with the other parent
- the the reports of appropriate professionals if used when legal custody or physical placement is contested
- any other relevant factors

Wisconsin's medical insurance guidelines: Generally, the decision as to which parent is going to provide medical insurance coverage for the child and how medical bills will be paid is set out in the marital settlement agreement. If it is not, then the courts may require either parent to provide health insurance coverage for the child. Usually, if a reasonable medical insurance plan is available through one of the parent's employment, they are required to cover their child on it.

How permanent are the provisions for Wisconsin child support and custody? Court orders providing for support and custody of children are subject to change or modification to reflect significant changes in income, and/or living arrangements of the children. While all orders concerning the children are modifiable in the future, we encourage you to not enter into an agreement based on the idea that it can always be changed or modified later.

Wage garnishment for child support payments: Most states, including Wisconsin, have a provision for withholding child support directly from the earnings of the parent who has been ordered to provide support. The payments are withheld much like income tax is withheld from earnings payments. This way of paying and receiving child support is generally easier for both parties and considered a very dependable solution. The way it typically works is, once the support is withheld, it

106

is then sent to the state agency authorized to receive and disburse payments. Once it has been verified that the support was paid, it is then sent to the parent designated to receive the support.

If a non-custodial parent can show that they are providing more than 50 percent of the support for dependents not included in the court order from a second marriage, and is not in arrears, no more than 50% of their disposable income can be attached if they cannot pay the full court-ordered amount of both orders. That number goes to 55% if the non-custodial parent is in arrears, 60 percent for a person only providing support to dependents under the current order, and 65% for a person who is in arrears and paying only on the current order.

How does joint custody work? Joint custody is now widely recognized by parents, courts and state legislatures as the preferred parenting plan in much of the nation. Specifically, joint custody is a form of custody of minor children that requires both parents to share the responsibilities of the children, and for both parents to approve all major decisions related to the children.

While joint custody is a 50-50 sharing of responsibilities and major decisions affecting the children, it rarely works out to be a 50-50 sharing of time with the children. Often one parent is named as the primary joint custodian and the other parent is granted visitation. The primary joint custodian typically retains the decision making power to determine the child's primary residence and school and to designate things such as the child's primary physician.

How Wisconsin determines child visitation: Generally, parents are free to visit with their children at all times that are mutually agreed to by both parents. When the courts have not awarded the parents with the equal-time alternating residential care provision, and the parents cannot agree to exactly when visitation will occur, the standard visitation schedule accepted most everywhere in the nation is: every other weekend; four to six (4-6) weeks during the summer; alternating holidays.

WYOMING: HOW CHILD SUPPORT IS DETERMINED

Either parent may be ordered to pay child support. The courts may appoint a trustee to invest the support payments and apply the income to the actual financial support of the children. There are official Wyoming Child Support guidelines, designed to be in the best interests of the child, that the courts use to help determine the correct amount of child support. Generally, the guidelines are determined by considering the combined income of both parents and the number of children to be supported. The child support obligation is divided between the parents in proportion to the net income of each. The non-custodial parent's chare shall be paid to the custodial parent through the clerk of the court. The guidelines will be followed, unless the parents have agreed to a child support amount approved by the courts, or the courts determine the guidelines are unjust for a particular case.

At what age does child support payments end? Generally, the obligation ends when the child reaches 18 years of age or the child graduates from high school, whichever occurs later. A child will also automatically be ineligible for child support if that child marries, is legally emancipated, dies or enters military service.

Wyoming's custody guidelines: Generally, the parents agree upon decisions about parenting and custody. If there is no agreement, then the courts will make these decisions. Joint, sole or shared custody may be awarded based on the best interests of the child. The courts also consider:

- the quality of the relationship each child has with each parent

- the ability of each parent to provide adequate care for each child throughout each period of responsibility, including arranging for each child's care by others as needed
- the relative competency and fitness of each parent
- each parent's willingness to accept all responsibilities of parenting, including a willingness to accept care for each child at specified times and to relinquish care to the other parent at specified times
- how the parents and each child can best maintain and strengthen a relationship with each other
- how the parents and each child interact and communicate with each other, and how such interaction and communication may be improved
- the ability and willingness of each parent to allow the other to provide care without intrusion
- geographic distance between the parents' residences
- the current mental and physical ability of each parent to care for each child
- any other factors the court deems necessary and relevant

In any proceeding in which custody of a child is at issue, the court shall not prefer one parent as the custodian solely because of gender. The court shall consider evidence of spousal abuse or child abuse as being contrary to the best interest of the children. At any time the court may require parents to attend appropriate parenting classes. If both parents are considered to be fit parents, then the court may order any form of custody that most encourages the parents to share in the rights and responsibilities of rearing the child.

Wyoming's medical insurance guidelines: Generally, the decision as to which parent is going to provide medical insurance coverage for the child and how medical bills will be paid is set out in the marital settlement agreement. If it is not, then the courts may require either parent to provide health insurance coverage for the child. Usually, if a reasonable medical insurance plan is available through one of the parent's employment, they are required to cover their child on it.

How permanent are the provisions for Wyoming child support and custody? Court orders providing for support and custody of children are subject to change or modification to reflect significant changes in income, and/or living arrangements of the children. While all orders concerning the children are modifiable in the future, we encourage you to not enter into an agreement based on the idea that it can always be changed or modified later.

Wage garnishment for child support payments: Most states, including Wyoming, have a provision for withholding child support directly from the earnings of the parent who has been ordered to provide support. The payments are withheld much like income tax is withheld from earnings payments. This way of paying and receiving child support is generally easier for both parties and considered a very dependable solution. The way it typically works is, once the support is withheld, it is then sent to the state agency authorized to receive and disburse payments. Once it has been verified that the support was paid, it is then sent to the parent designated to receive the support.

If a non-custodial parent can show that they are providing more than 50 percent of the support for dependents not included in the court order from a second marriage, and is not in arrears, no more than 50% of their disposable income can be attached if they cannot pay the full court-ordered amount of both orders. That number goes to 55% if the non-custodial parent is in arrears, 60 percent for a person only providing support to dependents under the current order, and 65% for a person who is in arrears and paying only on the current order.

How does joint custody work? Joint custody is now widely recognized by parents, courts and state legislatures as the preferred parenting plan in much of the nation. Specifically, joint custody is a form of custody of minor children that requires both parents to share the responsibilities of the children, and for both parents to approve all major decisions related to the children.

While joint custody is a 50-50 sharing of responsibilities and major decisions affecting the children, it rarely works out to be a 50-50 sharing of time with the children. Often one parent is named as the primary joint custodian and the other parent is granted visitation. The primary joint custodian typically retains the decision making power to determine the child's primary residence and school and to designate things such as the child's primary physician.

> **How Wyoming determines child visitation:** Generally, parents are free to visit with their children at all times that are mutually agreed to by both parents. When the courts have not awarded the parents with the equal-time alternating residential care provision, and the parents cannot agree to exactly when visitation will occur, the standard visitation schedule accepted most everywhere in the nation is: every other weekend; four to six (4-6) weeks during the summer ; alternating holidays.

PUERTO RICO: HOW CHILD SUPPORT IS DETERMINED

Either or both parents may be ordered to make periodic, lump sum or both types of child support payments. The factors the courts consider include.

- the age and needs of the child
- the ability of the parents to contribute to the support of the child
- the financial resources available for the child's support
- the amount of possession and access to the child
- the net resources of the parent who will pay support
- any childcare expenses necessary for the employment of a parent
- any other custody or child support obligations, or receipt of child support payments by either parent for another child
- the amount of alimony currently being paid or received
- health care and health care insurance provisions for the child
- any special educational or health care needs that the child has
- any benefits a parent receives from an employer
- the debt and obligations of the parents
- any wage or salary deductions of either parent
- the cost of traveling to visit the child
- any negative or positive cash flow from assets
- any extraordinary educational or health care expenses for a parent or the child
- expenses beyond secondary school
- any other relevant factors

There are official Puerto Rico Child Support guidelines, designed to be reasonable and in the best interests of the child, that the courts use to help determine the correct amount of child support. The guidelines will be followed, unless the parents have agreed to a different child support amount. The state guidelines are generally based on a percentage of the net income of the parent ordered to pay child support. For obligors with net resources under $6000 per month, the guidelines are as follows:

109

one child - 20%; two children - 25%; three children - 30%; four children - 35%; five children - 40%; six or more children - no less than the amount for 5 children.

At what age does child support payments end? Generally, the obligation ends when the child reaches 18 years of age or the child graduates from high school, whichever occurs later. However, a court can order the obligation to continue for an indefinite period if the child is disabled. A child will automatically be ineligible for child support if that child marries, is removed from disability status by a court order, or the child dies.

Puerto Rico's custody guidelines: Actually, parents are encouraged to agree on parenting and custody issues. If there is no agreement between the parents, or their agreement is not found to be in the child's best interest, then the courts will make these decisions. Custody is often called managing conservator ship. Joint or sole managing conservatorship may be awarded based on the best interests of the child and in some cases, considering the child's preference. The sex of the parents is not considered. Other factors the courts consider include: the age, circumstances, needs and best interests of the child; the parents' circumstances; any evidence of abuse; any other relevant factors

The courts now encourage joint legal custody whenever practical, based on their own considerations. The courts will not award joint custody if there is any credible evidence of spousal or child abuse. The courts will award joint custody if the parents have a written parenting agreement that:

- designates which parent has the exclusive right to establish the county of primary residence of the child
- establishes the geographic area of residence for the child
- states the rights and duties of each parent regarding the child's care, support and education
- includes ways to minimize disruption of the child's schooling, routine and association with friends
- was entered into voluntarily and knowingly
- is in the best interests of the child

Puerto Rico's medical insurance guidelines: Generally, the decision as to which parent is going to provide medical insurance coverage for the child and how medical bills will be paid is set out in the marital settlement agreement. If it is not, the courts may order a parent to provide health insurance coverage for the child and may include the cost in the computation of child support. Usually, if a reasonable medical insurance plan is available through one of the parents' employers, they are required to cover their child on it.

How permanent are the provisions for Puerto Rico child support and custody? Court orders providing for support and custody of children are subject to change or modification to reflect significant changes in income, and/or living arrangements of the children. While all orders concerning the children are modifiable in the future, we encourage you to not enter into an agreement based on the idea that it can always be changed or modified later.

Wage garnishment for child support payments: Most states, including Puerto Rico, have a provision for withholding child support directly from the earnings of the parent who has been ordered to provide support. The payments are withheld much like income tax is withheld from earnings payments. This way of paying and receiving child support is generally easier for both parties and considered a very dependable solution. The way it typically works is, once the support is withheld, it is then sent to the state agency authorized to receive and disburse payments. Once it has been verified that the support was paid, it is then sent to the parent designated to receive the support.

What exactly is joint custody and how does it work? Joint custody is now widely recognized by parents, courts and state legislatures as the preferred parenting plan. Specifically, joint custody is a form of custody of minor children that requires both parents to share the responsibilities of the children, and for both parents to approve all major decisions related to the children. While joint custody is a 50-50 sharing of responsibilities and major decisions affecting the children, it rarely works out to be a 50-50 sharing of time with the children. Often one parent is named as the primary joint custodian and the other parent is granted visitation. The primary joint custodian typically retains the decision making power to determine the child's primary residence and school and to designate things such as the child's primary physician.

How does joint custody work? Generally, parents are free to visit with their children at all times that are mutually agreed to by both parents. However, when parents cannot agree to exactly when visitation will occur, the standard visitation schedule accepted most everywhere in the nation is: every other weekend; four to six (4-6) weeks during the summer; alternating holidays.

VIRGIN ISLANDS: HOW CHILD SUPPORT IS DETERMINED

Either or both parents may be ordered to make periodic, lump sum or both types of child support payments. The factors the courts consider include:

- the age and needs of the child
- the ability of the parents to contribute to the support of the child
- the financial resources available for the child's support
- the amount of possession and access to the child
- the net resources of the parent who will pay support
- any childcare expenses necessary for the employment of a parent
- any other custody or child support obligations, or receipt of child support payments by either parent for another child
- the amount of alimony currently being paid or received
- health care and health care insurance provisions for the child
- any special educational or health care needs that the child has
- any benefits a parent receives from an employer
- the debt and obligations of the parents
- any wage or salary deductions of either parent
- the cost of traveling to visit the child
- any negative or positive cash flow from assets
- any extraordinary educational or health care expenses for a parent or the child
- expenses beyond secondary school
- any other relevant factors

There are official Texas Child Support guidelines, designed to be reasonable and in the best interests of the child, that the courts use to help determine the correct amount of child support. The guidelines will be followed, unless the parents have agreed to a different child support amount. The state guidelines are generally based on a percentage of the net income of the parent ordered to pay child support. For obligors with net resources under $6000 per month, the guidelines are as follows:

- one child - 20%; two children - 25%; three children - 30%; four children - 35%; five children - 40%; six or more children - no less than the amount for 5 children.

111

At what age does child support payments end? Generally, the obligation ends when the child reaches 18 years of age or the child graduates from high school, whichever occurs later. However, a court can order the obligation to continue for an indefinite period if the child is disabled. A child will automatically be ineligible for child support if that child marries, is removed from disability status by a court order, or the child dies.

Virgin Island's custody guidelines: Actually, parents are encouraged to agree on parenting and custody issues. If there is no agreement between the parents, or their agreement is not found to be in the child's best interest, then the courts will make these decisions. Custody is often called managing conservator ship. Joint or sole managing conservatorship may be awarded based on the best interests of the child and in some cases, considering the child's preference. The sex of the parents is not considered. Other factors the courts consider include: the age, circumstances, needs and best interests of the child; the parents' circumstances; any evidence of abuse; any other relevant factors

The courts now encourage joint legal custody whenever practical, based on their own considerations. The courts will not award joint custody if there is any credible evidence of spousal or child abuse. The courts will award joint custody if the parents have a written parenting agreement that: designates which parent has the exclusive right to establish the county of primary residence of the child; establishes the geographic area of residence for the child; states the rights and duties of each parent regarding the child's care, support and education; includes ways to minimize disruption of the child's schooling, routine and association with friends; was entered into voluntarily and knowingly; is in the best interests of the child.

Virgin Islands's medical insurance guidelines: Generally, the decision as to which parent is going to provide medical insurance coverage for the child and how medical bills will be paid is set out in the marital settlement agreement. If it is not, the courts may order a parent to provide health insurance coverage for the child and may include the cost in the computation of child support. Usually, if a reasonable medical insurance plan is available through one of the parents' employers, they are required to cover their child on it.

How permanent are the provisions for Virgin Islands child support and custody? Court orders providing for support and custody of children are subject to change or modification to reflect significant changes in income, and/or living arrangements of the children. While all orders concerning the children are modifiable in the future, we encourage you to not enter into an agreement based on the idea that it can always be changed or modified later.

Wage garnishment for child support payments: Most states, including Virgin Islands, have a provision for withholding child support directly from the earnings of the parent who has been ordered to provide support. The payments are withheld much like income tax is withheld from earnings payments. This way of paying and receiving child support is generally easier for both parties and considered a very dependable solution. The way it typically works is, once the support is withheld, it is then sent to the state agency authorized to receive and disburse payments. Once it has been verified that the support was paid, it is then sent to the parent designated to receive the support.

How does joint custody work? Joint custody is now widely recognized by parents, courts and state legislatures as the preferred parenting plan. Specifically, joint custody is a form of custody of minor children that requires both parents to share the responsibilities of the children, and for both parents to approve all major decisions related to the children.

While joint custody is a 50-50 sharing of responsibilities and major decisions affecting the children, it rarely works out to be a 50-50 sharing of time with the children. Often one parent is named as the primary joint custodian and the other parent is granted visitation. The primary joint custodian typically retains the decision making power to determine the child's primary residence and school and to designate things such as the child's primary physician.

How Virgin Islands determines child visitation: Generally, parents are free to visit with their children at all times that are mutually agreed to by both parents. However, when parents cannot agree to exactly when visitation will occur, the standard visitation schedule accepted most everywhere in the nation is: every other weekend; four to six (4-6) weeks during the summer; alternating holidays.

CHAPTER 3
KNOW SOME HELPFUL PRELIMINARY INFORMATION YOU'D NEED TO HAVE TO BE ABLE TO PURSUE A CHILD SUPPORT-RELATED CASE

If you have access to the internet, there is a listing of CSE agencies at:
http://ocse3.acf.dhhs.gov/int/directories/ext/IVd_list.cfin
State CSE websites often give the addresses and telephone numbers for local offices:
http://www.acf.hhs.gov/programs/cse/extinf.htmitfexta
There is a listing of tribal CSE agencies at:
http://ocse3.acf.hhs.gov/int/directories/tribaldirectors.cfm
Un listado de las agencias de CSE en espanol se puede encontrar en:
http://ocse3.acf.hhs.gov/int/directories/ext/Espanol IVdlist.cfin

La informacion de la ayuda del nino en espanol esta disponible en:
http://www.acf.hhs.gov/programs/cse/int/childspan.pdf
http://www.acf.hhs.gov/programs/cse/spanish/booklet.pdf

A. Who can get help?

Any parent or person with custody of a child who needs help to establish a child support or medical support order or to collect support payments can apply for child support enforcement services. People who have received assistance under the Temporary Assistance for Needy Families (TANF), Medicaid, and Federally assisted Foster Care programs are automatically referred for child support enforcement services.

Either parent can get help to have a child support order reviewed at least every three years, or whenever there is a substantial change of circumstances, to ensure that the order remains fair. An unmarried father can apply for services to establish paternity — a legal relationship with his child.

A non-custodial parent whose case is not in the CSE Program can apply for services and make payments through the Program. Doing so ensures that there's record of payments made.

Location services are made available for non-custodial parents whose children have hidden from them in violation of a custody or visitation order.

Although the majority of custodial parents are mothers, keep in mind that either the mother or father may have primary custody of the child.

B. Where can you apply for help in obtaining child support?

You can apply through me state or local child support enforcement (CSE) office. Usually, applying to your local CSE agency is most effective, and however, you have the right to apply to another tribunal if that will result in more efficient service. The telephone numbers for state CSE Agencies can be found in telephone directories, usually under the state/county social services agency, at the end of this Handbook, or on the state's child support website. These sites are linked at:
http://www.acf.hhs.gov/programs/cse/extinf.htm#exta

C. Is there an application fee?

People receiving assistance under Medicaid, Foster Care, or cash assistance programs do not have to pay for CSE services. For all others, a fee of up to $25 is charged, although some states absorb all or part of the fee or collect payment from the non-custodial parent.

D. Are there any other costs?

Because child support agencies may recover all or part of the actual costs of their services from people who are not in a public assistance program, there may be other costs to parents. These can include the cost of legal work done by agency attorneys, costs of establishing paternity, and costs of locating a non-custodial parent. The costs may be deducted from the child support payment before it is sent to you or may be collected from the non-custodial parent. Not all states recover the costs of their services. Your local CSE office can tell you about the practices in your state.

E. My state recovers costs from the custodial parent. How will I know how much will be deducted from my support checks?

Your caseworker should be able to estimate the costs involved in your case, and give you an idea of how much they will deduct from each check before sending it to you.

F. Will there be an extra cost if the enforcement agency is dealing with the enforcement agency in another state?

There may be extra costs if more than one tribunal is handling your case. Ask your caseworker to estimate these costs, if any.

G. Will the enforcement agency keep track of my child support payments to make sure they keep coming? I am not in a cash assistance program.

CSE offices are required to monitor payments to make sure they are made regularly and fully. But you should inform the agency if payments are late, in the wrong amount, or if you receive payments directly. When you monitor your case, you can keep the CSE office informed so that it can act quickly if needed.

H. What does the child support enforcement agency need to know

No matter where you start - establishing paternity, finding a non-custodial parent, establishing or enforcing a support order -- the CSE office must have enough information to work on your case effectively. All information you provide will be treated in confidence. The more details you provide, the easier it will be to process your case and to collect child support payments for your children.

I. What documents do I need to bring to the enforcement agency?

Bring as much as you can of the following information and documents. This will help the CSE office to locate the parent, establish paternity, and establish and/or enforce your child support order.

- Information about the non-custodial parent
- name, address and Social Security number
- name and address of current or recent employer
- names of friends and relatives, names of organizations to which he or she might belong
- information about his or her income and assets - pay slips, tax

returns, bank accounts, investments or property holdings

115

- physical description, or photograph, if possible

- birth certificates of children

- if paternity is an issue, written statements (letters or notes) in which the alleged father has said or implied that he is the father of the child

  - your child support order, divorce decree, or separation agreement if you have one

  - records of any child support received in the past

  - information about your income and assets

  - information about expenses, such as your child's health care, daycare, or special needs

You play a big role in getting the child support your children deserve.

J. The non-custodial parent lives across the state. I cannot afford to take the time off from work or to travel there for a child support hearing. How can I get enforcement of my child support?

Most local CSE offices handle enforcement in different jurisdictions in the same state without your having to travel outside your own jurisdiction. Ask your local CSE office for details about how enforcement would work in your case.

K. I am applying for TANF. Do I have to provide information about the father?

To be eligible for assistance programs, you must provide information to help to identify the father and collect child support from him. Any child support collected will be used to help support your children — going either directly to you or to repay the state for your assistance grant. Your state CSE agency will explain how the child support will be used.

L. I don't have any way to support my baby without help, but her father is dangerous. I'm afraid to tell the caseworker who he is.

If you think that you or the baby would not be safe if you try to establish paternity or collect child support, and you need to be in a cash assistance program, you can talk with your caseworker about showing good cause for not naming the father. There are safeguards in place to protect you such as a family violence indicator that can be placed in your records so that your personal information is not released to anyone who is not authorized to view it.

M. My children and I need money now. The non-custodial parent left us ten years ago. Can the CSE office still take my case?

If you apply for services, the CSE office will try to find the non-custodial parent to establish or enforce a child support obligation. Be sure to give your caseworker all the information you have that might help find the parent.

CHAPTER 4
FINDING THE NON-CUSTODIAL PARENT: LOCATION

In most cases, to establish the paternity of a child, to obtain an order for support, and to enforce that order, the Child Support Enforcement (CSE) agency must know where the other parent lives or works. When one person makes a legal claim against another, the defendant must be given notice of the legal action taken and the steps necessary to protect his or her rights. To notify the non-custodial parent in advance under the state's service of process requirements - for example, by certified mail or personal service - child support enforcement officials need a correct address. If you do not have the address, the CSE office can try to find it. The most important information that you can provide is the non-custodial parent's Social Security number and any employer that you know about.

State/tribal CSE agencies, with due process and security safeguards, have access to information from the following:

- State and local government:

  vital statistics
  state tax files
  real and titled personal property records
  occupational and professional licenses and business information
  employment security agency
  public assistance agency
  motor vehicle department
  law enforcement departments

- Records of private entities like public utilities and cable television companies (such as names and addresses of individuals and their employers as they appear in customer records)

- Credit bureaus

- Information held by financial institutions, including asset and liability data.

- The State Directory of New Hires, to which employers must report new employees
- The Federal Parent Locator Service (FPLS)

The FPLS, which includes the Federal Case Registry (FCR) and the National Directory of New Hires (NDNHJ, has access to information from:

- The Internal Revenue Service (IRS), the Department of Defense, the National Personnel Records Center, including quarterly wage data for Federal employees, the Social Security Administration, and the Department of Veterans Affairs

- State Directories of New Hires (SDNH)

- State Workforce Agencies (SWAs)

117

The FCR includes all 1V-D child support cases from the 54 states and territories and non-IV-D support orders established after October 1998. The NDNH contains new hire records, quarterly wage records for almost all employed people, and unemployment insurance claims.

If you have access to the internet, there is information about the FPLS at: http://www.act'.hhs,gov/programs/cse/newhire

1. I think the non-custodial parent is still in the area. What information will the enforcement office need to find him?

Most important are the Social Security number and any recent employer's name and address. Also helpful are the names, addresses and phone numbers of relatives, friends, or former employers who might know where he/she works or lives. Unions and local organizations, including professional organizations, might also have information.

2. What if I don't have the Social Security Number?

Social Security numbers are now required on applications (not the licenses themselves) for professional licenses,-drivers' licenses, occupational and recreational licenses, and marriage licenses; on divorce records, support orders, and paternity determinations or acknowledgements; and on death records

If none of these is available, or the Social Security number was not yet required when the document was issued, the CSE office can subpoena information about bank accounts, insurance policies, credit cards, pay slips, or income tax returns. If you and the other parent filed a joint Federal income tax return in the last three years, the CSE office can get the Social Security number from the IRS.

Your caseworker may be able to get the Social Security number with at least three of the following pieces of information: the parent's name, place of birth, date of birth, his/her father's name, and his/her mother's maiden name.

3. What if the non-custodial parent cannot be found locally?

Your CSE office will ask the State Parent Locator Service (SPLS) to do a search. Using the Social Security number, the SPLS will check the records of state agencies such as the motor vehicle department, S WAs, state revenue department, law enforcement agencies, and correctional facilities. If the SPLS finds that the parent has moved to another state, it can ask the other state to search, and send a request to the Federal Parent Locator Service (FPLS).

4. Can my lawyer or I ask the FPLS to find an address for the other parent?

Not directly. However, you or your attorney can submit a request to use the FPLS through the local or state CSE agency.

5. If I hire a private collection service, can the state CSE agency provide location and income information?

Yes. The private service must provide a guarantee in writing that the information is to be carefully safeguarded and only used for child support purposes, and it must have an agreement that meets state requirements for acting as an "agent of the child"

6. Can state and Federal location efforts be made at the same time?

Yes. For instance, a search can be initiated by the state to another jurisdiction and to the FPLS at the same time. The FPLS matches child support case data with data in the FCR and with the employment data in the NDNH and has access to information from other Federal agencies. Locate information is returned to the state(s) for processing.

7. Can enforcement agencies use the Federal income tax return to find out where the non-custodial parent lives and what he or she earns?

Yes. Under certain conditions, the IRS, working through the Federal Office of Child Support Enforcement (OCSE), may disclose to the child support office information that income providers submit on IRS Form 1099. This information is a valuable tool to help find a non-custodial parent and determine his or her financial assets. The information may only be used for the purpose of enforcing child support payments.

Information available through Form 1099 includes both earned and unearned income, including wages, earnings on stocks and bonds, interest from bank accounts, unemployment compensation, capital gains, royalties and prizes, and employer and financial institution addresses. Even very small businesses submit 1099 asset information to the 1RS, so this can be a good source of information. Any information obtained from the IRS must be verified through a second source, such as an employer or bank, before the CSE agency can use it.

8. What will happen when the caseworker has the current address of the non-custodial parent?

The worker will verify the home and work addresses, and take the next appropriate action on the case, which may include asking the non-custodial parent to come to the CSE office for an interview^, or notifying him/her that legal action may be taken.

9. The father of my child is in the military, but I don't know where he is stationed. Can the enforcement agency find him?

Yes. The FPLS can provide the current duty station of a parent who is in any of the uniformed services.

10. If the CSE office can't find the non-custodial parent, does that mean I can't get cash assistance?

No. You can get assistance from the TANF program if you are trying to help find the non-custodial parent. Your state or local CSE agency will tell you what information they will need you to provide in order to get assistance.

CHAPTER 5
ESTABLISHING FATHERHOOD: PATERNITY

A. Ways Which the Paternity of a child can be established.

A father can acknowledge paternity of a child by signing a written admission or voluntary acknowledgement of paternity. All states have programs under which birthing hospitals give unmarried parents of a newborn the opportunity to acknowledge the father's paternity of the child. States must also help parents acknowledge paternity up until the child's eighteenth birthday through vital records offices or other offices designated by the state.

Paternity can also be established at a court or administrative hearing or by default if the man was served notice of a paternity hearing but did not appear. Parents are not required to apply for child support enforcement services when acknowledging paternity. An acknowledgment of paternity becomes a finding of paternity unless the man who signed the acknowledgment denies that he is the father within 60 days. Generally, this finding may be challenged only on the basis of fraud, duress, or material mistake of fact.

If it becomes necessary to seek child support, a finding of paternity creates the basis for the obligation to provide support. A support order cannot be established for a child who is born to unmarried parents until paternity has been established.

It is important to establish paternity as early as possible. While Child Support Enforcement (CSE) offices must try to establish paternity for any child up to the child's 18th birthday, it is best to do it as soon after the child's birth as possible. If a man is not certain that he is the father, the CSE agency can arrange for genetic testing. These tests are simple to take and highly accurate.

Even if the parents plan to marry after their baby is born, establishing paternity helps to protect the relationship between the child and the father from the very start.

B. What are the benefits of establishing paternity?

In addition to providing a basis for child support, paternity establishment can provide basic emotional, social, and economic ties between a father and his child. There are strong indications that children whose fathers take active roles in their upbringing lead more successful lives.

Once paternity is established legally, a child gains legal rights and privileges. Among these may be rights to inheritance, rights to the father's medical and life insurance benefits, and rights to social security and possibly veterans' benefits. The child also has a chance to develop a relationship with the father, and to develop a sense of identity and connection to the "other half of his or her family. It can be important for the health of the child for doctors to have knowledge of the father's medical history.

120

C. What will the CSE agency need to know to try to establish paternity?

The caseworker needs as much information as you can provide about the alleged father and the facts about your relationship with him, your pregnancy, and the birth of your child. Some of these questions may be personal, but states must keep the information that you give confidential.

The caseworker will also want to know whether he ever provided any financial support, or in any other way acknowledged - through letters or gifts - that that the child was his. A picture of the alleged father with the child is helpful, as well as any information from others who could confirm your relationship with him.

D. What if he denies he is the father, or says he's not sure?

Paternity can be determined by administrative procedures which take into account highly accurate tests conducted on blood or tissue samples of the man, mother and child. Genetic test results indicate a probability of paternity and can establish a legal presumption of paternity. These tests can exclude a man who is not the biological father and can also show the likelihood of paternity if he is not excluded. Each party in a contested paternity case must submit to genetic tests at the request of either party or the CSE agency.
Because genetic testing is so accurate now, states are struggling with the question of what to do if paternity was established by acknowledgement or because the child was born during a marriage, but later testing proves that the man is not the biological father. Some states have procedures for disestablishing paternity. Often, though, when a father/child relationship has been established, states are reluctant to break that bond. State laws and practices determine whether or not paternity can be disestablished.

E. If genetic tests are necessary, who pays for them?

If the state orders the tests, the state must pay the cost of the testing. If the father is identified by the tests, some states will charge him for their costs.

If a party disputes the original test result, he or she can pay for a second genetic test and the state must then obtain additional testing.

F. What happens if 1 am not sure who the father is?

If the father could be one of several men, each may be required to take a genetic test. These tests are very accurate, and it is almost always possible to determine who fathered a baby and to rule out anyone who did not.

G. My boyfriend is on a military base abroad and I am about to have his baby. How can 1 establish paternity and get an order for support?

You can apply for child support enforcement services at your local CSE office. If he is willing to sign documents to acknowledge paternity and agree to support, then enforcement can proceed by an income withholding order. If the man is on a naval ship or lives on a military base abroad and will not acknowledge paternity, it may be necessary to wait until he returns to the United States for genetic testing to be done.

H. The father of my child said I would never get a paternity judgment on him because he'd just leave the state. What happens in this case?

If the accused father fails to respond to a formal complaint properly served upon him, a default judgment may be entered in court. The default judgment establishes paternity. At the same time, a court order for support may be issued. If the parent has disappeared, state and Federal

Parent Locator Services can be called on to help find him. States must give full faith and credit to paternity determinations made by other states in accordance with their laws and regulations,

I. My boyfriend and I are still in high school, and our baby is 6 months old. Why should legal paternity be established if the father has no money to support the child?

When the father gets older and starts working, he will be able to support the child. Having paternity established legally, even if the order for support is minimal or delayed, means collecting child support will be easier later. Aside from establishing a financial commitment from the father, establishing paternity fosters a personal relationship between the father and child.

Some states have laws enforcing child support obligations with respect to minor parents. If a custodial parent is receiving TANF assistance, the parents of the non-custodial minor parent may be responsible for paying child support. Check with your CSE agency to see if your state enforces "grandparent liability."

J. My baby's father lives out of state. Can I still have paternity established?

Yes, you can. For example, if the baby was conceived in your state, if the father used to live there, or there is another basis for exercising personal jurisdiction, your state can claim "long arm" jurisdiction over him, and require that he appear for paternity establishment. If your state cannot claim jurisdiction, the CSE agency can petition the state where he lives to establish paternity. Your caseworker will be able to tell you what needs to be done in your case.

J. What happens after paternity is established?

If it becomes necessary to establish a child support order, a CSE caseworker may discuss the child's financial and medical needs with the father and what he is required to pay for child support according to the state child support guidelines. If a court issues a child support order later,
it may also include the exact terms of custody, visitation, and other parental rights.

L. I don't want my daughter's father in our lives. I'd rather work two jobs and support my child myself than have him establish paternity. As long as I don't receive public assistance, why does establishing paternity matter?

There are few situations when it is not in children's best interest to have paternity established. Knowing their father and having his emotional and financial support is very important to children. In the future, information may be necessary for medical reasons, and paternity establishment may make obtaining appropriate medical attention easier. Also, remember, the child's father has the right to request genetic testing to prove that he is the father and he can then establish the legal right to a relationship with his child.

M. My child's father wants to declare paternity. Is there an easy way for him to do this?

All states offer parents the opportunity to voluntarily acknowledge a child's paternity until the child reaches the age of 18. Forms are available at the hospital or from the state vital records agency. More information is available from the CSE agency.

CHAPTER 6
ESTABLISHING COURT ORDER FOR CHILD
SUPPORT: SUPPORT OBLIGATION

If child support enforcement becomes an issue, it is necessary to have a legal order for child support spelling out the amount of the obligation and how it is to be paid. Establishing a support order depends on how much success you and your caseworker or lawyer have in several critical areas, such as locating the non-custodial parent, if necessary; identifying what he or she should pay; and determining the financial needs of the child.

All states have child support guidelines (a calculation of how much a parent should contribute to the child's financial support) that must be used to establish support orders unless it is shown, in writing, that doing so is not in the best interest of the child. Most state guidelines consider the needs of the child, other dependents, and the ability of the parents to pay. States must use the guidelines unless they can be shown to be inappropriate in a particular case.

Current law requires every 1V-D child support order to include a provision for health care coverage, and the Child Support Enforcement (CSE) agency is required to pursue private health care coverage when such coverage is available through a non-custodial parent's employer. Medical support can take several forms. The non-custodial parent may be ordered to:

- provide health insurance if available through his/her employer,

- pay for health insurance (health care coverage) premiums or reimbursement to the custodial parent for all or a portion of the costs of health insurance obtained by the custodial parent, and/or

- pay additional amounts to cover a portion of ongoing medical bills or as reimbursement for uninsured medical costs.

States today can have arrangements for establishing the support order by an administrative procedure or other expedited legal procedure. The hearing may be conducted by a master or a referee of the court, or by an administrative hearings officer. An order approved by this kind of procedure, whether contested or made by agreement between the parties, must be based on the appropriate child support guidelines for setting a child support order and generally has the same effect as one established in court. It is legally binding on the parties concerned.

If an agreement for support is made between the parents, it should provide for the child's present and future well-being. It may be useful to discuss these issues together if you can, or with a mediator or family counselor. You may call your CSE office or visit the state's website to find out about your state's child support guidelines:
http://www.acf.hhs.gov/programs/extinf.htmfexta

A. What is the most important action that a custodial or non-custodial parent can take to ensure that the order amount is fair?

The most important action is to appear at the support order hearing with the documents requested in the notification of the hearing. When both parents appear and bring the necessary documents, the tribunal making the determination will be able to make a fully informed and fair decision.

123

B. How docs the caseworker find out about the other parent's income or assets?

The caseworker will make every possible effort to identify the parent's employment, property owned, and any other sources of income, or assets. This information must be verified before the support order is final. Under certain situations, the Internal Revenue Service may provide financial information about the parent's earned and unearned income, such as interest payments and unemployment compensation. Employers are now required to report hiring people to the state, and the state then provides the information to the National Directory of New Hires (NDNH), which is a part of the Federal Parent Locator Service (FPLS). The FPLS can provide income information from the NDNH and from states' quarterly wage records. The state CSE agency now has-access to financial institution data, such as bank accounts and credit bureau data, which may provide information about employers and/or assets.

C. I'm sure the other parent is willing to pay support. Can we make an agreement between ourselves and present it to the court?

Laws vary from state to state, but parents who can work out a fair support agreement between themselves can avoid the discord that may occur with contested support hearings. You can get help from a lawyer, mediator or family counselor to present your proposal to the court or administrative hearing officer. The court's sole interest in your agreement is to sec that it is fair to all parties, that the welfare of the children is protected, and that the agreement reflects the guidelines.

D. Are the earnings of both parents considered in setting support awards?

Some states base their guidelines on both parents' incomes (an income-share model), some only on the income of the non-custodial parent (a percentage model). In the models based only on the non-custodial parent income, it is presumed that the custodial parent is contributing towards the child(ren)'s needs by providing care, food, clothing, and shelter.

E. My wife and I are working out a joint custody agreement. How would the court decide the amount of child support for each of us?

That depends a lot on the terms of your custody agreement and on your state's child support guidelines: Some states have guideline formulas that take joint custody into account. The same factors would apply: state guidelines, each parent's ability to pay, and the needs of the child.

F. My husband's income is enough to support the children and me without a drop in our standard of living after the divorce. Do the courts consider this?

These decisions, again, are based on the state's guidelines. However, when one or both parents have high income, the tribunal may decide that strict application of the guidelines is not in the best interest of the children. Such a decision may result in a higher and more appropriate support amount than the amount recommended by the guidelines.

G. I have custody and I just heard that my son's mother has had three promotions in the last four years but the child support is still like it was six years ago. Is there some way to find out when she has a raise?

CSE offices will review child support orders at least every three years, or if there is a significant change of circumstances, if either parent requests such a review. Some states have a procedure for an automatic update. Ask your caseworker for information about reviewing and, if appropriate, modifying your child support order. As part of the review, the caseworker will verify the current income of the non-custodial parent. States can adjust child support orders according to child support guidelines, a cost of living adjustment, or automated methods determined by the state.

124

H. What can I do to get my support increased if it is too low?

Check with your CSE office to see if your support order should be modified. The agency will consider the income and assets of the non-custodial parent; and, in many states, your financial situation; and any special needs of the child. If your support amount is found to be low based on the current financial situation, the agency can seek a legal modification.

I. My ex-husband has remarried and has another family to support. How will this affect the support that my children are due?

Even though the non-custodial parent has a second family, this does not eliminate responsibility to the first family. In some states, the judge may grant the non-custodial parent a decrease in the obligation based on application of the child support guidelines. You must be notified beforehand and given an opportunity to contest the proposed change. Other factors that could lower the support order include increases in your earnings, or poor health or decreased earning ability of the non-custodial parent. If your child leaves school and becomes employed, that can reduce, or stop, child support payments, too.

My children's father is divorcing again and will have another child support order. He lives in another state and I'm afraid that this other order will be enforced before mine. State guidelines may indicate how child support is to be shared when there is more than one support order. If his income will not provide for both orders, the amount of support for your children may be reduced, but you will receive a share of the support collected. For orders enforced by income withholding, states must have a formula for sharing the available income among the support orders. Each family must receive a portion of the available money, and current support has priority over arrearages. Depending on your state child support guidelines, it is also possible that the second support order may be grounds for his requesting a modification of your order. Ask your caseworker for more information.

J. I am the custodial parent. I can't get health insurance with my job but my ex-wife gets good benefits where she works. Can she be required to put the children on her insurance?

Yes. The CSE agency must petition the court to include medical support in any order for child support when employment related or other group health insurance is available to the non-custodial parent at a reasonable cost. Unless a custodial parent has satisfactory health insurance for the children other than Medicaid, he or she should petition the tribunal to include health insurance in new or modified support orders when health insurance is, or may be, available to the non-custodial parent at reasonable cost.

If a custodial parent has access to better health insurance, the support order may increase the non-custodial parent's obligation to offset the cost. Court orders can also be modified to include health care coverage.

States must have laws that should make medical support enforcement easier. For example, insurers can no longer refuse to enroll a child in a health care plan because the parents are not married or because the child does not live in the same household as the enrolled parent. In addition, child support agencies can require an employer to include a child on a medical insurance plan when the non-custodial parent participates in a group health plan but does not enroll the child. This law provides that custodial parents can obtain information about coverage directly from an insurer, submit claims directly to the insurer, and be reimbursed directly by an insurer. For specific information about these laws in your state, contact the CSE office.

125

CHAPTER 7
MAKING SURE SUPPORT PAYMENT IS PAID: ENFORCEMENT

A. A main objective of the Child Support Enforcement (CSE) Program

A main objective of the Child Support Enforcement (CSE) Program is to make sure that child support payments are made regularly and in the correct amount. While non-custodial parents who are involved in their children's lives are usually willing to pay child support, lapses of payment do occur. When they do, a family's budget can be quickly and seriously threatened. Some non-custodial parents do not pay regularly, and some spend a lot of effort and energy evading their responsibility for their children. The anxiety the custodial parent feels when payments are not regular can easily disrupt the family's life.

For this reason, Congress decided that immediate income withholding should be included in all child support orders. (States must also apply withholding to sources of income other than wages, such as commissions and bonuses; and to worker's compensation, disability, pension, or retirement benefits.) For child support orders issued or modified through state CSE Programs, immediate income withholding began on November 1, 1990. Immediate income withholding began January 1, 1994 for all initial orders that are not established through the CSE Program. The law allows for an exception to immediate income withholding if the tribunal finds good cause, or if both parents agree to an alternative arrangement. In these cases, if an arrearage equal to one month's payment occurs, that will automatically trigger withholding.

If the non-custodial parent has a regular job, income withholding for child support can be treated like other forms of payroll deduction, such as income tax, social security, union dues, or any other required payment.

If payments are skipped or stop entirely, especially if the non-custodial parent is self-employed, moves or changes jobs frequently, or works for cash or commissions, the CSE office will try to enforce the support order through other means. Subject to due process safeguards, states have laws which allow them to use enforcement techniques such as: state and Federal income tax offset, liens on real or personal property owned by the debtor, freezing of bank accounts, orders to withhold and deliver property to satisfy the debt, passport denial, or seizure and sale of property with the proceeds from the sale applied to the support debt.
These methods can be used by the CSE office without directly involving the courts.

All states have agreements with financial institutions doing business in their state for the purpose of conducting a quarterly data match known as the Financial Institution Data Match (FIDM). The purpose of FIDM is to identify accounts belonging to non-custodial parents who arc delinquent in their child support obligations. Once identified, these accounts may be subject to liens and levies issued by state or local child support enforcement agencies. An institution doing business in two or more states (multi-state financial institution) has the option to conduct the quarterly data match with OCSE or with the states where the institution does business. States are responsible for issuing levies to the financial institutions to collect the past-due child support.

Under the Passport Denial Program, states certify cases in which an obligor owes more than $5,000 in unpaid child support. The Office of Child Support Enforcement transmits the information to the Department of State so that a U.S. passport will not be issued, or renewed, to someone who is not supporting his or her children. Passports can be seized if the holder requests a change, such as a new address or an additional dependant. In some cases, the CSE

126

agency can help to obtain a Federal warrant. The Department of State can then start procedures to revoke the passport or arrest the obligor at the border when he or she returns to the United States.

If actions available through the CSE program are not successful, state CSE agencies can take cases to court for other enforcement actions such as show cause hearings, contempt of court proceedings, and criminal prosecutions.

B. The noncustodial parent refuses to pay child support, but owns a good deal of property in the county. Can a lien be issued on the property?

Yes. However, a lien on property does not by itself result in the immediate collection of any money. It only prevents the owner from selling, transferring, or borrowing against the property until the child support debt is paid. Even so, the presence of a property lien may encourage the non-custodial parent to pay the past-due child support in
order to get clear title to the property. States are now required to give full faith and credit to liens issued by another state.

C. Is it possible to collect the support payments from personal property?

Under some state laws, the enforcement official can issue an order to withhold and deliver. The order is sent to the person, company, or institution that is holding property belonging to the debtor, such as a bank account, investments, or personal property. The holder of the property must deliver it either to the enforcement agency or court that issued the support order. Some states permit the property to be attached or seized and sold to pay the debt. Some states require non-custodial parents with a poor payment history to pledge property as a guarantee of payment. Non-payment results in forfeiture of the property.

D. Can I have the income withholding applied to my existing child support order?

Yes, you can apply for the income withholding through your local CSE office or your attorney. Though there are limits on how much of a person's check can be withheld, income withholding can be used for both ongoing support and arrearages. Ask the CSE agency how this can be done.

E. Why can't my attorney work on my child support problem while I am receiving services from the child support program?

Your attorney (if you choose to have one) can work with the child support program. For best results, the attorney and staff in the CSE agency should coordinate their efforts to prevent duplication of services and conflicting enforcement decisions.

F. My child's mother works for a big company and has moved several times in her job. Can income withholding work in this case?

Yes. States must recognize the income withholding orders from other states, and continue the income withholding as ordered, without regard to where the non-custodial parent or the custodial parent and children live.

G. My ex-husband has a good job and is willing to have the payments deducted from his paycheck, but his employer won't do it. What can I do?

Under every state's law, an employer must withhold the support if ordered to, or if the non-custodial parent requests it. If you run into problems with an employer, seek the assistance of your CSE office. The state CSE agency staff will send the employer a withholding notice which is binding on the employer. An employer who fails to withhold (he income in accordance with the notice is liable for the accumulated amount that should have been withheld from the non-custodial parent's income. Employers who have questions about income withholding can find

127

information and contacts on the Office of Child Support Enforcement (OCSE) website: http://www.acf.hhs.gov/programs/cse/newhire/employer/home.htm

H. The children's father works irregularly and is paid in cash. Income withholding won't work for me. What will?

Automatic billing, telephone reminders, and delinquency notices from your CSE office might convince him to make regular payments. Other techniques, such as property attachment, credit bureau reporting, tax refund offset, and liens might work for the arrearages. States can suspend or revoke drivers, professional, occupational, and recreational licenses if an arrearage develops. If none of these is successful, your enforcement office can take the case to court for stronger enforcement methods.

I. My ex-wife has her own computer programming service. How can the CSE office find out how much she earns, and how can they collect the money?

The CSE office has access to information from the Internal Revenue Service to determine her income and assets. This information will help to set the support order amount.

Cases involving self-employed non-custodial parents can be challenging to work, and often take more time and effort. If it is not possible to arrange for an allotment or withholding, it may be possible to secure liens on her payments from regular clients or to garnish her bank account. If her business depends on having a license, she may make arrangements to pay rather than risk losing her license. Knowing that arrears will be reported to a credit bureau may give her a strong incentive to comply with the order. Provide your caseworker with as much information as you can about the business and her clients.

J. My children's father owns a cross-country moving van. Why won't the child support office put a lien on it?

Most states will not attach property which a person needs to make a living. Talk to your caseworker about what kinds of property are available for liens and attachment in your state.

K. Can past-due child support be taken from the state income tax refund?

All states with state income tax must have laws that require the offset of state income tax refunds to collect past-due child support. The money first goes to satisfy current support due for that month, next for past-due support owed to families, and finally to states to repay cash assistance provided the family.

L. How docs the non-paying parent find out that his or her state tax refund will be taken?

The state must notify the non-custodial parent in advance of taking the action. The notice specifics the amount owed in arrears and the amount to be offset. It also tells whom to contact if the person wants to contest the offset.

M. Can Federal income tax refunds be offset the same way?

Yes, states can request an offset of Federal income tax refunds for past-due support of over $500 owed on behalf of minor children not receiving cash assistance as well as over $150 owed to states that have provided assistance. Collections from Federal tax offset must go first to repay the state and Federal governments for assistance provided before they are distributed to families who arc owed past-due support. Congress has been considering a proposal for distributing collections to pay family arrearages before money owed the government is paid.

N. My ex-spouse is in the Army. How do I go about having child support payments deducted from a paycheck? And can I get medical coverage for my child?

Members of the military are subject to the same income withholding requirements as other public or private employees. If a service member is not meeting a support obligation, an income withholding order can be sent to the Defense Finance and Accounting Service (DFAS) Center in Cleveland, Ohio. Ask your CSE office for information on how to start this action. There is information on the OCSE website at:
http://www.acf.hhs.gov/programs/cse/fct/militaryguide2000.htm

DFAS also has useful child support information: http://www.dfas.mil/money/garnish/supp-qa.htm http://www.dfas.mil/money/garnish/

To get medical coverage for a child of a military member, the child must be enrolled in the Defense Enrollment Eligibility Reporting System (DEERS). There is information available at:
http://www.tricare.osd.miiydeers/general.cfm

Contact the Defense Manpower Data Center support office for enrollment information.

800-334-4162 (California only) 800-527-5602 (Alaska and Hawaii only) 800-538-9552 (all other states)

O. My children's father retired from the Navy when he was only 40, just before our divorce. Can his military retirement check be garnished for back child support?

Yes, it is possible to garnish the income of retired members of the military. With the assistance of your caseworker or lawyer, you can get a garnishment order from the court and send it with a certified copy of your child support order to DFAS (as above). Your local enforcement office can tell you the exact procedures and follow through on your behalf.

P. The children's mother works for the Federal government. She was recently transferred and stopped making payments. What Do 1 have to do to get them started again?

All Federal employees are subject to income withholding, and there is a central payment office for each Department, so moves within the Department should not affect an income withholding order. If you do not have a formal support order, ask a child support office or an attorney about establishing one. If you have a child support order, your CSE office or attorney can help you to secure payments by income withholding. If she has moved to a different Department, the Federal Parent Locator Service (FPLS) can provide her new location.

Q. My child's father is a contractor who receives payments from the Federal Government. Can the Federal payments be seized for back child support?

Various types of payments can be seized through Administrative Offset to pay child support. They include both recurring and one-time payments. Types of payments that can be intercepted include payments to private vendors who perform work for a government agency, federal retirement payments, and relocation and travel reimbursements owed to federal employees. Some payments cannot be intercepted through this program. They include Veterans Affairs (VA) disability benefits, federal student loans, some Social Security payments. Railroad Retirement payments, Black Lung benefits, and payments made under certain programs based on financial need, or those that are excluded by the head of the Federal agency that administers them.

A case is eligible for an Administrative Offset when the non-custodial parent owes at least $25 in past due support and is at least 30 days delinquent in his or her child support payments. People who owe child support debts subject to Administrative Offset will be notified via a Pre-Offset Notice, which also includes information about the Federal Tax Refund Offset and Passport Denial programs. The Pre—Offset Notice also provides information about how to contest the debt amount.

129

States must submit to OCSE those cases that meet the criteria for the Federal Tax Refund Offset Program. The states use the same process to submit to the Administrative Offset Program. When a match occur between the records of people who owe child support debts and the payment records for Federal payees, the Financial Management Service (FMS) in the Department of the Treasury will seize the amount and transmit it to the state, through OCSE. FMS will also send a notice to the non-custodial parent explaining the type of offset that occurred and referring him or her to the appropriate child support agency for further information.

R. The father of my child is in jail. Can I get support?

Past-due support may accumulate while the father is in jail. But unless he has assets, such as property, bank accounts, or any income such as wages from a work-release program, it is unlikely that support can be collected while he is in jail. You might write to the warden of the prison and ask if any provision is made for a prisoner to provide support for his children. Depending on state law, your support order may be modified so that payment is deferred or forgiven until he is released and working. (Some states will do this so that the arrearage when he is released is not so great that he might hide, but will seek work and resume payments.)

If he is in a Federal Correctional Facility, in addition to seizing available outside assets and income, if any, there also is a possibility that you can get child support payments from the inmate's prison account. According to the Bureau of Prisons instruction, the withdrawal of funds from an inmate's account is strictly voluntary. Child support obligations are listed as the fourth priority of funds that can be withdrawn. You, or your caseworker, will need to find out who the inmate's case manager is and write a letter to that person. Any correspondence to the case manager needs to specifically indicate that child support obligations are to be considered pursuant to the Inmate Financial Responsibility Program. If funds are not received, it may be due to the fact that the inmate has refused to make payment, or that the inmate is making payments that have priority over the child support payments. Contact with the case manager can verify whether or not the inmate is cooperating and willing to meet the child support obligations. (The Bureau of Prisons website has information about locating a prisoner: http://www.bop.gov/)

S. The children's father lost his job and is collecting unemployment compensation. Can child support payments be deducted and sent to me?

Yes. Unemployment Compensation, and other state and Federal benefits can be tapped for child support. Ask your caseworker about the procedures, and make sure you tell your caseworker immediately if you learn about changes in the father's employment situation.

T. By my own calculation, my ex owes me $3,475 in past due child support. Can the enforcement agency try to collect it for me?

If this support was owed before the CSE office became involved in your case, the CSE office will have to verify the amount owed, and you may have to present evidence of the debt to a court before collection procedures can start. While the debt is being verified, the agency can try to collect support payments for current months.

U. 1 heard that my children's father is buying a very expensive car. He owes over $5,000 in back support. Can the credit agency be told this?

Yes. By law, the CSE office must periodically report the amount of past-due child support to credit reporting agencies. Consult your caseworker for more information.

V. The other parent does not work regularly and keeps falling behind in child support payments. Is there any way to establish regular payment?

As mentioned at the beginning of this section, property liens and attachments might work. In certain cases, state law also authorizes that the parent be required to post security, bond, or other guarantees to cover support obligations. These guarantees may be in the form of money or property. Ask your enforcement caseworker if other forms of payment might be applied to your case.

W. My ex-wife has declared bankruptcy and says she doesn't have to pay child support. Is that true?

Child support payments generally cannot be discharged in bankruptcy. This means that the parent who owed child support cannot escape this duty by filing for bankruptcy. As of October 1994, bankruptcies do not act as a stay, or hold, on actions to establish paternity or to establish or modify child support obligations. The relationship between child support and bankruptcy is complex, and you may need the help of someone familiar with bankruptcy law. Ask your caseworker how the CSE office can help.

X. My daughter's father says that since he gives her gifts and money he does not have to pay child support.

An order for support specifies how support is to be paid and gifts or payments made outside the order are generally not considered a credit against the ordered child support amount. If he is not paying as ordered, check with the CSE agency about enforcing the order. If you do not have a support order, you can talk with staff in the CSE agency about establishing one.

Y. The child support office is not enforcing my case. Can I take it to the Federal Court?

If your caseworker and state CSE office have had no response to their requests for enforcement in another jurisdiction, it is possible for the case to be heard by a Federal court. This is not done often, and the decision to use a Federal court will be made by Federal investigators with help from the referring child support agency. The U.S. Attorney that has jurisdiction in your area makes the final decision about whether to prosecute. If you are not satisfied with the services you are receiving in your local CSE office, you may ask your state CSE agency for help. State agency addresses and phone numbers are listed at in Appendix B at the end of this Handbook. They are also provided on the OCSE website where the agency tries to post any changes reported as soon as they learn of them:
http://ocse3.acf.dhhs.gov/int/directories/ex.t/IVd_list.cfm
In Section VI: Working Across Borders, there is information about Federal enforcement in cases in which the non-custodial parent lives in another state and is actively evading a support obligation.

Z. My children are over 18 and don't get child support any more, but there is still a £10,000 arrearage owed to me for support that was never paid. Will the CSE office collect that money for me?

State statutes of limitations determine how long the CSE Office can try to collect on a child support debt. Within this period, the CSE office is required to collect verified back support. Ask your CSE office for more information.

1. Can my children be provided for if my ex-husband dies?

In most cases, the estate of the deceased non-custodial parent may only be responsible for satisfying any past-due support. In addition, the child may already be a beneficiary of that estate. See your local CSE office for assistance or guidance on filing an appropriate claim in probate court. Continued future support should be planned for by both parents and, in addition to verifying eligibility for Social Security and similar survivor benefits, parents should consider drafting appropriate wills and securing appropriate life insurance policies.

2. My ex-husband inherited a house and a sizeable amount of money from his parents. He already had some income and property. Now he doesn't have to work, and he put everything into his brother's name and got his child support reduced to the state minimum.

His action may constitute a "fraudulent transfer." Check with the state CSE agency to see if it would be considered as such under state law and if the property transfer can be voided. In addition, courts can establish a support order based on imputed income — the amount that someone would be able to pay if he or she had not voluntarily lowered his income or transferred his or her assets. Your CSE agency can provide information about a possible review of the order if the amount was reduced because of his actions.

3. My case is difficult and the state is having a hard time collecting from my ex-spouse. I'm thinking about contacting a private collection agency. What information is available about them?

A private collection agency (PCA) is a privately owned, for-profit business that, for a fee, helps parents collect child support. CHJSE recognizes a parent's right to choose to work with a PCA. However, parents should make informed choices. If you hire a PCA, make sure that you understand your rights and obligations under the contract before you sign. If you have access to the internet at home or at a public library, OCSE has developed an Information Memorandum that includes information that you might consider if you are thinking of using a PCA. hrtp://www.acf.hhs.gov/programs/cse/pol/IM/im-02-09a.htm

4. Do I have to close my case with the state CSE agency to hire a PCA?

The state cannot require you to close your case simply because you hired a PCA. A PCA may require that you close your case with the state as a condition of your contract. If you do close your case with the state, the following collections services may not be available: tracking changes in the non-custodial parent's employment through the National Directory of New Hires; interception of state and Federal tax refunds and lottery winnings; passport denial; and license revocation or suspension.

132

CHAPTER 8

DISTRIBUTION: HOW THE STATE DISBURSEMENT UNIT DISTRIBUTES THE MONEY COLLECTED TO THE CUSTODIAL PARENT

It is important that families receive their child support payments as quickly as possible. Any delay can quickly and seriously threaten a family's budget. For this reason, states are required to distribute most payments within two days of their receipt. When two states are involved, each one must send payments out within two days. Each state has established a State Disbursement Unit (SDU) — a single unit to receive and send out payments for child support. These SDUs are intended to get payments out with a minimum of turnaround time. They have the additional advantage of providing a single place in the state to which employers can send child support payments collected from their employees.

State SDUs are responsible for:

- receipt and disbursement of all payments;

- accurate identification of payments;

- prompt disbursement of the custodial parent's share of any payment;

- furnishing to any parent, upon request, timely information on the current status of payments under a support order; and

- maintaining a statewide record of support orders.

Families who receive public assistance, under the Temporary Assistance to Needy Families (TANF) programs, must assign their right to child support to the state. Some states "pass through" a portion of the child support collected to the family and may reduce the assistance payment.

After the family leaves the assistance program, the total current support collection goes to the family. Amounts collected beyond the amount ordered as current support are considered to be payments towards arrearages owed to the family and to the state/Federal Government. Under current laws, families receive their post-assistance arrears before the state collects money to repay the government for the assistance payments. (The new priorities will not affect collections made through the Federal Income Tax Offset Program, which will continue to reimburse Government assistance payments first.)

Will I receive the entire amount of support paid?

If you have not received cash assistance, you will receive the total child support payment (less any fees the state may collect). If you are receiving cash assistance, check with your state CSE agency. Some states will pass some or all of the child support payments through to you and may reduce your assistance payment; others will use the entire amount to repay the money provided to your family. If you are not receiving cash assistance now but did in the past, and if amounts are still owed to the state, any support collected beyond the amount ordered for current support and for arrearages owed to you may be used to reduce the arrearages owed to the state.

133

1 am working with a private collection service. Can the collection agency ask to have my child support payments sent there?

Orders established after 1993 require that wage withholdings are sent through the State Disbursement Unit (SDU). State IV-D programs can send payments in the custodial parent's name to the address that he or she provides, including a private agency that you delegate to be the agent of your child for collection purposes, unless otherwise prohibited by state law.

My child's father told me weeks ago that his tax refund was taken for child support. When will get the money?

It usually takes three to five weeks from the time the money is offset from the obligor's tax refund until the state receives it. The Department of the Treasury has encouraged states to hold collections from joint tax returns for up to six months in case the obligor's spouse who does not owe child support files for his or her share of the refund. The Office of Child Support Enforcement and Treasury Department will be working together to provide information to the states if the spouse has filed a claim for his or her part of the refund and has received the money. Slates will be able to distribute the offset to the family when they receive that information. Check with your CSE agency to see if the money has been collected and, if so, when you can expect to receive it. Keep in mind that any money owed for cash assistance provided to the family must be repaid first.

CHAPTER 9
THE ACF HEALTHY MARRIAGE INITIATIVE

A. What is the Children and Families Healthy Marriage Initiative

The U.S. DHHS (Department of Health & Human Services) Administration for Children and Families (ACF) Healthy Marriage Initiative began in 2003. Its mission is to help couples who choose to get married to gain greater access to marriage education services that will enable them to acquire the skills and knowledge necessary to form and sustain a healthy marriage.

Research indicates that children in stable two-parent families do better, on average, than those from single-parent households. Section 1115 of the Social Security Act (Act) authorizes the Secretary to test new uses of child support funds if he determines that these uses are likely to further the objectives of the Act, improve the financial well-being of children, or otherwise improve the operation of the child support program.

Section 1115 authorizes the Secretary to conduct demonstration projects designed to meet the objectives of the Child Support Enforcement program, such as:

- locating absent parents;

- establishing paternity when needed;

- establishing child support orders; and

- enforcing child support orders when needed.

One of the main activities of the demonstration projects will be teaching skills to help couples to communicate better, manage their emotions more effectively when they disagree and be better parents for their children. Skills that help parents work cooperatively should also increase voluntary paternity establishment for children born out of wedlock. Even when couples are unable to sustain a healthy marriage, parents who can work together are more likely to agree to fair support orders and to provide financial and emotional support for their children.

B. What is the connection between Child Support Enforcement and the ACF Healthy Marriage Initiative?

The purpose of the Healthy Marriage Initiative is to test new strategies in communities to strengthen the child support program's ability to promote the financial well-being of children by integrating healthy marriage and healthy parental relationship skills building into the existing range of child support enforcement activities. Funded projects will provide information and skills primarily to couples with children who are considering marriage. It is important for unmarried parents to realize that voluntarily establishing paternity is a giant step towards ensuring that a child can depend on both parents. It is not the beginning of an adversarial child support proceeding. These programs will explain to parents that paternity establishment does not mean abandoning the hope of marriage. Couples can get the information and skills they need to make good decisions about getting married and establishing paternity. These are compatible actions, both of which are important aspects of taking responsibility for one's family.

135

C. Will funding of these projects divert funds from establishing and collecting child support?

No. There is no reduction in the amount of Federal or state funds dedicated to supporting the services currently being provided by the IV-D program to families and children as a result of these projects. The Federal funds for the project will add to the total being spent on the 1V-D program. The state funds to provide matches for these federal funds are donated funds. They do not come from state child support enforcement agency funds that would otherwise be used to operate the child support program. Section 1115 allows the Department of Health and Human Services to treat donated funds as state funds to be matched with the federal funds.

D. How will the outcomes of these projects be measured?

These projects are designed to produce positive outcomes, but it is precisely the purpose of Section 1115 projects to test ideas that hold the promise of increasing paternity establishment and financial support of children. The Department will conduct a comprehensive, high quality evaluation to assess just how these programs affect families and children, and the operation of the Child Support Program. The evaluation will be designed in partnership with research organizations, academic researchers, foundations and the states and local entities conducting the projects.

E. Does the Healthy Marriage Initiative risk pushing women into unhealthy marriages?

No. Healthy marriage projects are intended to help people form healthy and respectful relationships and marriages that reduce the risk of abuse and violence. Domestic abuse and violence are serious problems. Healthy Marriage projects do not push people into marriages, but help them understand how healthy relationships and marriages work and help them assess their own relationships realistically. All ACF supported activities must include appropriate attention to potential issues of domestic violence, and every opportunity must be taken to ensure the safety of victims or potential victims.

CHAPTER 10
COLLECTING OR PAYING CHILD SUPPORT ACROSS BORDERS:
COOPERATION BETWEEN STATES, TRIBES, COUNTRIES

A. Interstate/Inter-jurisdictional Enforcement

It has been difficult to collect child support when the parent obligated to pay child support lives in one jurisdiction and the child and custodial parent live in another. However, all state and tribal/K-D Child Support Enforcement (CSE) agencies are required to pursue child support enforcement, including location, paternity establishment, and establishment of support obligations, as vigorously for children who live outside their borders as for those under their own jurisdiction.

With the enactment of the Full Faith and Credit for Child Support Orders Act, and the Federal mandate that all states enact the Uniform Interstate Family Support Act (UIFSA), interstate enforcement of child support obligations is improving. Tribes have not been required to enact UIFSA in order to receive Federal funding for child support programs as states have been required to do. However courts of all United States territories, states and tribes must accord full faith and credit to a child support order issued by another state or tribe that had jurisdiction over the parties and the subject matter. UIFSA includes a provision designed to ensure that, when more than one state is involved, there is only one valid child support order which can be enforced for current support. The law also includes a provision that allows a IV-D agency to work a case involving an out-of-jurisdiction obligor directly if certain conditions are met.

UIFSA has procedures under which an enforcement official (or private attorney) can refer a case to another tribunal within the United States. The laws can be used to establish paternity and to establish, modify, or enforce a support order

Interstate income withholding can be used to enforce a support order in another jurisdiction if the noncustodial parent's employer is known. Under UIFSA, income withholding can be initiated in one state and sent directly to an employer in another without involving the CSE agency in that state. Laws vary and you will need to ask your caseworker whether this option is available in your case.

State CSE Agencies all have an office called the Central Registry to receive incoming interstate child support cases, ensure that the information given is complete, send cases to the right local office, and respond to inquiries from out-of-jurisdiction CSE offices. Standard forms make it easier for state and tribal caseworkers to find the information they need to enforce a case, and to be sure they are supplying enough information for another jurisdiction to enforce their case.

B. I know the out-of-state address of my children's father, and my caseworker sent a petition to establish my support order there. That was three months ago, and still no support payments. What's wrong?

It may be any number of things: enforcement officials may not be able to serve notice on the non-custodial parent due to inadequate address information; if a hearing is necessary, it may take a while to get a court date. Generally speaking, a state must complete service of process to begin an action within 90 days of locating the non-custodial parent, and the majority of orders should be established within six months from the date of service of process. Continue to keep in touch with your caseworker to resolve any delay or to provide any new information you may have.

C. I need to establish paternity for my child, and the father lives in another part of the country. How does this work?

The fact that you and the person presumed to be the father live in different jurisdictions will not keep you from pursuing a paternity establishment action. Your state may be able to claim jurisdiction and establish paternity if the father has lived there, the child was conceived in your state, or there is another basis for the exercise of personal jurisdiction. Otherwise your state can petition the other jurisdiction to establish paternity under their laws. Often, genetic tests will be ordered to help prove paternity. Ask your caseworker for specific information about the laws in your state and the state where the other parent lives.

D. My case worker filed an interstate petition for paternity. The father denied it, and the other court just dismissed the case. What wend wrong?

A responding CSE office should not dismiss a case without asking for the information it needs. The initiating state is required to provide that information within 30 days. (Tribal IV-D agencies do not have this requirement.) Either party in a contested paternity action can request blood or genetic testing. Ask your caseworker to reopen the case. You have the right to establish paternity until your child's 18th birthday.

E. If paternity is established in another state, will the support order also be entered in that state?

Yes, UIFSA procedures cover establishing paternity and establishing an enforcing child support orders when more than one tribunal is involved. Ask your caseworker how this is done.

F. Will location and enforcement services cost more if my agency dealing with another state or jurisdiction? I am not receiving cash assistance.

Possibly. It depends on what the CSE office has to do to find the non-custodial parent and to establish regular payment. The more solid information and leads you provide, the more efficiently your case can be conducted. For non-assistance cases, service fees vary in different states. Your caseworker should be able to tell you more about these costs in your particular case. (See discussion in the Introduction section of this Handbook., and in Chapter 4)

G. I don't have a support order. Can 1 have one established by petitioning the court where my ex-husband lives?

Yes. This can also be done by your CSE office. Depending on the facts, it could be handled in your jurisdiction or referred to another jurisdiction under UIFSA. An affidavit of the facts, indicating the name and address of the responsible parent, details of your financial circumstances, and the needs of the child, will be included. The petition will be mailed to the enforcement agency, the court, or the interstate official where the father lives. The responding jurisdiction will review this information together with information about the father's ability to pay, and set the amount to be paid.

H. I have had to wait several months for my enforcement agency to get a reply to its request for location assistance in another state. Why does it take so long to get an answer?

Even though they try to be responsive, enforcement agencies have a very high demand for their services. An agency's ability to act rapidly depends on the characteristics of the case, the quality of information received, and the amount of staff and other resources they have to devote to it. Be sure to follow up regularly with your caseworker to make sure that each jurisdiction is actively working your case.

138

I. As soon as the children's father is notified about enforcement, he moves. How will I ever be able to collect my support?

It is difficult to enforce child support payments when the non-custodial parent intentionally moves to avoid paying. Try to be an active participant in your own case. Whenever you learn that the non-custodial parent has moved or has a new job, you should tell your caseworker as soon as possible. All states are required to have a State Directory of New Hires, and employers are required to report hiring new employees within 20 days. The information, in turn, is sent to a National Directory of New Hires. This helps locate the non-custodial parent quickly if he/she moves onto a new job.

J. Isn't there a law now that makes it a Federal crime to not pay child support if the child lives in another state?

The Child Support Recovery Act of 1992 (CSRA) made it a Federal . crime to willfully fail to pay support for a child living in another state if the arrearages exceed $5,000 or are unpaid for longer than a year. That law was strengthened in 1998 by Public Law 105-187, which added new categories of felonies with stronger penalties for more blatant child support evaders. Because successful prosecution depends on extensive investigation, the U. S. Attorney's offices are very selective about the cases they accept. Priority is given to cases: (1) where there is a pattern of moving from state to state to avoid payment; (2) where there is a pattern of deception (e.g., use of false name or Social Security number); (3) where there is failure to make support payments after being held in contempt of court; (4) where failure to make support payments is connected to some other federal offense such as bankruptcy fraud. The U.S. Attorneys may also require that it can be shown that the nonpayer has financial resources and is able to pay.

In nearly all cases, U.S. Attorneys ask that cases be reviewed and forwarded to them by the state CSE offices. When a CSE office has screened and referred the case, the U.S. Attorneys can be reasonably sure of receiving significant information about the case and that civil and state criminal remedies are exhausted. Check with your caseworker to see if prosecution under this Act would be available in your case. The final decision about whether to prosecute, is with the U.S. Attorney, relying heavily on information provided by the CSE agency.

K. My former wife lives in another state. She owns an expensive car, jewelry, and several pieces of property. Would the CSE Program be able to attach this property for child support?

An interstate CSE action may be filed on your behalf to ask the other state to attach this property.

L. The children's mother lives in another state and every time the kids come home from there, they talk about her new car or stove or something, but she still won't pay her child support. Why can she get credit if the courts know she owes her kids so much?

CSE office staff must report child support arrearages to credit bureaus, so that information is available to people/offices that offer credit. Also, the state notifies the noncustodial parent if the debt will be reported to the credit-reporting network. Sometimes, that is enough to encourage payment of the overdue support.

M. Tribal Cases

The Department of Health and Human Services recognizes the unique relationship between the Federal government and Federally recognized Indian tribes, and acknowledges this special government-to-government relationship in the implementation of the tribal provisions of the Personal Responsibility and Work Opportunity Reconciliation Act (PRWORA). For the first time in the history of the title IV-D program, PRWORA authorized tribes and tribal organizations to operate child support enforcement programs like states do.

Before enactment of PRWORA, only the states were authorized to administer IV-D services. However, within much of tribal territory, the authority of state and local governments is limited or non-existent. The Constitution, numerous court decisions, and Federal law, clearly reserve to tribes important powers of self-government, including the authority to make and enforce laws to adjudicate civil and criminal disputes including domestic relations cases, to tax, and to license. States have been limited in their ability to provide IV-D services on tribal lands and Native American families have had difficulty obtaining services from state IV-D programs. Cooperative agreements between tribes and states have helped bring child support services to increasing numbers of Indian and Alaska Native families.

The tribes that are operating child support programs at the time of the printing of this Handbook are listed at the end of the booklet. Tribal programs are also listed on CSE website at: http: http://ocse3.acf.hhs.gov/int/directories/tribaldirectors.cfm

1. My ex-husband is a Native American who lives and works on an Indian reservation. Can the CSE Program help get child support for my children?

If your ex-husband is a member of a tribe with a IV-D program, this will not be a problem. The state office should contact the tribal IV-D office and work cooperatively with them to get the child support you need. You may also want to consider applying for child support services directly from the tribal child support office.

If your ex-husband is a member of a tribe that does not have an agreement with OCSE to operate a CSE program, your caseworker should contact the tribal court and ask about the tribal procedures for child support. Most tribes have an office that handles child support enforcement cases even if they do not have a cooperative agreement with OCSE to operate a child support enforcement program.

2. My ex-husband is not a Native American, but he works on a reservation. Will his employer withhold income from his cheek to make the child support payment?

If the tribe is operating a IV-D CSE program, your caseworker should send the income withholding order through the tribal IV-D agency. The tribal IV-D agency will present the income withholding Order to the tribal enterprise for processing and income withholding.

If the tribe does not have an agreement with OCSE to operate a child support enforcement program, your caseworker should contact the tribal court and ask about the tribal procedures for honoring an income withholding order. In must instances, the tribal enterprise will honor the withholding order, but it must be processed through the tribe's procedures.

3. I am a Native American mother of a 3-year-old and I live on a reservation. His father is not a Native American, does not live on the reservation, and does not fall under the jurisdiction of tribal court. How can I get him to help support his son?

If your tribe has a CSE agency, work through that office to establish and enforce an order. You can also apply for child support services with the appropriate state office. There is nothing that precludes you from applying for services with both the tribe and the state. States and tribes work cooperatively to ensure that the children get the support that they need.

N. International Cases

1. The father of my child has left the United States. How can I get my court order for child support enforced?

The U.S. government has negotiated Federal-level reciprocity declarations with several countries and is negotiating declarations with others on behalf of all U.S. jurisdictions. The government website lists countries with which the U.S. has agreements at this website: http://www.acf.hhs.gov/programs/cse/international/index.html

If there is not a Federal level agreement, check with your state CSE agency. Many state CSE agencies have agreements with foreign countries to recognize child support judgments made in other countries. Interstate Roster and Referral Guide of the U.S. Office of Child Support Enforcement, includes information provided by the states about countries that they work with, at: http://ocse3.acf.hs.gov/ext/irg/sps/selectastate.

These international child support agreements specify procedures for establishing and enforcing child support orders across borders. While requirements for getting enforcement action may vary, depending on the other nation involved, generally a parent will be asked to provide the same information as in a domestic case, including as much specific information, such as address and employer of the non-custodial parent, as possible.

If a non-custodial parent works for an American enterprise, or for a foreign company with offices in the U.S., income withholding might work even if the country he or she lives in does not have any agreement to enforce an American state's order. Even in cases where the non-custodial parent is living and working in a country that has no reciprocity agreement, approaching the foreign employer directly for help might prove successful.

2. What if you've checked with the CSE office, but the country in which your child's father lives has no agreement with any state to enforce child support obligations. Is there anything else to try?

The Office of Citizens Consular Services may be able to give you information about how to have the support order enforced in that country and how to obtain a list of attorneys there. The address where to inquire is: U.S. Department of State, Office of Citizens Consular Services, Washington D.C. 20520

3. My child's mother is still in the U.S., but I understand that she is planning to live abroad with her new husband. She owes me $14,000 in child support. I s there anything the CSE Office can do?

147

State CSE Agencies can certify child support arrearages of more than $5,000 to the Secretary of Health and Human Services, who, in turn, will transmit the certification to the Secretary of State for denial of passports. The passport can also be seized if she asks for any change – change of address, a new visa, addition of a child, etc. In addition, you should ask your caseworker if the court can impose a bond to secure payment of the arrears and future support.

CHAPTER 11
RIGHTS OF NON-CUSTODIAL PARENTS

A. Child's Best Interest Is Served When BOTH Parents Are Involved

Both research and observation give clear and convincing evidence that children benefit greatly if both parents are actively involved in their lives. It is critical to children as they grow and develop. Bringing a child into the world means making a commitment to care for him or her throughout childhood – ensuring the best possible environment to grow in. Children need safe places to live, nourishing food, education, and a solid foundation of values. Mothers and fathers bring different, but equally important, qualities to their children. In a divorce or non-marital situation, either parent may be granted custody of the child - or both may share equally in the physical custody and/or decision-making responsibilities.

Because traditionally men are less likely to have custody, and because the role of fathers is so important, the Department of Health and Human Services (HHS) has established a Fatherhood website at: http://fatherhood.hhs.gov/index.shtml

B. I'm getting a divorce and my spouse wants me to pay child support directly to her. Can 1 insist on paying through the CSE office?

A non-custodial parent can apply for child support services if the case is not being enforced through the Child Support Enforcement (CSE) program, unless the support order requires you to pay her directly. Since January 1994, support orders must include a provision for income withholding unless both parents and the courts agree on another payment method. If your order does not call for income withholding, you can request this service. If you do, you will have a record that you have made payments as required. If you are self-employed, you may be able to arrange for an automatic transfer of funds to the child support agency through electronic Funds transfer (EFT). Either parent can apply for CSE services, which include collecting and distributing payments.

C. I'm the non-custodial parent. I love my kids. I pay my child support. About hall the time when I go to pick them up for my weekend, my ex-wife has made other plans for them. It's not fair that the state will enforce my child support obligation but not do anything about my right to see my kids.

Although the CSE Program lacks authority to enforce visitation, many state or local governments have developed procedures for enforcing visitation orders. Also the Federal government has made funding available to states for developing model programs to ensure that children will be able to have the continuing care and emotional support of both parents. Check with your local CSE agency and clerk of court to see what resources are available to you and to find out about laws that address custody and visitation.

143

D. After I pay my child support, I don't even have enough money for decent food. When my child support order was set, I was making about $300 a month more than I am now. Can I get the order changed?

Either parent can request a review, and adjustment, if appropriate, of a child support obligation at least every 36 months, or sooner if there has been a substantial change in circumstances such as reduced income of the obligated parent or a change in medical support provisions. Check with your CSE office to see if your child support obligation is in line with state guidelines and ask how to request a review.

If your case does not meet the state's standards for review, either because the order has been reviewed within your state's review period or the change in income is smaller than would merit an adjustment under state standards, you may still be able to petition the courts for a hearing. In this case, it may be helpful to have the services of an attorney. Your local legal aid society may be able to advise you about finding low-cost counsel if you cannot afford a private attorney. Also, a number of states have information about how to handle your case pro se (a legal term for representing yourself) to have the courts determine if your support obligation should be changed. Contact your local CSE office or the clerk of the court for more information.

E. Is there a limit to the amount of money that can be taken from my pay check for child support?

The amount that can be withheld from an employee's wages is limited by the Federal Consumer Credit Protection Act (FCCPA) to 50 percent of the disposable income if an obligated parent has a second family and 60 percent if there is no second family. These limits are each increased by 5 percent (to 55% and 65%) if payments are in arrears for a period equal to 12 weeks or more. State law may further limit the amount that can be taken from a wage earner's paycheck.

F. I can't find my child and the custodial parent. What can I do?

One of the services of the Office of Child Support Enforcement is helping to locate children in parental kidnapping cases. Federal law allows the use of the Federal Parent Locator Service (FPLS) in parental
kidnapping or child custody cases (including cases in which the custodial parent has hidden the child in violation of a visitation order) if: 1) a civil action to make or enforce a custody order has been filed in the state courts; or 2) a criminal custodial interference case is being investigated or prosecuted.

Requests for information from the FPLS in custody and parental kidnapping cases must come from a state CSE agency. State CSE agency telephone numbers and addresses are at:
http://ocse3.acf. dhhs.gov/int/di rcctories/ext/IVd_listcfm (English)
http://ocse3.acf.dhhs.gov/int/dircctories/ext/Espanol IVd list.cfm (Spanish)

State CSE agency web site links are available on our web site at:
http://www.acf.dhhs .gov/programs/cse/extinf.htm#exta

States may collect a fee from people using the service to cover processing costs

G. I just found out that I was named the father of a child I never even knew about. How can that happen and what can I do about it?

If you have received papers naming you as the father of a child, and providing information about attending a hearing, contacting the CSE agency or some other tribunal, or other action that you must take, it is very important to follow up as required by the document you received. Check with the CSE agency to see how to request genetic testing, or to learn about paternity establishment in your state.

There are cases in which a man can be determined to be the father of a child if he was "properly served" notice of a paternity hearing but did not go. What constitutes "proper service" is determined by the state – it may be in the form of a registered letter, a notice delivered to the person's legal residence, or even a notice delivered to the person's legal residence, or even a notice published in the newspaper. Check with the CSE agency in the state where paternity is established to see what can be done. If paternity was established by fraud, duress, or material mistake of fact, it may be possible, depending on state law, to challenge the paternity finding.

Also, there are cases in which the alleged father is misidentified - if names are closely similar, for example. There, too, your best information about resolving this will come from the state CSE agency. Contact information is at the end of this Handbook if it was not provided in the notice that you received about the paternity.

H. How long do I have to pay?

Emancipation and the age of majority for termination of child support are determined by the states. Some states have provision for child support payments while a child is in college. If you have access to the internet, there is state-specific information on our web site, at http://ocse3.acf.dhhs.gov/ext/irti/sps/selectastate.cfm.

You can also check with the state CSE agency. Telephone numbers and addresses are listed at the end of the Handbook,

For particular situations - if a child leaves school before reaching the age of majority, is still in school but is emancipated, or is enrolled but not attending classes, for example – check with the child support agency to see how the state handles them.
If a child is handicapped, parents may be required to pay support after that child becomes an adult. Also, if a child was determined to be disabled before reaching the age of majority, states can still collect arrearages through tax refund offset.

I. I pay child support every month. I buy extras like school clothes and pay for field trips, why can't I claim my child as a dependent?

Under domestic relations tax provisions set forth by the Internal Revenue Code, for divorced or separated parents, the parent who has custody for a greater portion of the calendar year is entitled to the dependency exemption for the child (See 26 U.S.C. 152(e). In some cases a court or administrator will address the issue of who can claim dependency. Also, the parent with custody can provide the other parent with a written statement that he/she may take the exemption for a given year. The non-custodial parent can then attach the statement to the income tax form, using IRS Form 8332, and claim the child(ren) as dependents for a given tax year. To obtain IRS Form 8332 and other IRS Forms and Publications, visit the IRS Web site at http://www.irs.gov/formspubs/index-html

In the case of parents who have never married, the IRS gives information about who can be claimed as a dependent in their Form 501: http://www.irs.gov/pub/irs-pdf/p501.pdf
Generally, that would be a child for whom you had provided more than 50% of the support over the year.

145

J. My current wife is working and when we filed our taxes, the whole refund was taken.

If a couple filed a joint return and only one of them is liable for child support payments, in non-community property states the other spouse can file an amended return to receive his or her share of the tax refund. The person who is not responsible for the child support debt can file tax Form 8379, the Injured Spouse Claim and Allocation. You can get Form 8379 by calling the IRS (listed in your telephone directory) or by visiting the Treasury Department's website at: http://www.irs.ustreas.gov. Follow the instructions on Form 8379 carefully and provide the required documents.

K. I tried to get a passport for a business trip abroad. The State Department denied it because of child support. 1 don't know which state they say I owe child support. How do I find out?

If you do not know which state certified your case, or if you have never owed back child support, check the list provided with the Department of State denial letter for the contact information it gives for the state where you currently live. If you don't have the list, the staff in the state agency can check with the Federal Office of Child Support Enforcement to see which state certified the case and can get you contact information for resolving any problem. State agency addresses and telephone numbers to call are in Appendix B of this manual.

CHAPTER 12

SOME LESSONS LEARNED FROM DECADES OF
CHILD SUPPORT ENFORCEMENT

A. The four different Kinds of non-custodial parents

The Child Support Enforcement Program was established as a part of the Department of Health and Human Services (HHS) in 1975 (see Chapter 1, Section A) with the basic objective of ensuring that children receive financial support from parents who arc not living in their household. Since then, four general types of non-custodial parents have emerged:

- ✓ Those who are willing and able to pay,
- ✓ those who are willing but unable,
- ✓ those who are unwilling but able, an
- ✓ those who are unwilling and unable to provide support for their children.

Learning to work with these groups is changing the program's ability to collect child support and its attitude about other ways to help children and families.

1. Parents who are willing and able to pay support have their children's best interests at heart. These children likely will flourish and grow to responsible adulthood. If the parents miss a payment, a caseworker's early telephone call will often reveal the reason - a change of job or other circumstance, an error in payment identification - and the problem usually can be resolved.

2. For parents who are willing but unable to pay, a number of states have started programs for teaching job skills or finding employment. States arc looking at the benefits of ensuring that child support orders are set at a realistic amount. Many states work with these parents effectively to ensure that child support debt docs not drive them away from their children.

3. Parents who are unwilling but able to pay face strong enforcement tools, such as wage withholding, tax offset, passport denial, and asset seizures. Just as important, parents who have a close relationship with their children are more inclined to pay child support: removing barriers to access may lead to increased collections, and to a better chance for children to have a secure, successful adulthood.

4. For parents who are unwilling and unable to pay, an ideal program would give them the skills to earn enough money to support their children and help them discover the satisfaction of parenting. Setting fair Support orders and helping these people acquire job and parental skills might help them to make their children's lives, and their own, more rewarding.

To help reach its ideal, the program has several efforts under way.
According to the federal and state government's pronouncements, the CSE program is primarily intent on ensuring that child support orders are fair – that non-custodial parents are not burdened by a debt they cannot pay - and that children receive the support that their parents can afford. According to them, they "want to ensure that people who bring a child into the world shoulder the responsibility that it entails."

B. Children need two involved parents:

Over the last four decades, the number of children growing up in homes without fathers has dramatically increased. In 1960, fewer than 10 million children did not live with their fathers. Today, the number is nearly 25 million. More than one-third of these children will not see their fathers at all during the course of a year. Studies show that children who grow up without responsible fathers are significantly more likely to experience poverty, perform poorly in school, engage in criminal activity, and abuse drugs and alcohol. Purely from the point of view of ensuring financial support, research suggests that there is a positive relationship between non-custodial fathers' involvement with their children and their payment of child support.

HHS supports programs and policies that reflect the critical role that both fathers and mothers play in building strong and successful families and in the well-being of children. Some programs reach out directly to fathers to promote responsible fatherhood and strengthen parenting skills. Other programs work to discourage young men from becoming fathers until they are married and ready for the responsibility. HHS also partners with states and with faith-based and community organizations to promote responsible fatherhood in local communities nationwide. And HHS researches the role that responsible fathers play in ensuring the healthy development of children. More information about many HHS initiatives promoting fatherhood is available at http://fatherhood.hhs.gov. Since fiscal year 1997, the sum of $10 million has been made available each year for grants to all 50 states, the District of Columbia. Puerto Rico, the Virgin Islands and Guam, to promote access and visitation programs to increase non-custodial parents' involvement in their children's lives. Each state is given flexibility in how it designs and operates these programs and may use these funds to provide such services as voluntary or mandatory mediation, counseling, education, development of parenting plans, visitation enforcement (including monitoring, supervision, and neutral drop-off and pick-up), and development of guidelines for visitation and alternative custody arrangements.

The 1996 welfare reform law recognized that two-parent, married families represent the ideal environment for raising children and therefore featured a variety of family formation provisions. HHS has approved grants and waivers for responsible fatherhood efforts designed to help non-custodial fathers support their children financially and emotionally. Under the Partners for Fragile Families demonstration, 10 states are testing ways for child support enforcement programs and community and faith-based organizations to work together to help young unmarried fathers obtain employment, provide financial support to their families, and improve parenting skills. Eight states have also received demonstration grants or waivers to allow them test comprehensive approaches to encourage more responsible fathering by non-custodial parents. In addition, President George W. Bush's Welfare Reform Reauthorization proposal includes up to $300 million for programs that encourage healthy, stable marriages. These programs would incorporate research and technical assistance into promising approaches-that work and may involve premarital education and counseling efforts.

C. Child support orders should be fair:

Child support orders that are set too high relative to low-income obligors' ability to pay contribute to child support arrears and, unfortunately, child support debt can drive a wedge between a parent and child. A number of states' guideline formulas rely on a "self-support reserve" for the basic living expenses of a non-custodial parent before a child support obligation is determined. The self-support reserve in most states, if it is used at all, can be considerably below the Federal poverty level for one person.

Another cause of child support orders not matching a parent's ability to pay is the establishment of orders by default. Default orders are written if a non-custodial parent fails to appear m the child support case being brought against him or her. All too often, a non-custodial parent will not get the notice of the proceedings, or will not understand that a fairer order might be written if he or she attends the hearing.

148

OCSE, with our various colleague agencies, is studying effective policies and practices for working with low-income non-custodial parents. Studies by the HHS Office of the Inspector General and others report on the large percentage of total arrears owed by low-income parents who may never have the resources to satisfy their debt. Preliminary outcomes have already reinforced beliefs that the most effective way to avoid arrears for low-income non-custodial parents is to make sure that they are a part of the order establishment process and that the process ends with a reasonable obligation.

States also may need to maximize access to and use of computerized wage data to find as much earnings information as possible for all cases, including cases established by default, and those in which a parent tries to hide income. Designing a system that sets fair and reasonable obligations to encourage rather than discourage child support payment will go a long way toward reaching that goal.

D. Enforcement, when required, should be effective:

In addition to actions that can be taken through law enforcement and judicial proceedings (such as citations for contempt of court, and filing of state and Federal criminal charges), over the years, Congress has provided the Child Support Enforcement Program with strong enforcement tools including: wage withholding, offsetting of Federal and state income tax refunds, and the ability to secure liens on property. In recent years, more tools have been added:

- *An expanded Federal Parent Locator Service:* Provisions in the 1996 bipartisan welfare reform

legislation established a Federal Case Registry and National Directory of New Hires to track delinquent parents across state lines. This legislation also required that employers report all new hires to state agencies for transmittal to the national directory and expanded and streamlined procedures for direct withholding of child support from wages.

- *Financial Institution Data Matching:* In 1998, Congress made it easier for multi state institutions to match records by using the Federal Office of Child Support Enforcement. Accounts of non-payers can be seized or frozen to help satisfy a child support debt.

- *Project Save Our Children:* An initiative on criminal child support enforcement, Project Save Our Children, is succeeding in its pursuit of chronic delinquent parents who owe large sums of child support. Multi-agency regional task forces, involving Federal and state law enforcement agencies, work together to obtain convictions in interstate cases.

- *Passport Denial:* When a parent falls $5000 behind in child support payments, the State Department is notified and, if that person applies for a passport, or tries to renew or update it, the
passport will be denied until the state that submitted the case is satisfied that the debt is paid or a satisfactory plan is agreed to.

As can be seen from the above described measures, the government seems to be continually learning new lessons with every passing year. Hopefully, the Child Support Enforcement Program will serve the families who need it well: that children will have all of the love and the support - both emotional and financial - that both parents, working together, can provide for the

E. CONCLUSION

Here's the simple theory of child support collection or payment that you should always remember: The amount or degree of success you'll have, if you're a custodial parent seeking child

149

support, in obtaining regular, adequate, and full child support payments, can often depend on how well you can make the full child support enforcement system that's generally in place work for you. And the same will be true, as well, for the amount or degree of success you're likely to get in obtaining your normal parental rights as a non-custodial parent who has to pay child support – your right to a fair support amount, to a fair hearing and reasonable treatment in the courts, and to proper visitation and good relationship with your children, etc. They both depend, to quite a great extent, on how well you "know" or can master the child support enforcement system and how it works, and be able to utilize the methods and options available to you in the system to your advantage.

At the same time, there's one cardinal point that is of the utmost importance that you always remember in child support matters, namely: that not all the solutions to your child support problems are within your control. Always bear it in mind that the legal rights and welfare of all parties - the custodial parent as well as the non-custodial parent, and, even more importantly, the children, and others - under the law, must be strictly respected and exercised by all parties, and that the more each party is able to exercise such rights and responsibilities under the law, the more successful you will be in obtaining the support that rightfully belongs to your children, or the parental rights to which you're rightfully entitled. As you proceed with your enforcement case, it is a good idea to keep a written account of the actions taken and the outcomes of those actions. Do not hesitate to ask questions and make suggestions to your enforcement caseworker. If you are not satisfied with the actions taken on your behalf, you have recourse to appeal your case to the head of the local CSE office as well as to the director of the state or tribal Child Support Enforcement agency. Keep in mind that it is always best to communicate the problem in writing, than merely orally.

An informed parent can help make the child support enforcement system work. This, together with improvements that state enforcement programs, legislatures, and the courts are making, can benefit millions of parents like you and their children.

In sum, use the treasury of tools and information provided you in this guidebook to better "know" the child support enforcement system and how exactly it works, and to make the system work for you and the child(ren) in the best interest of all.

Chapter 13

INFORMATION & RESOURCE MATERIALS FOR PARENTS WHO COLLECT CHILD SUPPORT, OR PAY SUPPORT.

The following are sources, websites, agencies, support groups and agencies (both government, private and non-profit), which you may further contact for assistance or additional information either in filing for or collecting child support, or in handling a child support case against you with the other parent, or the court or child support enforcement agencies.

A. General Information, resources, and contacts that will be of help to parent on child support payment or collection issues

CSE agency web site links are available at:
http://www.acf.dhhs.gov/programs/cse/extinf.htm#exta; and
http://www.ocse3.acf.dhhs.gov/int/directories/ext/IVd_list.cfm
http://www.supportguidelines.com

http://www.supportguidelines.com/links.html [Links to U.S. (Federal) & State Child Support Guidelines and Child Support Enforcement Agencies for every state and the division of child support for each state].

http://www.childsupport.cc

http://www.child-support-collections.com (General information on child support collection laws of each state, child support calculator facilities, paternity, child support enforcement and resources).

http://www.childsupportoptions.org (National coalition for child support options).

http://www.csdpls.com (Web detectives, free people search and finder, private investigations, etc).

B. Child Support Calculator Web Sites.

These are sites that can use your state Guideline calculator to determine your proper monthly child support obligation for every state.

http://www.allLaw.Com/calculators/html

http://www.divorceLawInfo.com

http://www.arrearsCalculator.com

http://www.divorcehq.com/calculators.html

C. Aid and Support groups or information for FATHERS who are having trouble making child support payments

http://www.brainwashingkids.com

http://www.childsupporthelp.com (Non-custodial Fathers of America).

http://www.ancpr.org (alliance for Non-custodial Parents Rights, family law, child support, fathers' rights, false allegations of abuse and custody, father and child reunion).

http://www.childsupport.com (Fathers child support help line)

http://www.fatherscustody.org/

http://www.longdistanceparenting.org

D. Aid and Support groups or information for MOTHERS who are having trouble collecting child support

http://www.singleparents.about.com

http://www.childsupport-aces.org (Association for children For Enforcement of Support, Inc – ACES)

http://www.childsupportrecovery.com

http://www.deadbeatparents.com

http://www.nationalchildsupport.com ("specializes in helping custodial parents get the child support payments they are legally entitled to receive.")

http://www.supportcollectors.com (helping women get child support)

http://www.childsupportnow.com (Support for Children, Inc).

http://www.spencefoundation.org
Nonprofit organization dedicated to "exposing and finding deadbeat dads."

E. Related But Useful Resources

Site catering to single moms http://www.singlemom.com

The Single Parent Network http://www.makinglemonade.com/

Resource for Single Mothers http://www.singlerose.com/

Single Mothers Online for single moms by choice or chance http://www.singlemothers.org/

Parenting Toolbox for Traditional and Nontraditional Families http://www.parentingtoolbox.com/

F. Resources For Collecting Child Support From a Non-custodial parent Who Lives In A Foreign Country

See the information in Chapters 3 & 10 of the guidebook.

APPENDIX 1

GLOSSARY OF CHILD SUPPORT ENFORCEMENT TERMS

Adjudication - the entry of a judgment, decree, or order by a judge or other decision-maker, based on the evidence submitted by the parties.

Administration for Children and Families (ACF) - the agency in the Department of Health and Human Services that houses the Office of Child Support Enforcement.

Administrative offset - seizure of a tax refund or other Federal payment to satisfy a child support debt.

Administrative procedure - method by which support orders are made and enforced by an executive agency rather than by courts and judges.

Agent of the child - person, usually a parent, who has the legal authority to act on behalf of a minor.

Arrearage - unpaid child support for past periods owed by a parent who is obligated to pay.

Assignment of support rights - the legal procedures by which a person receiving public assistance agrees to turn over to the state any right to child support, including arrearages, paid by the obligated parent in exchange for receipt of a cash assistance grant and other benefits. The money is used to defray the public assistance

Child Support Enforcement (CSE) agency - agency that exists in the 54 states and territories and several Native American tribes, established by title 1V-D (Four-D) of the Social Security Act, to locate non-custodial parents, establish paternity and establish 'and enforce child support orders.

Child Support Enforcement Program - the Federal/state/local partnership established under Part D of the Social Security Act to locate parents, establish paternity and child support orders and to enforce those orders.

Complaint - written document filed in court in which the person initiating the action names the persons, allegations, and relief sought.

Consent agreement - voluntary written admission of paternity o responsibility for support.

Consumer Credit Protection Act (CCPA) - Federal law that limits the amount that may be withheld from earnings.

Continuing Exclusive Jurisdiction (CEJ) - doctrine that only one support order can be in effect at one time and that only one state has jurisdiction to modify the order.

Custodial parent - person with legal custody and with whom the child lives; may be a parent, other relative, legal guardian (JPS) or someone else.

Custody order - legal determination which establishes with whom a child shall live.

Default - failure of a defendant to appear, or file an answer or response in a civil case, after having been served with a summons and complaint.

Default judgment - decision made by the tribunal when the defendant fails to respond.

Defendant - person against whom a civil or criminal proceeding is begun.

Disestablishment - procedure by which a court or tribunal can nullify an order or a determination of paternity generally.

Disposable income - income remaining after subtracting mandatory deductions such as: Federal, state and local taxes; PICA and Medicare taxes; unemployment insurance, workers' compensation insurance; state employee retirement systems; additional deductions mandated by state law.

Electronic finds transfer (EFT) - transfer of money from one bank account to another or to a CSE agency.

Enforcement - obtaining payment of a child support or medical support obligation.

Establishment - the process of determining paternity and/or obtaining a child support order.

Family violence indicator - a notation in the case documents that that information about a family's whereabouts cannot be released without a court order.

Federal Case Registry (FCR) — a program under the Federal Office of Child Support Enforcement which makes available to state CSE agencies a route for securing a tax refund of parents who have been certified as owing substantial amounts of child support.

Federal Income Tax Offset Program - a program under the Federal Office of Child Support Enforcement which makes available to state CSE Agencies a route for securing the tax refund of parents who have been certified as owing substantial amounts of child support.

Federal Parent Locator Service (FPLS) - a service operated by the Federal Office of Child Support Enforcement to help state CSE agencies locate parents in order to obtain child support payments; also used in cases of parental kidnapping related to custody and visitation determinations. The FPLS obtains address and employer information from Federal agencies.

Federally assisted Foster Care - a program, funded in part by the Federal government, under which a child is raised in a household by someone other than his or her own parent.

Financial Institution Data Match (FIDM) - a quarterly data match for the purpose of identifying accounts belonging to parents that owe past due child support.

Finding - a formal determination by a court, or administrative process, that has legal standing.

Full Faith and Credit - doctrine under which a state must honor an order or judgment entered in another state.

Garnishment - a legal proceeding under which part of a person's wages and/or assets is withheld for payment of a debt.

Genetic testing - analysis of inherited factors (usually by blood or tissue test) of mother, child, and alleged father which can help to prove or disprove that a particular man fathered a particular child.

Good cause - a reason for not trying to collect support from the father, usually because the father may be a threat to the mother and child(ren).

Guidelines - a standard method for setting child support obligations based on the income of the parent(s) and other factors as determined by state law.

IV-D (Four-D) Child Support Enforcement Program - the Federal/state/local and tribal child support programs established under title IV-D of the Social Security Act.

Immediate income withholding - automatic deductions from income which start as soon as the agreement for support is established (sec income withholding).

Judgment - the official decision by the tribunal in authority on the rights and claims of the parties to an action.

Jurisdiction - legal authority which a court has over particular persons, certain types of cases, and in a defined geographical area.

Legal father - a man who is recognized by law as the male parent.

Lien - a claim upon property to prevent sale or transfer until a debt is satisfied.

Long arm statute - a law that permits one state to claim personal jurisdiction over someone who lives in another state.

Medicaid program - Federally funded medical support for low-income families.

Medical support - legal provision for payment of medical and dental bills.

National Directory of New Hires - a national repository of employment, unemployment insurance, and quarterly wage information.

Noncustodial parent - parent who does not have primary custody of a child. Obligation – amount of money to be paid as support by the responsible parent and the manner by which ii is to be paid.

Offset - amount of money taken from a parent's state or Federal income tax refund to satisfy a child support debt

Parentage - the legal mother-child relationship and/or father-child relationship as determined by the state.

Paternity judgment - legal determination of fatherhood.

Plaintiff - the person who brings an action, complains or sues in a civil case.

Presumption of paternity - a rule of law under which evidence of a man's paternity (e.g., voluntary acknowledgment, genetic test results) creates a presumption that the man is the father of a child. A rebuttable presumption can be overcome by evidence that the man is not the father, but it shifts the burden of proof to the father to disprove paternity.

Probability of paternity - the probability that the alleged father is the biological father of the child as indicated by genetic test results.

Pro se - when a party represents themselves in a legal matter.

PRWORA (Personal Responsibility and Work Opportunity-Reconciliation Act) - legislation that was passed in 1996, which is also known as Welfare Reform.

Public assistance - money granted from the state/Federal government to a person or family for living expenses; eligibility is based on need.

State Parent Locator Service (SPLS) - a service operated by the state Child Support Enforcement Agencies to locate non-custodial parents to establish paternity, and establish and enforce child support obligations

State Workforce Agencies (SWAs) - agencies that provide Quarterly Wage and Unemployment Insurance Compensation data to the NDNH.

Statute of limitations - the period during which someone can be held liable for an action or a debt; statutes of limitations for collecting child support vary from state to state.
A Stay - an order by a court that suspends all or some of the proceedings in a case.

Temporary Assistance to Needy Families (TANF) – assistance payments made on behalf of children who don't have the financial support of one of their parents by reason of death, disability, or continued absence from the home. The program provides parents with job preparation, work and support services to help them become self-sufficient.

Tribal Organizations - organizations run by Native American tribes.

Tribunal - a court, administrative agency or quasi-judicial entity authorized to establish, enforce or modify support orders or to determine parentage.

Uniform Interstate Family Support Act (UIFSA), and Uniform Reciprocal Enforcement of Support Act (URESA) - laws enacted at the state level which provide mechanisms for establishing and enforcing support obligations when the non-custodial parent lives in one state and the custodial parent and the children live in another.

Visitation - the right of a non-custodial parent to visit or spend time with his or her children.

Voluntary acknowledgment of paternity - an acknowledgment by a man, or both parents, that the man is the father of a child, usually provided in writing on an affidavit or form.

Wage withholding - procedure by which automatic deductions are made from wages or income to pay some debt such as child support; may be voluntary or involuntary.

For more information on how the child support system works in your state, contact your state Child Support Enforcement agency. For general information about the Child Support Enforcement Program, contact the Office of Child Support Enforcement, 370 L'Enfant Promenade, Washington, D.C. 20447, or visit the website at; http://www.acf.hhs.gov/progTams/cse

APPENDIX II
STATE CHILD SUPPORT ENFORCEMENT OFFICES

ALABAMA

Department of Human Resources Division of Child Support, 50 Ripley St, Montgomery, AL 36130-1801 (334) 242-9300 (334) 242-0606 FAX I-800-284-4347[1]

ALASKA

Child Support Enforcement,

550 West 7th Avenue, Suite 310, Anchorage, AK 99501-6699 (907] 269-6800 (907) 269-6813 FAX 1-800-478-3300

ARIZONA

Division of Child Support Enforcement, P.O. Box 40458 Phoenix, AZ 85067 (602) 252-4045 (no toll-free number)

ARKANSAS

Office of Child Support Enforcement, Department of Finance and Administration, P.O. Box 8133 Little Rock, AR 72203 Street. Address: 400 E Capitol Little Rock. AR 72203; 501-682-8398; 682-6002Fax 1-800-264-2445 (payment) 1-800-247-1549 (program)

CALIFORNIA

Department of Child Support Services. Rancho Cordova, CA 95741 -9064 (866) 249-0773
www.childsup.cahwnet.gov

COLORADO

Division of Child Support Enforcement, 157 5 Sherman St., 5th Floor, Denver, CO 80203-1714 (303) 866-4300 (303) 866-4360 FAX (no Ioll-free number) http://www.childsupport.state,co.us

CONNECTICUT

Department of Social Services Bureau of Child Support Enforcement
25 Sigourney Street Hartford, CT 06106-5033 (860) 424-4989 (860) 951-2996 FAX 1- 888-233-7223[1] (information/payments)

DELAWARE

Division of Child Support Enforcement, Delaware Health and Social Services, 84A Christina Road, PO Box 904, New Castle, DE 19720. (302) 577-7171; (302)326-6239 Fax. 1-800-273-9500

DISTRICT OF COLUMBIA

Child Support Services, Division Office of the Attorney General Judiciary, Square 441 Fourth Street., KW, 5th Floor Washington, DC 20001. (202) 442-9900; (202) 724-3710 FAX (no toll-free number)

FLORIDA

Child Support Enforcement, Program Department of Revenue P.O. Box 8030Tallahassee, FL 32314-8030; (850)488-4401 (FAX) I-800-622-5437

GEORGIA

Child Support Enforcement, Department of Human Resources, 2 Peachtree Street, Suite 20445, Atlanta, GA 30303-3142 (404)657-3851 (404) 657-3326 FAX 1-800-227-7993 (for area codes 706 & 912). For area codes 404 & 770, dial code + 657-2780.

GUAM

Department of Law, Office of Attorney General] Family Division, Ada's Commercial Building Suite 103B, 130 East Marine Drive, Hagatna, GU 96910. (671)475-3360 (no toll-free number)

HAWAII

Child Support Enforcement Agency, Department of Attorney General, 601 Kamokila Blvd., State Office Building Kapolei, HI 96707 808-692-2865 (O'ahu); 808-243-5241 (Maui); 808-241-7112 (Kauai)

IDAHO

Bureau of Child Support Services Department of Health and Welfare P.O. Box 83720 Boise, ID 83720 0036. (208) 334-5500; 1-800-356-9868

ILLINOIS

Division of Child Support Enforcement Illinois, Department of Public Aid, 509 South 6th Street, 6" Floor, Springfield, IL 62701. (217)782-1820; (217) 524-4608 FAX. 1-800-447-427K 1-877-225-7077' (payments)

INDIANA

Child Support Bureau Division of Family and Children, 402 W Washington Street. K Indianapolis, IN 46204. (317)232-4885 (317) 233-4925 FAX 1-800-840-8757

IOWA

Bureau of Collections, Department of Human Services, 400 SW 8th St., Suite M, Des Moines, IA 50309-4691. 515-242-5530; 515-242-5514 FAX, 1-888-229-9223

KANSAS

Child Support Enforcement Program, Dept. of Social & Rehab. Services, PO Box 497, Topeka, KS 66601. 975-296-3237; 785-296-5206 FAX

KENTUCKY

Division of Child Support Enforcement, Cabinet for Human Resources , PO Box 2150, Frankfort, KY 40602; 502-564-2285; 502-564-5988 FAX. 1-800-248-1163

LOUISIANA

Support Enforcement Services, Office of Family Support, PO Box 94065, Baton Rouge, LA 70804-4065. 225-342-4780; 225-342-7397. 1-800-256-4650 (payments)

MAINE

Division of Support Enforcement & Recovery, Bureau of Family Independence, Dept. of Human Services, 268 Whitten Rd. – 11 State House Station, Augusta, ME 04333 207-287-2886; 207- 287-5096. 1-800-371-3101

MARYLAND

Child Support Enforcement Administration, Dept. of Human Services, 311 West Saratoga St. Baltimore, MD 21201. 410-767-7934; 410333-8992FAX. 1-800-332-63-47

MASSACHUSETTS

Child Support Enforcement, Dept. of Revenue, P.O. Box 9561, Boston, MA 02114-9561 617-877-7540 FAX. 1-800-332-2733

MICHIGAN

Office of Child Support, Family Independence Agency, PO Box 30478, Lansing, MI 48909-8078
Street Address: 235 S. Grand Ave, Lansing, MI 48909-8078, 517-241-7460; 517-241-7442 FAX

MINNESOTA

Child Support Enforcement Division, Department of Human Services, 444 Lafayette Rd., St. Paul, MN 55155-3846. (651)215-1714; (615) 297-4550 Fax.

MISSISSIPPI

Division of Child Support, Dept. of Human Services. PO Box 352, Jackson, MS 39205. (601) 359-4861; (601) 395-4415 Fax. 10800-434-5437 (Jackson). 1-800-354-6039 (Hines, Rankin & Madison Counties).

MISSOURI

Dept. Of Social Services, Division of Child Support Enforcement, PO Box 2320, Jefferson City, MO 65102-2320. (573) 751-4301; (573) 751-8450 Fax. 1-800-859-7999.

MONTANA

Child Support Enforcement Division, Dept. of Social and Rehabilitation Services, PO Box 202943, Helena, MT 596620, (406) 444-6856; 1-800-346-5437. (Outside of Helena & Helena area) 406-444-9855; 406-444-1370 Fax.

NEBRASKA

Child Support Enforcement Office, Dept. of Health and Human Services, PO Box 94728, Lincoln, NE 68509. (402) 479-5555; (402) 479-5543. 1-877-631-9973.

NEVADA

Welfare Division, 1470 East College Parkway, Carson City, NV 89706-7942; (775) 684-0704; (775) 684-0712 Fax. 1-800-992-0900 x 4744.

NEW HAMPSHIRE

Division of Child Support Services, Dept. of Health and Human Services, 129 Pleasant Street, Concord, NH 03301. (603) 271-4427; (603) 271-4787 Fax. 1-800-852-3345 ext. 4427.

NEW JERSEY

Division of Family Development, Bureau of Child Support & Paternity Programs, Dept. of Human Services, PO Box 716, Trenton, NJ 08625. (609) 588-2915; (609) 588-3369 Fax. 1-800-621-5437; 1-877-655-4371 (automated system).

NEW MEXICO

Child Support Enforcement Division Department of Human Services P.O. Box 25 110 Santa Fe, NM 87504 Street Address: 2009 S. Pacheco Pollen Plaza Santa Fe, NM K75O4 (505) 476-7045 FAX
1-800-288-7207 1-800-585-7631

NEW YORK

Child Support Enforcement Division Office of Temporary and Disability Assistance 40 North Pearl Street, 13th Floor Albany, NY 12243-0001 (518)474-9081 (518)4S6-3127FAX 1-888-208-4485

NORTH CAROLINA

159

Child Support Enforcement Section, Division of Social Services, Department of Human Resources, P.O. Box 20800 Raleigh, NC 27619-0800 (919)225-3800 (919)212-3840 1-800-992-9457

NORTH DAKOTA

Child Support Enforcement Agency, Department of Human Services, P.O. Box 7190 Bismarck, ND 58507-7190 (701)328-7509 (701) 328-6575 FAX 1-800-755-8530

OHIO

Office of Child Support Enforcement Department of Human Services 30 Fast Broad Street, 30th Floor Columbus, OH 43266-0423 (614) 752-6561; 614-752-9760 (Fax) 1-800-686-1556

OKLAHOMA

Department of Human Services, P.O. Box 53552, Oklahoma City, OK. 73152. Street Address: 2409 N. Kelly Avenue
Annex Building Oklahoma City, OK. 73152 (405)522-5871 (405) 522-2753 FAX 1-800-522-2922

OREGON

Oregon Department of Justice, Division of Child Support Enforcement, 494 State Street, SE
Salem. OR 97301. (503)986-6090 (503) 986-6297 FAX 1-800-850-0228 1-800-986-2400 (rotary)

PENNSYLVANIA

Bureau of Child Support Enforcement, Department of Public Welfare, PO Box 8018, Harrisburg, PA 17105. (717) 783-5184; (717) 787-9706; 1-800-932-0211.

PUERTO RICO

Administration for Child Support, Department of Social Services, P.O. Box 9023 349, San Juan, PR 00902-3349 Street Address: Majagua Street Bldg. 2 Wing 4, 2nd Floor, Rio Pedras, PR 00902-9938, (787) 767-1500; (787) 723-6167 FAX

RHODE ISLAND
Rhode Island Child Support Agency, 77 Dorrance Street, Providence, RI 02906. (401] 222-2857 (401) 222-3835 FAX (no toll-free number)

SOUTH CAROLINA

Department of Social Services Child Support Enforcement Division P.O. Box 1469 Columbia, SC 29202 1469. (803) 898-92 10; (803) 898-9126 FAX; 1-800-768-5858; 1-8OO-768-6779 (payments)

SOUTH DAKOTA

Division of Child Support, Department of Social Services,7110 Governor's Drive, Pierre, SD 57501-2291
(605)773-3641 (605) 773-7295 FAX 1-800-286-9145 (Active Cases)

TENNESSEE

Child Support Services Department of Human Services Citizen Plaza Building - 12th Floor 400 Deadrick Street, Nashville, TN 37248-7400 (615)313-4880; (615) 532-2791 FAX

TEXAS
Child Support Division, Office of the Attorney General, P.O. Box 12017
Austin, TX 78711-2017. (512)460-6000 I-800-252-8014

UTAH

Bureau of Child Support Services, Department of Human Services, P.O. Box 45033, Salt Lake City, UT 84145-0033 (801)536-8500 (801) 536-8509 Fax. 1-8OO-257-9156² http://www.Ors.utah. gov

VERMONT

Office of Child Support -103 South Main Street, Waterbury, VT 05671-1901
(802)241-2313 (802) 244-1483 FAX 1-800-786-3214

VIRGIN ISLANDS
Paternity and Child Support Division, Dept. of Justice, Nisky Center, 2nd Fl. Suite 500 St. Thomas, VI 00802

VIRGINIA
Division of Child Support Enforcement, Dept. of Social Services, 7 North Eight Street, Richmond, VA 23219. (804)726-7000; (804)692-1438 Fax 1-800

WASHINGTON

Division of Child Support, Dept. of Social and Health Services, PO Box 9162, Olympia, WA 98507. Street Address: 712 Pear Street, SE., Olympia, WA 98507. (360) 664-5113; (360) 438-8520 Fax. 1-800-457-6202

WEST VIRGINIA

Bureau of Child Support Enforcement, Dept. of Health and Human Resources, 350 Capitol Street, Room 147, Charleston, WV 25301-3703. (304) 558-3780; (304) 558-4092 Fax. 1-800-249-3778.

WISCONSIN

Bureau of Child Support Enforcement, Department of Workforce Development, 201 E. Washington, Room E200, PO Box 7935, Madison, WI 53707-7935. (608) 266-9909; (608) 267-2824 Fax

WYOMING

Division of Child Support Enforcement, Department of Family Services, 2300 Capital Avenue, Hathaway Building, Room 374, Cheyenne, WY 82002-0490. (307) 777-6948; (307) 777-7747 Fax.

TRIBAL GRANTEE CONTACT INFORMATION

Chickasaw Nation, Child Support Enforcement Dept., P.O. Box 1809, 125 South Broadway, Ada, OK 74821. (580) 436-3419; (580) 436-3460 Fax

Navajo Nation, Dept. of Child Support Enforcement, PO Box 7050, Window Rock, AZ 86515. (928) 871-7194; (928) 871-7196.

Port Gamble S'Klallam Tribe, Child Support Program, 31912 Little Boston Road, NE Kingston, WA 98346. (360) 297-9641; (360) 297-7097

Lac du Flambeau Band of Lake, Superior Chippewa Indians, LDF Tribal Child Support Agency, PO Box 1198, Lac du Flambeau, WI 54538. (715) 588-4236; (715) 588-9240.

Sisseton-Wahpeton Oyate, Office of Child Support Enforcement, PO Box 808, Agency Village, SD 57262. (605) 698-7131; (605) 698-7170.

Puyallup Tribe of Indians, Child Support Enforcement Program, 1850 Alexander Ave., Tacoma, WA 98421. (253) 573-7808; (253) 573-7929.

Menominee Indian Tribe of Wisconsin, Menominee Dept. of Administration, PO Box 910, Keshena, WI 54135. Main: (715) 799-5290; 715) 799-5154; 715) 799-4525.

Lummi Nation, Lummi Nation Child Support Enforcement, 2616 Kwina Road, Belligham, WA 98226. (360) 384-2326; (360) 384-1734.

Forrest County Potawatomi Community, FCPC Tribal Child Support Agency, 8000 Potawatomi Trail, PO Box 340, Crandon, WI 54520. (715) 478-7260; (715) 478-7442.

REGIONAL OFFICES OF THE OFFICE OF

CHILD SUPPORT ENFORCEMENT

REGION I – CONNECTICUT, MAINE, MASSSACHUSETTS, NEW HAMPSHIRE, RHODE ISLAND, VERMONT

OCSE Program Manager, Administration for Children and Families, John F. Kennedy Federal Building, Room 2000, Boston, MA 02203. (617) 565-2440.

REGION II – NEW YORK, NEW JERSEY, PUERTO RICO, VIRGIN ISLAND.

OCSE Program Manager, Administration for Children and Families, Federal Building, Room 4114, 26 Federal Plaza, New York, NY 10278. (212) 264-2890.

REGION III – DELAWARE, MARYLA ND, PENNSYLVANIA, VIRGINIA, WEST VIRGINIA, DISTRICT OF COLUMBIA.

OCSE Program Manager, Administration for Children and Families, 150 South Independence Mall West, Suite 864, Philadelphia, PA 19106-3499. (215) 861-4000.

REGION IV – ALABAMA, FLORIDA, GEORGIA, KENTUCKY, MISSISSIPPI, NORTH CAROLINA, SOUTH CAROLINA, TENNESSEE

OCSE Program Manager, Administration for Children and Families, Federal Center, 61 Forsyth Street, SW, Suite 4M60, Atlanta, GA 30303-8909. (404) 562-2960.

REGION V – ILLINOIS, INDIANA, MICHIGAN, MINNESOTA, OHIO, WISCONSIN

OCSE Program Manager, Administration for Children and Families, 233 North Michigan Ave., Suite 400, Chicago, Il 60601-5519. (312) 353-4863.

REGION VI – ARKANSAS, LOUISIANA, NEW MEXICO, OKLAHOMA, TEXAS

OCSE Program Manager, Administration for Children and Families, 1301 Young Street, Room 914 (ACF-3), Dallas, TX 75202. (214) 767-9648.

REGION VII – IOWA, KANSAS, MISSOURI, NEBRASKA

OCSE Program Manager, Administration for Children and Families, 601 East 12th Street, Federal Building, Suite 276, Kansas City, MO 64106.

REGION VIII – COLORADO, MONTANA, NORTH DAKOTA, SOUTH DAKOTAM UTAH, WYOMING

OCSE Program Manager, Administration for Children and Families, Federal Office Building, 1961 Stout Street, 9th Floor, Denver, CO 80294-3538. (303) 844-1132.

REGION IX – ARIZONA, CALIFORNIA, HAWAII, NEVADA, GUAM

OCSE Program Manager, Administration for Children and Families, 50 United Nations Plaza, Room 450, San Francisco, CA 94102. (415) 437-8400

REGION IX – ALASKA, IDAHO, OREGON, WASHIGTON

OCSE Program Manager, Administration for Children and Families, 2201 Sixth Avenue, Mail Stop RX-70, Seattle, WA 98121. (206) 615-2547.

163

APPENDIX III
PUBLICATIONS FROM DO IT YOURSELF LEGAL PUBLISHERS & SELFHELPER LAW PRESS

The following is a list of publications from Do-It-Yourself Legal Publishers/SelfhelperLaw Press of America.
CUSTOMERS: For your convenience, just make a **PHOTOCOPY** of this page and send it along with your Order. Please, **DO NOT** tear or rip off the page! Just make a photocopy.

1. How To Draw Up Your Own Friendly Separation/Property Settlement Agreement With Your Spouse
2. Tenant Smart: How To Win Your Tenants' Legal Rights Without A Lawyer (New York Edition)
3. How To Probate & Settle An Estate Yourself Without The Lawyers' Fees ($35)
4. How To Adopt A Child Without A Lawyer
5. How To Form Your Own Profit/Non-Profit Corporation Without A Lawyer
6. How To Plan Your 'Total' Estate With A Will & Living Will Without a Lawyer
7. How To Declare Your Personal Bankruptcy Without A Lawyer ($29)
8. How To Buy Or Sell Your Own Home Without A Lawyer or Broker ($29)
9. How To File For Chapter 11 Business Bankruptcy Without A Lawyer ($29)
10. How To Legally Beat The Traffic Ticket Without A Lawyer (forthcoming)
11. How To Settle Your Own Auto Accident Claims Without A Lawyer ($29.95)
12. How To Obtain Your U.S. Immigration Visa Without A Lawyer ($31.95)
13. How To Do Your Own Divorce Without A Lawyer [10 Regional State-Specific Volumes] ($35)
14. How To Legally Change Your Name Without A Lawyer ($26.95)
15. How To Properly Plan Your 'Total' Estate With A Living Trust Without The Lawyers' Fees ($35)
16. Legally Protect Yourself In A Gay/Lesbian Or Non-Marital Relationship With A Cohabitation Agreement
17. Before You Say 'I do' In Marriage Or Co-Habitation, Here's How To First Protect Yourself Legally
18. National Home Mortgage Reduction Kit. How to Cut Your Mortgage in Half & Own Your Home Free & Clear in Just a Few Short Years
19. National Mortgage Qualification Kit. How to Qualify for and Obtain Your Mortgage Money 99% of the Time ($24.95)
20. So You Really Want to Sue Your Doctor. Here's When and How You May Do It. ($24.95)
21. Pet Trusts & Wills: How to Legally Guarantee that Your Pet Will be Protected & Cared for If You Are Incapacitated or Gone
22. How to Legally Collect Your Child's Fair Child Support Dues. Or to Fight Payment When You Need to. ($24.95)
23. The Select Proven Ways by Experts Guaranteed to Boost Your Auto Fuel Economy & Cut Your Gas Costs by at Least 50%. (forthcoming) ($19.95)

Prices: Each book, except for those specifically priced otherwise, costs $28, plus $5.00 per book for postage and handling. New York residents please add 8% sales tax. **ALL PRICES ARE SUBJECT TO CHANGE WITHOUT NOTICE**

ORDER FORM

CUSTOMERS: Please make and send a photo copy of this page with your orders) TO: Do-it-Yourself Legal

DO-IT-YOURSELF LEGAL PUBLISHERS
1588 Remsen Avenue, Brooklyn, N.Y. 11236.

Please send me the following:
1. _____ copies of _____
2. _____ copies of _____
3. _____ copies of _____
4. _____ copies of _____

Enclosed is the sum of $_____ to cover the order. *Mail my order to:*
Mr./Mrs.//Ms/Dr. _____
Address (include Zip Code please): _____
Phone No. and area code: (   ) _____ Job: (   ) _____
* New York residents please add 8% sales tax.

IMPORTANT: Please do **NOT** tear or rip out the page. Consider others! Just make a **PHOTOCOPY** and send it.
Thank you.

INDEX

10/'11 replaced torn out pg. 46